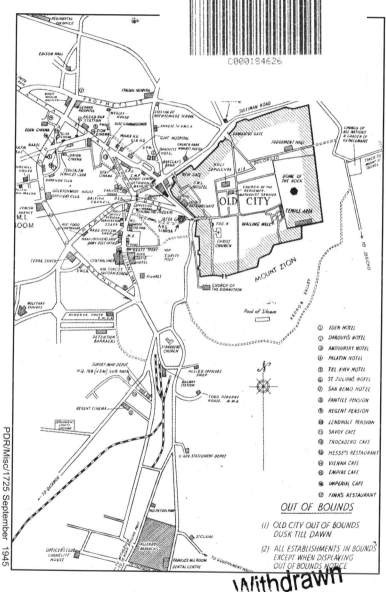

① EDEN HOTEL
② DAROUTI'S HOTEL
③ ANDOURSKY HOTEL
④ PALATIN HOTEL
⑤ TEL AVIV HOTEL
⑥ ST. JULIANS HOTEL
⑦ SAN REMO HOTEL
⑧ PANTILE PENSION
⑨ REGENT PENSION
⑩ LENDHOLT PENSION
⑪ SAVOY CAFE
⑫ TROCADERO CAFE
⑬ MESSE'S RESTAURANT
⑭ VIENNA CAFE
⑮ EMPIRE CAFE
⑯ IMPERIAL CAFE
⑰ FINK'S RESTAURANT

OUT OF BOUNDS

(1) OLD CITY OUT OF BOUNDS
    DUSK TILL DAWN

(2) ALL ESTABLISHMENTS IN BOUNDS
    EXCEPT WHEN DISPLAYING
    OUT OF BOUNDS NOTICE

PDR/Misc/1725 September 1945

JAFFA – TEL AVIV

POPULATION
TEL AVIV...... 162,000
JAFFA.......... 110,000

SCALE

| METRES | 0 | 500 | 1000 | 1500 | METRES |

| MILES | 0 | ¼ | ½ | ¾ | 1 MILE |

TABLE OF DISTANCES

TEL AVIV	TO	CAIRO	356 MILES
"	"	BEIRUT	159 "
"	"	TIBERIAS	107 "
"	"	NAZARETH	86 "
"	"	HAIFA	63 "
"	"	DEAD SEA	65 "
"	"	GAZA	52 "
"	"	JERUSALEM	40 "
"	"	NATANYA	28 "
"	"	REHOVOTH	14 "
"	"	LYDDA AIRPORT	12 "
"	"	SARAFAND	10 "

N

STADIUM
LEVANT FAIR
YARKON RIVER
ROWING BOATS FOR HIRE
R.A.F. CON. CAMP
NORTHERN POL. STA.
AMERICAN OFFICERS CLUB
FIELD SECURITY
HABERT HOUSE
C.M.P.
ZOO
RITZ OFFICERS' CLUB
E.F.I. CANTEEN
TOWN H.
SCOPUS CLUB
MILITARY BUS STOP
RAF DAP.M. SERVICES CLUB & ARK.
OFFICERS' AND SISTERS' HOSTEL
MILITARY CAR PARK
GAN RENA CINEMA
EITHER CINEMA
P.A. CENTRE
MIGDALOR CINEMA
MOGRABI CINEMA
MUNICIPALITY
HABIMA
SARONA
ALLENBY CINEMA
MUNICIPAL INFORM OFFICE
APAK POL STA.
U.S.A. CMP.
TURKEY DEPT.
AMAMI CINEMA
OPHIR CINEMA
J.I.B.
INDERUSH CINEMA
AMERICAN RED CROSS CLUB
CHURCH OF SCOT. CLUB POLISH HQ.
TRAFFIC OFFICE
BARCLAYS BANK
KEIHER TAXI STA.
NAVY TAXI STA.
MUSEUM
GREEK DAP.M.
CITRUS HOUSE TOWN MAJOR CANTEEN M.I. ROOM
EGGED TAXI STA.
RAILWAY STATION
EDEN CINEMA
G.P.O.
GOV. OFFICES
ST ANDREW'S HOSTEL
CENTRAL BUS STATION
RAILWAY STATION
HOUSE OF SIMON THE TANNER
DISTRICT POLICE HQ
WAR COMFORTS HOSTEL
G.P.O.
GOVERN. OFFICES
BARCLAYS BANK
BUS STA.
TRAFFIC OFFICE
GAZA BUS STA.
LYDDA AIRPORT
MUNICIPALITY
JERUSALEM
OFFICERS' CONVALESCENT HOME
JAFFA CLUB (OFFICERS)

OUT OF BOUNDS

PDR/Misc/1725 July 1945

Reporting
from Palestine

The sword is without, and the pestilence and the famine within: he that is in the field shall die with the sword; and he that is in the city, famine and pestilence shall devour him.

Make a chain: for the land is full of bloody crimes and the city is full of violence.

EZEKIEL **VII 15 & 23**

Reporting from Palestine 1943–1944

Barbara Board

Edited by Jacqueline Karp

Five Leaves Publications

www.fiveleaves.co.uk

Reporting from Palestine
1943-44
Barbara Board

Published in 2008
by Five Leaves Publications,
PO Box 8786, Nottingham NG1 9AW
info@fiveleaves.co.uk
www.fiveleaves.co.uk

Cover image courtesy of the Khan Museum, Hadera

ISBN 978 1 905512 32 4

Five Leaves acknowledges financial support from
Arts Council England

Five Leaves is a member of Inpress
(www.inpressbooks.co.uk),
supporting independent publishers

Typeset and design by Four Sheets Design and Print
Printed in the UK

British Mandate Palestine

"I have written this book because I believe it will help in some measure towards a better understanding of the Palestine problem. I have told all that I have seen and heard during several years in that unhappy land — facts, opinions, demands — in an attempt to give a true picture of what is happening.

When I returned to England from Jerusalem, I was met with this question from my friends: "Are you pro-Jewish or pro-Arab?" It seemed inconceivable to them that I could have lived in Palestine without becoming a protagonist for one side or the other.

I hope this book supplies the answer."

Barbara Board

Contents

11

About the Author

Barbara Board (1916–1986), my mother, started working as a reporter in 1935 on the *Southern Times*, a west of England newspaper group. She did her first assignment abroad in 1936 and for the next ten years was to send regular dispatches from the Middle East to London and Canadian papers, first for the *Daily Sketch*, then freelance, mostly to the *Daily Mirror* and the *Toronto Star*.

After matriculation, she left Dorchester High School for Girls, where she had developed a love of botany. She wrote the "Nature Notes column" for the *Southern Times*, and flowers were to creep into every description she made of the Palestine landscape, the heliotrope trees, the scarlet anemones that bloomed on the hills around Jerusalem, the neat gardens in Hadera, where she lived in 1943.

Her mother was a primary school teacher from Taunton. But her inspiration was her father, William E. Board, who ran a commercial school in Weymouth, taught her shorthand and typing, and wrote short stories. His passion for St Paul's journeys as well as for languages inspired her to travel. Her father taught himself Esperanto, although its creator, Zamenhof, is the only link I can find between him and my paternal Bialystoker family.

Her most important early assignment was a murder trial. It changed her from a provincial reporter into an international journalist. In June 1936, the prospect of a woman being hanged brought the national press flocking to Dorchester Assizes, and a woman journalist was still so unusual that the *World Press News* remarked on it:

"After all the fuss there's been in World Press News *about women covering assignments which might be regarded as the men's province, I wasn't surprised last week at the*

Bryant murder trial at Dorchester to see a lone female presence in the Press *contingent...* [alongside representatives of the national press].

She was Barbara E. Board, who, apart from taking a turn with two men colleagues on the actual note-taking, was doing a human angle story for her group, Dorset County Chronicle, Southern Times, Sherborne Post *and* Poole and Parkstone Standard."

The *Dorset Chronicle* had by-lined her only as "a *Dorset Chronicle* Woman Reporter". The *World Press News* report named her. It was her breakthrough. Within two weeks, under the heading "Doomed mother's sacrifice" she was covering Charlotte Bryant from outside Exeter prison where she was due to hang, but this time for the national *Daily Sketch*. A few months later, she was in Palestine for the *Sketch*, who also by-lined her simply as "our Jerusalem correspondent". She had been sent out to cover the Royal Peel Commission, set up in November 1936 to investigate the causes of Arab unrest in the Mandate.

Board wrote her first book, *Newsgirl in Palestine* (Michael Joseph, 1937) during that period. It was a crucial time. The Mandate, created after the end of World War I, was going through its second serious bout of serious unrest. The anti-Semitic Nuremburg laws passed in 1935 were sending German Jews in their thousands in search of refuge to Palestine, where Jews the world over hoped the National Home that Lord Balfour had promised them in 1917 would become a reality. At the same time, this new influx made the majority Arab population fear both for the loss of their land and for loss of employment. Board's first book includes interviews with the Emir Abdullah I of Jordan, with Henrietta Szold and Golda Meir, still Goldie Meyerson at the time. She reported from Bethlehem women's prison and denounced the British Government's use of criminal prisons as detention centres for illegal immigrants awaiting deportation.

NEWSGIRL IN PALESTINE

BARBARA BOARD

a girl of 20, went to Palestine to live among the 👉

*Barbara Board meets the Emir Abdullah I of Transjordan,
November 1936*

She next covered King Farouk's coronation, and collected material for her second book, *Newsgirl in Egypt*,
published in 1938 (also Michael Joseph). Both in the *Daily
Sketch* and in her book, she was critical of the young king
bowing to Muslim pressure to abandon his honeymoon
and to place his western-educated bride in the royal
harem. She continued to cover Egypt on an occasional
basis — until a front page article in the *Daily Mirror* on
February 26, 1946, criticising Premier Sidky Pasha for
denying Egypt's responsibility in violent rioting that
shook Cairo the previous week, led to her being given *per-
sona non grata* status.

After a period of work in London, which included
reporting on the 1939 Round Table Conference on
Palestine, she returned to the Middle East. In the spring
of 1940, she married the author Michael Roy Hastings
(1907–1980), who was posted as a Flight Officer to RAF

Ramleh, near Tel Aviv. Board sailed from Marseille to Haifa in April — Palestine was not at war, so accompanying wives were allowed.The marriage was shortlived, but Board remained working in the area throughout the war and afterwards.

Reporting from Palestine 1943–44, originally entitled *The Sword Without* by Board in reference to the sombre Ezekiel quotation which introduces the text, was her third book. It covers the critical period in Mandate history, when the British Government was unable to appease either Arab or Jew with its continued White Paper policy on Jewish immigration. For the Jewish population, desperate to save as many Jews as possible from Nazi Europe, the quotas were grossly insufficient. For the Arabs, who feared a population imbalance, they were still too generous.

Originally, Board had signed an agreement with her publishers, Michael Joseph, to produce a third manuscript by 1942, but she had trouble getting past the government censor and obtained a delay. She then chose to concentrate on a far more critical period, the lead-up to and the aftermath of the Government White Paper deadline for all Jewish immigration, March 1944. The wartime paper shortage, however, was acute, and when she returned to England with the manuscript Michael Joseph finally turned it down, on those grounds alone. Another publisher, Methuen this time, then accepted it, but this time my mother withdrew it. Was it, as she wrote on the folder, because she had signed a short-term contract with the *Daily Mirror* and had to return to Palestine, which she did in October 1945? So close to events, was the subject matter, to use modern jargon, too time-sensitive to wait?

My mother in later life followed closely every development in the emerging state of Israel and always harboured the hope that one day she would return to work there as a journalist. Whatever the reason for her withdrawing this present text in 1945, she held on to it, together with a second complete manuscript, *This Land is Mine*, which covers the period from the Tel Aviv riots of November 1945 until the aftermath of the King David Hotel explosion in July 1946, and which I am still editing.

By the spring of 1943, my mother was living in the coastal town of Hadera, to which several chapters are devoted. Hadera is also where my parents met. My father, Jack Karp, formerly Goldblatt, a British Army officer in the Pioneer Corps in Palestine, came from a Russian Zionist family running a clothing business in Liverpool. They had an orange grove in Karkur-Pardess Hanna, just outside Hadera, where my father, in charge of Arab labour

Celebrating the first orange harvest, 1930s, Pardess Hanna. Front left: Jack Karp, far right: his parents, Sophia and Wolff Karp

20

on army installations, was posted at the time. My father also knew Palestine well and in his teens had gone to agricultural college in Haifa.

Board worked as a journalist and radio broadcaster (broadcasting to occupied Eastern Europe) and remained in Palestine until late 1946. My father was not demobilised until the following March. Meanwhile my grandfather had sold the orange-grove where they had hoped to live and with regret, they settled in Southport. In the post-war recession, freelances were mercilessly shed. Cut off in small town Lancashire from regular access to Fleet Street, and with me, still a toddler, on her hands, she was never published again.

During her lifetime, I had no idea this writing even existed. Before she died, in 1986, she meticulously cleared her small apartment but left everything connected with her truncated writing career stacked under the bed: her published books, her two unpublished manuscripts, her press cables and newspaper cuttings, covering the King David Hotel explosion, the refugee boats, (she travelled on the *Ocean Vigour* from Jaffa to Cyprus and reported from the refugee camp in Famagusta) and other crucial events in the last years of the Mandate.

As soon as I started reading, I began to search for a publisher. There was a lull of interest in the Middle East in the late 1980s, with the world caught up in the end of the Cold War, but now, things are different. In the post-Arafat, post-Sharon, uncertain US road map era, when no one can see clearly how or whether permanent peace could at last come of the aborted negotiations and renewed confrontations that have become the daily fare of both Israel and the Palestine Authority, eyes are once more riveted on the area. The striking similarity between events then and today — take the date away, change the actors, and you could at times be reading today's press — have made these manuscripts something I wanted to share.

In the twenty years since I found the original typescripts, word-processing and Internet have radically changed and facilitated the editing process and enabled me to find trace of people met or mentioned by my mother. There have been emotional moments. Seeing old photos of the hotel where she lived in Hadera, and finding the son of the mukhtar who invited her to dine with Jewish friends in the Arab village of Irtah, south of Tulkarm. But my job has essentially been to add footnotes to events for the modern reader and, as far as possible, correct information

The Irtah courtyard, where Barbara Board dined in 1943, show-ing Fareed Shehadeh, the 83 year old son of Sheikh Dheeb, the mukhtar who invited her
(Photo: Abed Alkhaliq Jebara)

which an on the spot reporter could not have known at the time. The spelling of personal and place names remains as she wrote them, in keeping with the period.

Much has been written from the point of view of Jew and of Arab about the Mandate period. Less from a non-Jewish British stance. Less still from the stance of a British woman journalist. Board shunned the colonial trappings of Palestine life which a reading of the *Palestine Post* for the period reveals.[1] The horse races, the concerts, the balls and the garden parties were not her scene. While working as a journalist, she chose to live among and seek out ordinary people, to try and understand the fiercely-held opinions on all sides. Some of her personal fears may seem excessive and ill-founded today, as for example, her comparison between fascism and the Yishuv's May Day youth parades, but she feared above all an excess of militancy being inculcated into children on both sides. In 1943, this was, I think, understandable and I hope, excusable. Many other reports of the period are coloured by full knowledge of what happened in Europe. Board did not have the benefit of hindsight. She was there in the thick of it, sifting information on a day-to-day basis. She wanted above all to remain unswayed by one argument or another, while asking many questions which people did not dare ask and for which, even today, there is no single clear cut answer. As we now know from later historians, even the Palestine press played down the scale of what was happening in Europe. More recently, the research of Israel's new historians, *Ha'aretz* journalist Tom Segev[2] among them, has made us aware, not only of differences of opinion among the Arab population regarding immigration and partition, but also among Zionists and non-Zionists in the different Yishuv communities.

Sixty years since the creation of the state of Israel, it seems to me still important to look back and see how life appeared to an outsider as the Mandate drew to a close. Nina Rodin, the curator of the Khan Museum in Hadera, says on the museum website that there is little written trace of the lives of early female pioneers in Hadera at the beginning of the twentieth century. Board's testimony manages to capture the lives of some of the later migrants who came to the village in the 1930s and early 40s, fleeing the start of the next and even more terrible wave of anti-Semitism... Sixty years on, this on-the-spot journalism has become in its turn valuable archive material.

Both my parents narrowly escaped death in Jerusalem. My father, from an Irgun attack on the Syrian Orphanage in Jerusalem where he was stationed, my mother, during the King David's Hotel explosion when a policeman threw her to the ground and lay on top of her to save her from falling masonry. This did not stop either of them intensely loving the country. But, as she set out to show in this book, my mother steadfastly refused to take sides. And even today, were she still alive, I know she would not do otherwise.

Jacqueline Karp
Vaux-sur-Mer, October 2007

Chapter One
April 1943

Village in the plain — Arab and Jewish terrorism —
Slaughter of defenceless colonists — Jewish power to strike
back — Irgun Zvai Leumi and the Stern gang — Are the
Jews a nation? — Hebrew as a modern language — Jews
wanting to return to Europe — Old Ma Dubrowsky.

I had a penthouse in Palestine — on the roof of a hotel in
the village of Hadera, set between the dunes of the
Mediterranean and the gaunt flanks of the Judean Hills.

Hadera was once a nameless swamp — a forbidden fever
area where the malarial mosquito and the sand fly bred
undisturbed. Today, fifty years after the first pioneers gave
their lives fighting to drain the land, Hadera is a self-supporting village with its own council, cinema and shops. Two
main streets carry the Haifa-Tel Aviv traffic; in each, there
are at least a dozen cafés — "Soldier's Home," "Real English
Food," "Egg and Chips. Beer. Gazouz. Tea." — each catering for passing service vehicles. One is run by a Jewess from
Liverpool, others by Jews from Poland and Germany,
Austria and the Balkans. In summer, the cafés are black
with flies, dusty and hot. In the brief winter, their stone-
tiled floors are like ice.

In the east, out of the grey hulk of the Judean Hills,
looking like a tumbled mass of old eiderdowns, rise the
pink minarets of Tulkarm, pencil-thin, cutting the air like
stilettos above the flat Arab houses, placed in open country far from police block-houses. Nearer, in the plain, the
red roofs of the Jewish colonies, like child's bricks amid
toy fir trees. And beyond, to the west, hidden by the sand
dunes, the columns of the hippodrome of Caesarea, containing the scandals of that Roman holiday resort.

This then was Hadera. Cooking steak on my primus stove while the first orange blossom of the year unfolded in the grove below and Malka, my Russian maid, said *Da* and did the opposite.

From my penthouse, I could watch the life of the village unfolding below me. People who came to see me said, "Why live here?" "Frankly," I told them, "I don't know, but I like it." And they would leave me again, thinking I had become as puggled as most English people in the Middle East. But I loved my penthouse. To be able to lean over the parapet and watch the incredible procession of Palestine life — that's what I loved. The street was never still. Buses and camels, perambulators, the village hearse, Arabs from the hills in striped nightshirts and white kaffiyehs, Jewish colony girls wearing what has become a traditional uniform — blue bloomers with white blouses; and punctuating the natural panorama of the village, more organised expressions of the community's life — processions and demonstrations, protests against British immigration policy. For friends, I had the people of Hadera, and for dumb friends, the birds who regarded the

May Day procession in front of the Ophir Hotel, Hadera, 1930s. Barbara Board's room is visible on the roof. (Khan Museum, Hadera)

26

roof as their legitimate resting-ground: sparrows nesting in the eucalyptus tree; carrion crows like wizened old men, waiting to pounce when the rubbish bin was raised.

Beneath me in the hotel,[4] there lived a variety of pioneers and refugees. Their doyenne, Old Ma Dubrowsky, had come from Poland to eke out her lingering years in the land of Zion. She would sit each afternoon on one of the lower balconies, wrapped in her lemon shawl, thinking of snow-swept Warsaw, as she gazed on the hot shadowless road. Kurt[5], who owned the hotel, came from Vienna. He was shaven-headed, squat and tireless. I would see him carrying bedsteads to the smithy for repair, fetching fish and vegetables. His one pleasure was tea, milkless and stale; the longer it had been stewing in the saucepan on the primus the better he liked it. Ruth, a taut girl in her late twenties, who helped with the hotel work, was from Transylvania. She had married a Jew with a Palestinian passport in order to enter the country and was in the process of divorcing him — a simple enough procedure under rabbinical law.

In the daytime, the hotel seemed to drowse in the heat. The desultory clatter of china from the kitchen and the slam of a door were like electric shocks in that sleepy atmosphere. At night, the character of the building changed. The tiled corridors echoed to the tramp of army boots as British soldiers on leave stopped for a few hours in what seemed like a little oasis in the dun expanse of the Sharon Plain.

It was said that those who came to Hadera always returned, as if the place held a charm, a fascination from which one never wholly recovered. Fascination there was, even for those who did not delve beneath the surface beauty of the trim white villas, the green banana fronds, the cerise splashes of bougainvillea, all clear cut under a cloudless sky from which the sun burnt down with steady fury. That was the physical picture; but beneath, there was something deeper which provided the fascination for me — a legacy of the pioneer spirit of half-a-century ago which had stamped on Hadera the imprint of hard-won success against tremendous odds. There was no lack of character about the village — a quality missing from many of the more recently constructed Jewish settlements. The people bore themselves proudly, as if all the time they were conscious of the achievements of their forefathers, who had carried out one of the most successful colonising experiments in Palestine long before the Jewish Agency had been established by the Zionists.

Because of this I found it all the more difficult to understand why these villagers were now allowing politics to seep into their daily lives and disrupt the comparatively even tenor of their way. Unwittingly, official Zionist propaganda was changing the character of the village, fostering dissatisfaction and encouraging demonstrations against the government. In a more clandestine way the forces of unofficial militant Zionism were at work, gaining supporters for the Jewish terrorist gangs who regarded themselves not as terrorists but as soldiers of a resistance movement deserving as much admiration and recognition as the troops of Marshal Tito or the patriots of the Maquis.

How hard it was to reconcile these facts with the bland smiling face of the village, to know that in the midst of the peace and contentment some house would be harbouring a member of the gangs — a Stern man or a "soldier" of the National Military Organisation (NMO) — who, securely hidden, was planning the next blow he would strike against the Mandatory Power. How incompatible the realisation that, as the sunlit days drifted on, families in the village would be forced to surrender hard-won savings to emissaries from those gangs in order to provide them with funds. Yet without such underground help the gangs could not function.

Looking over my roof parapet in the clear bright noon, thoughts of terrorism seemed wildly out of harmony with the picture beneath me. White villas, banana fronds — my mind wanted to butterfly away from the fact that it was April 1943, that little more than a year had passed since

28

the Stern gang, the self-styled Fighters for the Freedom of Israel[6] had perpetrated one of their most cold-blooded outrages in the streets of Tel Aviv. Prior to that, the gang had been conducting a series of successful bank robberies and had swiftly extended its list of wealthy Jews who could be blackmailed or coerced into providing funds. Many who refused to succumb to blackmail had been kidnapped and held to ransom.

In the Tel Aviv outrage — a cleverly timed land-mine explosion — three British police officers lost their lives. While the local newspapers blazoned the story in Hebrew, Arabic and English, the Palestine Police Force[7] carried out a ruthless search of the city, following up clues leading them to Jerusalem and Haifa — and finally back to Tel Aviv. A price of one thousand pounds was placed on the head of Abraham Stern, the thirty-year-old Polish leader of the gang; but he had found a safe refuge in the city and neither the substantial reward nor the fear of arrest for harbouring would induce his protectors to give him away. Meanwhile the police were successful in tracking down four members of his gang. They were traced to a house in Rehov Dizengoff Street, Tel Aviv, surrounded, and after a siege, wounded and captured. The days passed. One more Stern man was chased and caught. Later came news of another arrest — that of Joshua Zettler,[8] one of the most notorious of the gang's members. Zettler was sent down for fifteen years. He had taken part in the Anglo-Palestine Bank robbery in 1940.

So the weeks drifted.

Not till February 12th, 1942, was Stern himself finally driven to ground. He sought sanctuary in a house in the Florentin quarter of Tel Aviv and was preparing for a siege when the police broke into his apartment. He was shot dead as he drew his revolver.[9] But though the leader of the gang had been eliminated, the power of the Fighters for the Freedom of Israel was in no way diminished. Stern had died, but there were lieutenants to take his place. And there were Jews scattered throughout the country, as in

Hadera, who were forced to shelter the gangsters, feed them and protect them from the police.

How was it possible for such Jews, who according to all Zionist avowals were concerned only with the upbuilding of Eretz Israel, to become tools in the hands of the gangsters? To what extent were they being blackmailed? Or were they helping of their own free will? But to these questions no one could give an adequate answer.

In Britain and America, despite preoccupation with the war, people sympathetic towards the fate of Palestine could see in the outbursts of Jewish gangsterism the prophetic writing on the wall. Letters from England told me how friends of Zionism were shocked, bewildered and painfully unable to explain to those who only know the Palestine situation superficially why the Jews themselves were allowing terrorism to throttle the National Home and to encourage anti-Semitism at a moment when all Zionist efforts were bent towards gaining support for the establishment of a Jewish state.

Members of the Palestine Police, intensifying their efforts to discover the gangster hideouts, were adamant in private conversation that the gangs would not flourish if the Jewish community willed otherwise. A police inspector who had been stationed in Palestine more than eight years told me it was impossible for gangsters whose photographs were held by the CID to escape detection in a country little bigger than Wales, unless they were being helped and hidden voluntarily. If it were a question of blackmail, then throughout the months in which the gangsters had been operating someone would have found the courage to risk reprisal by informing.

There were others who felt that the Jews needed more than courage before they gave away the gang members — they needed to be convinced that they were doing right in betraying fellow Jews whose crime was no more than an over-fervent or militant interpretation of Zionism. I was told this by different Jewish families in Hadera who claimed that though their outlook might appear unreasonable to non-Jews it was a natural reaction to what had taken place in Palestine during the tense years before the war. In those difficult times from 1936 to autumn 1939, officially described as "the troubles," the terrorist Arabs were conducting their campaign against the Palestine Jews. They attacked indiscriminately. Jewish women and children were killed and wounded in raids on isolated and not-so-isolated colonies and settlements. Crops, sown on hard-won reclaimed land, were set on fire; orange groves were looted, orchards burnt. No colony was immune from attack, not even children's settlements. Few roads were safe, except for vehicles in convoy. The inland route from Haifa through Jenin and Nablus to Jerusalem was unusable. Only the coastal road could be travelled in comparative safety and that not by lone buses or cars.

Despite all the special measures taken by the police, despite punitive military expeditions and numerous arrests and military court trials, the Arab reign of terror continued. Jews, unarmed and defenceless, were shot in cold blood, and Britain seemed powerless or unwilling to exercise sufficient power, to stop the slaughter.

Month by month, week by week, stories of attacks on settlements, accounts of burial services on land farmed by those who had been killed, made headlines in the press of Britain and America. And as the months passed, letters of sympathy and gifts of money to help the bereaved families began to reach official Zionist bodies in Palestine. At that time, when it seemed that the Jewish colonists were facing a terror as bloody as that endured by the Middle West settlers from the Red Indian, there were even non-Zionist Jews in the Diaspora who wished to show practical sympathy. Unofficial Jewish emissaries from Palestine set out on journeys to Britain and America — journeys that were to have violent repercussions on the peace of Palestine. The emissaries travelled through Britain and America calling on Jewish families, irrespective of their Zionist or non-Zionist convictions, and pleading for funds to help the colonists buy arms with which to defend themselves against attack. Money there was — and plenty. The travellers returned to Palestine with sufficient capital to equip the majority of settlements with rifles and revolvers and in some cases with machine-guns.

The arms were obtained through various underground sources, mainly by smuggling across the Transjordan border.

Then began the rigorous training of the colony youths. Secret rifle ranges, camouflaged as part of the farm buildings, were set up and each Jewish youth was taught how to handle a rifle, to fire a revolver — and so protect the women and children of his colony when attacked. Slowly each colony formed its own special Haganah defence unit. By 1938, there were few settlements that could not put up a fight when necessary.

At last, stories of raids on colonies no longer ended with the details of the funeral of those who had fallen. The numbers of Arab attackers killed gave a more fitting climax and satisfied those Jews who had subscribed money for the protection of the colonists.

But this power to strike back at the Arabs, to avenge the death of loved ones, and to protect those still exposed to attack, had come too late. Already the clandestine forces of militant Zionism — the nationalist extremists amongst the Palestine Jews — had been at work. In 1937 the Irgun Zvai Leumi, or National Military Organisation (NMO), which later was to become notorious for its outrages, was set up by the ultra-nationalist Zionists under the leadership of Zeev Jabotinsky[10], despite the fact that he was then in exile and had to conduct the formation of the organisation through underground channels. Jabotinsky had been an open admirer of Mussolini and of the Italian brand of Fascism.

The Irgun Zvai Leumi had an immediate programme — retaliation; the ability to strike back at those who had so ruthlessly disrupted the happiness of the colonists, a happiness achieved after years of toil and struggle against disease, a strange climate and stranger surroundings. This programme, the Irgun Zvai Leumi claimed, was not anti-government. It was in fact implementing the desires of the government in a more forceful way than the government seemed capable of achieving by itself.

Not till the publication of the White Paper in 1939, under which all Jewish immigration into Palestine was to cease after the end of March 1944, did the policy of the organisation change. It then became openly anti-government and stood for a practical and militant interpretation of Zeev Jabotinsky's creed. This was the establishment by force of a Jewish state embracing not only Palestine but parts of Transjordan and Syria — a state in which the Arabs would be in a minority and Jews would be free to live safe contented lives, proud of their Jewish nationality and striving to make the land of Zion a forceful power in the councils of the world.

Yet this policy of establishing a state by force was apparently abandoned when war broke out. Both the Jews and the Arabs at that time made a tacit truce with the government and with each other for the duration. The truce was to be kept by the Irgun Zvai Leumi until 1944, when the terror campaign against the British Administration was launched in all its accumulated fury. In the meantime, however, the more militant members of the organisation broke away under their leader Abraham Stern to form the terrorist group that became known by the British as the Stern gang. By 1943, the membership of the gang — with Stern dead and numbers already under arrest — was, according to my Hadera informants, well over five hundred. All the gangsters were fully equipped with smoke and Mills bombs, machine-guns, rifles and revolvers.

Through what underground sources were they obtaining these arms, now that the frontiers were more closely guarded than in the months before the war? The answer, one of unhappy irony to many Jews in Britain and America, was simple. The bulk of the arms was being drawn from the unofficial Haganah armouries established on the settlements and colonies with funds subscribed by these British and American Jews. In some cases, the arms were taken from the colonies by force; in others by connivance with the extremist members of the settlements. They were often given to the gangsters by the colony mukhtars[11] themselves, who too readily believed that the aims of the gangs were purely those of retaliation against the Arabs and not of attack against the government.

From what sections of the Jewish community in Palestine were the gangsters drawn? Under what guise did they masquerade as a cover to their other activities? My Hadera informants gave me varied answers. Many of the gangsters, they told me, had come from the colonies themselves. They were potential criminal types who had avoided joining the armed forces in 1940 and had managed to resist Zionist pressure to enrol at the recruiting centres set up in the following months. These youths, ironically enough already trained in self-defence, found it an easy matter to work out operations for attack. They formed themselves into self-contained gangs. Then, not as individual members but as units, they allied themselves with Stern. Not all the gangsters however were ex-colonists. A large proportion came from the ranks of the unemployed — pitiful groups of derelict young Jews who between the beginning of the war and the opening of War Department installations in Palestine roamed the streets of Tel Aviv and Haifa, penniless and starving. They had provided ripe material for militant propagandists. Yet other members of the gangs, neither colonists nor unemployed, believed in terrorism as their national creed. They were fascists culled from varied sections of the Jewish community — sons of wealthy families, clerks, shop assistants, waiters, factory hands, labourers.

This, then, was the background to the drama that was to be played out in succeeding months...

Spring 1943 found the village of Hadera passive in the brilliant noon, shadowless, torpid. In that deceptive atmosphere was it possible to believe what my friends told me, to accept the words of a bleak young Jew from

Bucharest who the night before had assured me with a fatalistic resignation that the country faced one of the bloodiest civil wars of all time? "Not a straight civil war between two clearcut factions," he told me, "rather a massacre of brother by brother, father by son, of Revisionists by colonists and Zionists by anti-Zionists. And on the other side, the Muslims fighting against the Christian Arabs and inside the Muslim ranks, Nashishibis warring against Husseinis — Jews and Arabs slaughtered each by their own and by each other... Unholy hell in the Holy Land."

Looking over my parapet at the sun-splashed road, at the village women doing their shopping, at colony carts rumbling over the warm asphalt, I could not twist my thoughts to the gangsterism that was later to become a virulent menace to the social and political peace of the country.

In Hadera, there *was* peace. Baby sparrows tumbling out of their nests in the eucalyptus tree; the first blossom opening in the orange grove while the last golden fruit of the old crop was still clinging to the bough; giant purple thistles in the fields outside the village. And later, as the sun struck down like a crimson sword over the sand dunes, the fireflies becoming ephemeral flying diamonds against the darkening night.

* * *

That spring in Hadera was one of immense contrasts to me. I made friends; I grew to know and love the people who had settled down in the village, battled against all manner of hardships, endured and survived to enjoy if not happiness at least a tranquil satisfaction. I learnt to understand the difference between those who believed in Zionism, militant or passive, and in assimilation: to isolate the minority viewpoint from the welter of opinions, and to answer questions which had teased my mind since I had arrived in Palestine three years before. At that time, I had

had conversations with the political leaders of both sides, with Muslim and Christian Arabs, Zionist and non-Zionist Jews. But it was only by living amongst the people themselves as I was doing in Hadera that I could hope to dig beneath the official skin of Palestine and find the real flesh and blood — discover to what extent the people were behind the outpourings of their spokesmen.

By living amongst them — there was no better way than in my penthouse where, like a newly-arrived immigrant, I had to set up home, hire furniture, shop in the village, eat local food and to an extent share the everyday sufferings of the villagers: khamsin[12] headaches, jaundice, a common illness in Palestine, and sand fly fever.

Only by sharing in this way did I feel competent to analyse the outlook of the Palestine Jews and to believe myself right in trying to disprove one of the main contentions of the Zionists — that the Jews are a nation. Never did I find this less true than in Hadera, where each different nationality with which I came into contact seemed to underline its isolation from the next. Though the Stern gang and the Irgun Zvai Leumi (NMO) might be fighting for the establishment of a Jewish state; though official Zionist bodies proclaimed the ardent desire of Jewish Palestine to become a separate self-contained country, I found the majority of the villagers fearful about changing the status quo. There were few who felt that the ties binding them to each other were sufficient to justify a common nationality. Those who had been born in the village and those who were comparatively new immigrants shared this outlook. Yet there were not many who would willingly admit that the idea of a Jewish state was impractical. Such sentiments, from a Palestine Jew, would have been revolutionary. But the lives of the villagers were a testimony to their inner thoughts. At every turn, I found fresh proof that Jewish nationalism exists only in the minds of idealists. Poles, Czechs, Germans, Austrians, Russians — each nationality in Hadera kept itself apart from the other. Polish Jews associated with Polish Jews,

Czechs with Czechs. Each nationality treasured its individual European background and not a few retained a traditional dislike and distrust of former neighbours. Poles were careful to avoid dealing with Russians. Czechs would not enter German shops. Austrian Jews considered themselves culturally superior to German Jews. Such rifts in the community were constantly being illustrated for me.

Malka, my Russian maid, was a representative example. She had come to Palestine with her husband and son from Kharkov six years previously. They had rented a little wooden shack and found work in the village. They had come not as refugees but as emigrants from the Ukraine sharing the bond of a common religion with the other Jewish inhabitants of Hadera. The bond was not sufficient to allow them to become properly absorbed into the village. They had tried to discard their old associations, to stammer at each other in unfamiliar Hebrew, to give up Russian food for kosher dishes and to make friends with German and Polish Jews. But their attempts at friendship through the medium of an ancient unwieldy tongue and in the face of traditional contempt for each other's nationalities died awkward but natural deaths. The kosher food involved unnecessary work. In the end, only their son learnt to speak Hebrew and that at school. Shopping in the village, Malka would conscientiously stumble out her requests in Hebrew, and her husband working as a labourer could form the necessary sentences to show he understood the orders of his foreman. But in the privacy of their little shack, Malka's husband and son spoke the soft Ukrainian dialect, drank tea from a samovar, ate rich borscht soup with sour cream, lemon and sugar. At Jewish festivals, they shared their mourning or their rejoicings with other Russian Jews, just as the Poles shared their festivals with other Poles.

Over this question of the Hebrew language, I found much dissatisfaction in the village. Parents were not content that their children should learn it as their mother tongue. A few wealthy parents were making plans to send their sons and daughters to Europe when peace had been restored in order that they should study at continental universities where they would acquire fluency in a Western tongue and be more competent to hold their own in the Western world. Hebrew, an Asiatic language[13], seemed inadequate as a means of conversation, save in Palestine. Though it might have sacred inspiration for the idealists, I found it held little inspiration for realistic parents.

"They shall go back." I heard this sentiment not infrequently expressed as parents of Austrian and Czech nationality discussed with me their plans for their children's future. "They shall go back, and be brought up as we were brought up; they shall have the advantages of Western education in a Europe where discrimination against the Jews has been finally crushed." I heard such plans with a certain admiration because it needed tremendous courage on the part of those parents to face the flood of criticism and censure with which they would be surrounded by official nationalist bodies. For any immigrants to wish to return to Europe was a poignant admission of the failure of Zionism to satisfy their desires.

Several adult immigrants I spoke to who were waiting to return were afraid, not of their own capabilities to re-establish themselves in the lands of their birth, but of the power of official Jewry to prevent their being given visas by the government.

This wish to leave Palestine, this avoidance of using Hebrew — how tragic it was to realise that the bonds of common suffering and religious oppression were proving insufficient to make the present generation of European refugee Jews coalesce into a nation.

* * *

"It's no use, my dear," Old Ma Dubrowsky would say to me when we talked of the future of the village. "This place looks happy enough on the surface, that's the old pioneering spirit. It dies hard. But underneath, they're all becoming as unhappy as they can and that's the way they'll go on if the politicians and the terrorists continue to work on their susceptibilities. There isn't anyone can help them. The old folk, the ones who laid the foundations of the village, are dead and gone. And the young folk who've grown up here, they were happy enough until the Arabs started their attacks and the propagandists began working them up over retaliating. Now they're tired, disillusioned. As for the new immigrants, there aren't many families who've managed to settle down properly."

She'd wrap her lemon shawl a little tighter around her shoulders and wrinkle her old silken face as she nodded and said *"tak, tak"* with emphasis and went on staring down the hot road.

There were many who brought their troubles to Old Ma Dubrowsky; for she would always prefer to talk of other people's sufferings rather than her own. Sometimes she would let me peep into her tragic past — a past that should have made her an embittered old woman. There were gay pictures of ballrooms in Warsaw — of midnight skating on the frozen Vistula. There was the tenderness of her love for a Roman Catholic Pole whom her parents banished from their house and forbade her to marry. There was the vivid cruelty of stones thrown at her in the streets of the Warsaw ghetto for having associated with a Christian. Afterwards, the long unhappy story of her marriage to a Jew whom her parents had chosen and the ultimate dissolution of her family of eight children. Distance and death had come to separate her sons and daughters. One son had been killed in the Spanish war; two had emigrated to America; another, who had stayed in Warsaw, had given his life in the ghetto rising against the German conquerors. And of her daughters only one was still alive and she was a widow enduring racial discrimination in Fascist Italy. Two daughters had died in Nazi concentration camps and a third had committed suicide when her lover had been tortured to death by the Gestapo in the Vienna Grey House.

"The whole world is in agony," Old Ma Dubrowsky would say with a heavy shake of her head. "There is little comfort anywhere, except God's beauty — if one can find it: the sun for warming old bones and the flowers to reflect colour in tired eyes, like the heliotrope tree over there..."

But her resignation to fate was deceptive. She could still be stirred into anger by what she considered unnecessary dramatising of the plight of the Jews. Days which were chosen by the Zionists as "National Days of Mourning" would rouse her to immense wrath. I would find her shrugging her shoulders impatiently, saying: "There is already too much sadness. Our whole religion is sad, wearying, but it is not enough for some. We must have more drama, melodrama, we must organise our sadness. How mad the world is getting!"

At the beginning of April that year — when the Zionists ordered the Palestine Jews to wear yellow paper spots as a sign of mourning for those European Jews forced by the Nazis to distinguish themselves in this way, Old Ma Dubrowsky flamed into a passionate temper. Shaking her fist at the village road, she stumped off the balcony to spend the day indoors where she could no longer see "such stupidity".

She was not alone in her outlook. There were many in the village who agreed with her, who thought exhibition-ism one of the things most calculated to promote anti-Semitism and to antagonise those members of the government sympathetic towards Jewish aims. Only a few had the strength of conviction to abstain from buying the spots on sale in the village streets.

Chapter Two
Late April–June 1943

Sand and thunder — The storks fly north — Inflation and the black market — May Day processions in Hadera — The village synagogue — Night life of Hadera — Ruth and the Struma *disaster.*

The first khamsin came in the middle of the Passover.[14] One night a cool sharp breeze blew through my penthouse from the coast. By the morning, great sand clouds, the curse of Arabia, were billowing over the crests of the Judean Hills and moving across the Sharon Plain like a malignant wall. With the dust came wind, hot and stinging, tossing the blossoms of the heliotrope tree to the ground and coating the shiny leaves of the orange groves with a grey film. At six in the morning, the temperature was bearable. By noon, it had rocketed to ninety degrees. On the third day, my thermometer touched a hundred.

But the pressure was less endurable than the heat. The blanket of sand weighed down with suffocating heaviness. Breathing was an effort, physical work impossible.

Yet the life of the village went on. In the last hour before dusk, the streets were crowded as women who had stayed indoors behind shuttered windows slipped out to fetch their shopping.

Night came without bringing any alleviation. Darkness clamped down hot and thick. Pillows oozed heat. My rooftop shower gave hot water from the cold tap. Flies in their hundreds swarmed outside the swinging net curtains, while those that fought their way through the mesh clustered in dark masses on the electric flex of the fan, a fan that I kept going day and night but which served only to stir the warm air. There was no coolness anywhere, people became irritable and depressed; the old and the very young suffered from heart strain.

The first khamsin that spring came earlier than usual — before the last rains had fallen. On the sixth night, a great gale surged through the village carrying sand, dust, leaves, rubbish and everything before it. By dawn, the air was clear and once more, the sun was blazing down from a blue sky. Two more days... and as the Passover drew to its close blue-black thunderclouds rolled westwards from the hills. The festival ended amid the anger of the heavens and the staccato crack of hail on windowpanes. From my roof, I watched the storm dying down over the Sharon Plain. A double rainbow, the first I had seen in Palestine, stretched from the pink minarets of Tulkarm towards Pardess Hanna. Once again, the sparrows were twittering in the eucalyptus, and the orange-trees were clean and glossy.

A few days later, I saw the last storks passing on their long journey from Africa to Europe. They came in great black-and-white droves like camouflaged bombers, their wing beats as loud as the soughing of waves on a wild shore. Laggards were left behind in the fields and on rooftops. One circled my penthouse searching for a landing-ground and snapping his crimson beak as he looked for food. There was none. The titbits I had scattered for the sparrows had been stolen by the carrion crows. A piece of *matzot*[15] I threw hopefully across the cement was ignored as the powerful wings wheeled and carried their owner northwards with great speed on the tail of the main flight.

How tired one grew of eating *matzot*, or unleavened bread. Similar to water biscuit, it is produced in large squares about the size of a quarto sheet of paper, and with butter and honey, or cheese, is delicious. But it is no substitute for bread. British troops, served in Hadera's cafés with *matzot* as an accompaniment to ordinary meals found it thin fare; but the village bakeries were closed during the Passover and no bread was made even in private homes. *Matzot*, however, was more expensive than bread, though the poorest families scrupulously ate it throughout the festival. A pound of ordinary flour cost the equivalent of eight pence: a pound of *matzie*[16] sold at two shillings.

"Ach! It costs to be holy," Kurt would say to me as we chatted on the hotel balcony in the brief dusk, "It costs to be able to live at all in this country for that matter..." Then he would launch into a description of the misgovernment of Palestine, ending with a bitter denunciation of the rise in the cost of living.

"If inflation goes on at this rate," he'd say, "it will soon be a hundred per cent what it used to be. It will be terrible. The people, they will suffer, how they will suffer!" And he'd wipe a bead of sweat from the end of his nose and waddle off grumpily to the kitchen for another glass of stale tea.

I found Kurt was optimistic. Before eighteen months had passed, inflation in Palestine had sent the cost of living up to more than three hundred per cent its peacetime level. Already in the spring of 1943, homes were being split up as one by one sons and daughters, husbands and wives had to separate in order to find work and support themselves. People were selling household goods, heirlooms and treasures brought with them from Europe, old pictures, china, plate, even such family possessions as Hanukkah candelabra handed down from one generation to another. Townspeople were having to send their children to the colonies where they could work for their keep and be educated at the settlement schools.

My village grocer, a man of moderate and considered opinions, was ruthless in his condemnation of the government. "Everyone's seen it coming," he would say to me. "It isn't something that's happened overnight. The government could have legislated against it. In England despite the war, they've kept down wholesale inflation. Why couldn't they do it in Palestine? Why can't they do something now before it gets worse?"

Officially, of course, certain commodities were being sold at controlled prices, but most of these goods were in

43

reality on the black market — a market as black as that of any European country. Meat, vegetables, eggs, butter, clothes, medicines and drugs — there was nothing that could not be obtained through underground sources, whether from Arab or Jewish merchants. Wealthy people could live as comfortably as in peacetime. The poor learnt to feed themselves on root crops as their staple food. The rationing system, one based entirely on points, was impractical and open to abuse. In the cities, it was enforced to a certain degree. In country districts, it provoked permanent scorn for the government. Some villages came under the rationing system; others were immune. Arabs and Jews who could afford it journeyed from one to the other to obtain sugar, butter, cheese, flour, and other pointed commodities. The greatest hardship was endured by those who had neither money nor opportunity to travel out of rationed areas. With such an essential commodity as bread heavily pointed, they found themselves by midweek living on substitute bulk foods such as eggplant and pumpkin. A dreary vista of unsatisfying meals loomed before the majority of housewives and the government seemed powerless to ease the situation.

* * *

April slid into May in a crescendo of heat. Down the lanes, the mimosa trees were powdered with yellow pollen, and the fragrance hung sweetly in the still air. May Day itself was a blaze of furious sunshine. I spent it leaning over my parapet watching the many processions of colony boys and girls marching along, singing, bearing gay blue-and-white banners — the Zionist colours — with the Shield of David and Hebrew lettering embroidered in scarlet and gold. The banners were carried with the dignity and precision of a regiment bearing its colours. And the marching of the children, whose ages ranged from seven or eight to near the enlistment age, was as faultless as well-drilled infantry. With each procession, there came a sprinkling of Arabs —

children from the hill villages, whose white kaffiyehs and ankle-length striped garments made an odd contrast with the khaki shorts of the Jewish boys and the inevitable blue bloomers of the girls.

Rising on the clear air above the rooftops came the sound of Hebrew songs as the children marched past, and of rhythmic shouting as they kept impeccably in step. On either side, the road was lined with people from the village — parents, friends of the children who cheered as the columns went by.

Ruth, the hotel help, who came up to my rooftop to watch, said: "Ah, but it is beautiful..." And she leant over the parapet with an intense air of satisfaction.

I shook my head. The picture was certainly gay and colourful. But to me there was something deeper which made the May Day processions a symbol of militant Zionism. I wished that the three-abreast marching could become ragged, that just one small boy or girl would straggle out of the ranks and break the immaculate neatness of the columns.

Why, I asked myself, were the Jewish settlements bringing up their children in a free land in a way that emulated one of the worst practical expressions of a doctrine they had fled? In conversations with British Government officials and with Arabs, I had heard the Jews condemned for teaching their children to become militant, and I had been told by the Arabs that such training was deliberate because the colonies were preparing for the day when they should rise and seize Palestine by force; that together with this military preparation there was an equally careful mental training designed to convince the children that Palestine was their lawful heritage, that they had only to reach out and take it and Britain and America, faced with a fait accompli, would not interfere. They would, in fact, be satisfied that the Palestine problem had solved itself. Arabs had assured me that this was the Zionist educational policy and that already Jewish children born and brought up in Palestine sincerely believed that the Arabs had no right to the country and that only those who had reclaimed the soil, like the colonists, were the legitimate inheritors of the land.

"It reminds me," I told Ruth, as I watched with unhappy fascination another column passing along the road, "of a procession of boy Blackshirts I once saw marching over the cobbles of Trieste — kindergarten children carrying Fascist banners and moving faultlessly along the water-front past the Town Hall."

"Perhaps so," said Ruth. "But their parents have come from Fascist Europe; it is natural the children are brought up this way, with boys and girls in uniform, marching. And why not?" she said with a tilt of her head. "Uniforms? Even I like uniforms."

Ruth had been arrested by the Romanian Iron Guard. She had not escaped until after many weary months in a Transylvanian prison. I had thought that she would have had more reason than many to abhor militarism.

* * *

Talking to Old Ma Dubrowsky one afternoon, I found myself asking her what part the village synagogue played in the life of the community. The synagogue building was set on high ground like a village church, but from my rooftop, the great concrete structure seemed to bear little resemblance to a place of worship. It had, however, been built in the face of many difficulties and even at that time had not been properly completed.

"Synagogue?" said Old Ma Dubrowsky with a look of immense wisdom in her tired eyes. "Ah! Once upon a time..." And she was back in Warsaw, telling me of the synagogues in the ghetto and of how the Sabbath had been spent in her childhood. "In Hadera...?" she said as I brought her back to the present. "For the old, yes, it is a comfort. But not for the very old who are infirm, like me. For the young generation? But there's no comfort in it for them! Only the old go to the synagogue here and if you go

Hadera Synagogue under construction, 1930s
(Khan Museum, Hadera)

once and see for yourself what it's like, you'll understand why. It is sad, our religion, sad and ancient. There is already too much sadness, too much mourning, too little happiness. Why should young people endure more?"

Each Sabbath morning I had watched from my rooftop the straggling groups of village men walking up the incline, dressed in their Sabbath best and carrying the velvet cases in which they kept their prayer shawls. One Saturday I joined in the procession past the silent smithy to the synagogue entrance where, in a metal trough set in the outer wall, the men were washing their hands before entering the building. In the little crowd around the trough, there was every shade of village life represented —

rich and poor, artisan and labourer. Orthodox Jews wore long velvet or gaberdine coats reaching to their ankles with big plush hats edged with brown fur; the less orthodox were dressed in normal clothes; boys accompanying their fathers had their heads covered with the traditional black skullcaps reminiscent of paintings of medieval ghettos. Against this sombre background, the velvet shawl cases made vivid splashes of colour: amber, royal blue, maroon, chocolate, each case finely embroidered with gold Hebrew lettering.

There were no women entering the synagogue. After a moment's hesitation I stepped under the archway and found myself motioned to the left where behind a white cotton curtain extending in an arc around the northern side of the building a few old women were rocking themselves to and fro, whispering Hebrew from their prayer books. They looked at me oddly. Then one moved along the row of chairs to where I was standing and beckoned me to come and share her prayer book. I glanced down at the Hebrew characters and in the pauses between the prayers looked over the barrier of the curtain at the main part of the synagogue where the men and the boys were segregated from the women. The picture before me was one which was to engrave itself on my memory.

What had I expected? A certain dignity, a solemnity about the service. An atmosphere impressive through its ancient tradition, in short, a service from which although I could not understand the ritual, I might gain a quiet inspiration and feel that same spirit of dedication which is as much a part of the interior of a church or mosque as its architecture.

Yes, I found dignity and solemnity and that same spirit of dedication — but in a form that it was difficult for me to understand. My eyes refused to blot out the distraction of watching the prayer shawls with their cream and black bands perpetually slipping from the heads of the worshippers and the constant monotonous movement as the congregation rocked itself to and fro. In that atmosphere, I felt a stranger, as if scorn was being heaped on my attempts to understand the Jewish outlook. For though in the homes of the villagers I might be welcomed as a friend, here, in the synagogue, I was an outsider, and the faces I recognised seemed only to accentuate the barrier. There was my village grocer who had spoken to me about the inflation heaving his prayer shawl over his head as it slipped on to his shoulders, a figure which had suddenly become unfamiliar.

And other faces I knew, elderly village businessmen, contractors, traders... In the synagogue setting, they seemed transformed out of the present into an archaic past, and by that transformation to have divorced themselves from their Western culture. It was not difficult to understand why the youths and young men of the village did not attend the synagogue, nor to realise that after a few decades the congregation would have steadily shrunk until it consisted only of the male members of Orthodox and other observant families.

Standing there behind the white curtain and looking eastwards towards the sacred ark containing the Tables of the Law, I could not help asking myself why the Jews were allowing the great common bond of religion to play an increasingly diminishing part in their lives. One would have thought that the Zionists, side by side with their fostering of the spirit of nationalism, would have attempted some form of religious revival.

I came away from the synagogue with a feeling of hopelessness. Outside, the heat of the village was warmly assuring after the coolness of the great building. It was as if for a little while I had been entombed in the past and was now released into the reality of the present, where under the constant blue of the heavens there could be no hopelessness, however much the facts denied the illusion.

Walking back to my hotel each few steps in the hot sunshine seemed to lighten my feelings. The civilised picture of modern concrete villas, of lorries passing along the main road at the foot of the slope, of two colony girls walking past with a swinging stride — this was Hadera. The great build-

49

ing I had left behind me on the crest of the slope was not a living symbol of village life but a monument to the religious beliefs of the pioneer forefathers of the community.[17]

Ruth, whom I met on the hotel stairs as I climbed up to my rooftop, said: "Synagogue! Why I haven't been inside one for years! Leave that sort of thing to the old and the Orthodox. They find comfort in it. I shouldn't. Can't say I believe in praying for the restoration of the Temple. If the Temple was rebuilt it would only create something else for the Muslims to be up in arms about. No — my religion is not built around any ancient laws. I believe in a God. Most people believe in a God — a deity controlling our lives. But religion as such, even in prison I found little consolation in that."

* * *

Soon the summer would shrivel the last patches of grass and turn the countryside into a vast expanse of burnt soil with only the evergreen cypress to break the brown of the landscape.[18] Along the main street each day came the colony carts, sometimes driven by children, filled with the last green crops of the season, corn and fodder harvested before the sun drained them of moisture.

Before the sand dunes grew too hot and while the wadi banks were still green, I wanted to visit Caesarea. I had made friends with the police at Kfar Vitkin and they lent me Jimmy, a great sixteen-hand stallion with a mouth like silk, who galloped over the cliff tops and the sands with the abandon of a two-year-old.

One morning we set off down the sloping cliff paths into the bay where the streams that water Hadera's farm-steads empty themselves into the Mediterranean. There was no one in sight, just the police station on its cliff top behind me, nothing except the broad sweep of the coast and the rolling gold of the dunes rippled like water from the sea winds, broken here and there with stunted patches of scrub. In the middle of the bay, there was a wooden jetty. It seemed to have been stuck down there for no apparent purpose. Certainly not for fishing, for the Jewish fishing colony was next to Caesarea. Later, I learned that the jetty had been built several years before so that illegal immigrants who had managed to reach the Palestine coast in ships that were not allowed to berth in Haifa could still slip ashore at night on rafts and in dinghies. It was the job of the police force down the coast to stop such illegal entry into the country.

That brilliant May morning, for me it was just a jetty in the middle of nowhere.

Jimmy and I forded a stream and came to a beach café that had been hidden from view by eucalyptus and tamarisk. This was the beginning of Hadera's planned beach resort, a place that they told me in twenty years or more would have an esplanade rivalling Tel Aviv. I tethered Jimmy to a post and went inside. There were two Jewish youths playing chess. One got up and brought me tea. Then, ignoring me, he went on with his game.

Half an hour later, they told me I was the first customer for over a week. "No one comes down here," they said, "It's like living in a lighthouse." They stayed because their parents had invested capital in the seashore café and they had to guard it from being robbed by Bedouin or used as a safe storing place for arms by the Stern gang or as a hideout for illegal immigrants. "But one day," they told me "when this place becomes a holiday resort, we shall be rich."

They started another game of chess, as imperturbable as the sands surrounding them, as patient as only those who have suffered in Europe and found ultimate safety can be.

Jimmy and I rode away from the café along the beach where the shells were glossy with mother of pearl and the low escarpment blotted out the dunes. A few kilometres further north lay the pink houses of Caesarea, jutting out to sea like a miniature Acre.

Abu George had seen us coming. In his blood red tarbush, walking with the aid of a high stick, he came along the cliff

51

path to greet me. Caesarea is a difficult place to reach. There are only two means of access — one from the main road across fields and along twisty paths, and the other up the coast. There are few visitors in wartime except service people on leave. Tourists have not been seen there since 1939. Abu George, who revealed himself as the village guide, was scratching a living for himself and his two wives by being the "medicine man" for the Arab inhabitants and the half-settled Bedouin from the nearby tents.

He bowed to me and led the way along a narrow path between tumbled Arab dwellings into the village centre. Here was Cleopatra's well, which she had built, so he told me, out of thankfulness to God for having safely reached Caesarea on her journey southward. Cleopatra's well was busy. Village women, wearing long black dresses with coloured cummerbunds and cloths over their heads filled two-gallon petrol tins in an unending queue. Donkeys were waiting their turn to drink. Two village pye-dogs slunk over the mud surrounding the well. Balancing the tins on their heads, the women returned to their homes. How sad, I thought, that the ancient clay water jars should have given way to petrol tins.

Abu George took me to see the ruins of the hippodrome. Great basalt pillars lay broken and slimy beneath the water. What had once been a promenade for Roman matrons was now buried under the Mediterranean. An archway remained, and through this, I looked over Caesarea's bay, a smooth semicircle bordered with Arab brick and mud homes, all in the same dusty pink.

"Now you will come and take coffee," said Abu George, leading me past the well along narrow stale-smelling lanes to a door in a wall. I tied Jimmy's reins round the lintel and went inside.

The two wives came to welcome me. One was about fifty; the other a young girl, with the beautiful satin skin so typical of Arab women, and dark childlike eyes. The courtyard was crowded with cats, rubbish and chickens. Abu George directed me into a dark clean room that he kept for visitors. There was a bed and a small table. Presently he came back, bearing a tray of Turkish coffee and an English brand of cream crackers.

Then he sat down to entertain me with tales of the miracle cures he had worked in the village. Of how his main source of income was derived from magic herbs that he gave to childless women who were desperate because their husbands were threatening divorce.

Abu George sold these herbs at fabulous prices. He claimed to be the marriage-mender of Caesarea. I drank his coffee, laughed a lot, and rode away wondering how gullible the village women really were and how many of the tourists who had signed Abu George's visitors' book believed his tales.

* * *

When the heat of the day gave way to dusk I would sometimes wander through the village as far as the little marketplace where at open-air booths bright yellow pumpkins and Valencia oranges made a vivid burst of colour against the arid brown of the ground. Giant tomatoes would be piled high on the stalls. The glossy purple of eggplant and the grey-green of lady's fingers — small seed-pods eaten whole — gave depth to the canvas. One by one, the shutters of the booths would drop down as the villagers began to go home with their bulging string bags and the marketplace closed for the night.

Nearby, at the bus shelter where the grey Egged vehicles from Tel Aviv and Haifa disgorged their weary passengers, Jewish children would be selling the last scarlet poppies of the year. Clutched in warm damp hands, the flowers were thrust through the open windows or thrown on to people's laps almost before the buses had come to a standstill and brittle young voices, speaking Hebrew, would demand two piastres, fifteen mils, one piastre, until passengers in desperation threw them a handful of small coins and seized the flowers.

Then the village would become alive with movement as passengers and market sellers, café waitresses and shop-keepers wended their way home. And slowly the scents of the trees and flowers would gain ascendancy over the dust and fumes from the daytime traffic.

How lovely it was to walk in the perfumed air, to breathe the scent of nameless tropical night blossoms, to see the tobacco plants uncurling their white petals as the moths hovered overhead. Then the sounds of birds would begin to die in the treetops and wings cease fluttering among the flame-trees and tamarisk bushes.

The peace of the short twilight, the quiet sounds of colony carts returning home, the padding of camels moving inland towards Tulkarm, and the last hammer-blows on the smithy's anvil, these were the sounds I loved — ordinary sounds which by contrast made the nights a cacophony of alien noise.

How fiercely alive was the darkness! As the twilight dimmed, the pye-dog packs led by the jackals would come slinking into the village from the dunes and wastelands, prowling through the empty streets, moaning and howling in perpetual and uneven choruses as they searched for rot-ting food. From my rooftop, I could hear them baying in the grove at the back of the hotel. Then the cats that reared their families in the rubbish bins would start bawl-ing in terror, until it seemed as if the whole village must awake in protest.

Howls and bawls, and away on the village outskirts an ass punctuating the clamour with screams for its mate, or a clumsy barn owl screeching as it flew heavily away from my radio mast.

Some nights, before the sluggish trickles of water in the wadis had finally dried up for the summer, the bullfrogs would add to the tumult. Their barking would end as sud-denly as it began. One moment it sounded like litters of angry puppies trying out their voices for the first time. The mating calls might cease after a few minutes — they might last all night. Then the whole colony of bullfrogs

54

would silently migrate from the wadis to other breeding grounds further off.

On the rooftop itself, I had the friendly ticking of the cicadas, whose fragile bodies, like brown tissue paper, were indistinguishable against the cement, even when I searched for them with a torch. Click-click they would go from nightfall to daybreak. Click-click... click-click... like alarm clocks running down.

Once a rare silent visitor came into my penthouse — a praying mantis. He found a way through the mesh curtain and landed his green bulbous body on my table, where he hopped around holding his two hands tightly together as if asking God for something which needed a great deal of asking.

* * *

Medical services[19] in isolated parts of Palestine are as good as the government can make them. In the Jewish settlements, there are well-equipped clinics and sick quarters run by the colonists themselves, many of whom hold German or Viennese degrees and are specialists in Eastern diseases. In large Arab towns like Jaffa, there are Moslem and Christian Arab doctors who have studied at the Beirut University or in Stamboul.[20] But in isolated villages like Caesarea the people have to rely on local quacks or else journey perhaps many kilometres to the nearest Jewish colony for help. I have seen Arabs taking their wives and their children to these colony clinics and I have heard the English scoffing at the propaganda the Zionists make out it. Because it is publicised, they think it is untrue.

In Jewish villages like Hadera, the standard of medical services is of course high. Some of the best specialists from Europe have become country doctors in Palestine, and although there are too many of them for each to make a reasonable living, their wives and children help to support the home by taking work outside.

Some German friends of mine took me one day to visit a

children's specialist in Pardess Hanna, a nearby village that is one of the centres of the citrus industry. This doctor, I will call him Hans[21], was living on a handful of piastres a week. The children's parents were unable to afford to pay him, but he carried on his work, saving many for the unfortunate illnesses one gets in the country, and becoming a kind of fairy godfather to the neighbourhood.

Hans had held a practice in Hamburg, where he had amused his young patients with clockwork toys, trains, buses and trams. As a hobby, he had built a complete model of Hamburg's tramway system and convalescent children would go to his house to play all day with this fascinating game. Hans brought this same enthusiasm for model toys to Palestine with him. One day that summer, he went to Pardess Hanna railway station to copy down the train timetable. He was going to build a Palestine railway system for the children of his village. The Arab *ghaffir*[22] on duty at the station placed him under arrest for suspicious behaviour. Hans was taken to Hadera police. His notebook was confiscated. Forty-eight hours later, he returned home, disillusioned, to carry on his work of healing.

Today he is still in that village, looking after sick children and existing on an income below subsistence level.

* * *

The village postman in Hadera was usually a bearer of important tidings. Each morning he would deliver two or three Red Cross letters bringing news of relatives in Europe. Sometimes a family would be happy with rejoicings, as after months, even years, of silence they heard of parents still living safely in Germany as yet untouched by the Gestapo. But usually the Red Cross on an envelope meant tragic tidings and houses would be plunged into mourning for a brother or father, a sister or mother who had died in a German labour camp or been gassed in a death chamber.

Kurt had received a Red Cross letter early that spring giving news of a relative who had lost his life with other conscripted Todt labourers, building defences on the Orsha-Mogilev Fatherland Line in White Russia.

In June, the postman delivered a Red Cross letter for Ruth.

When I saw her later that day she was distracted with grief but by the next morning her grief had changed into an angry bitterness against the government, for the tragedy was one which could have been averted had the Palestine authorities acted with greater speed and with more courage.

Ruth's younger sister, Shoshannah, had died — and in a way which was no less terrifying than the extermination methods of the Germans. She had gone down in the *Struma*. The letter, from an uncle in Budapest, had taken five months to reach Ruth. He himself had been trying to trace Shoshannah for nearly a year. She had last been heard of in Constanza in December 1941 when she had been waiting with other refugees to board the ship that was to take them to Palestine. Ruth's uncle had now confirmed that Shoshanna had actually sailed on that ill-fated voyage.

The story of the *Struma* is one that will never be forgotten by the Jews of Palestine. At the time of the disaster, and in succeeding months, it evoked more bitterness against the government and more distrust of the immigration authorities than any other similar happening, including the refusal to let the *Patria*[23] passengers land at Haifa. Questions about the *Struma* were asked in the House of Commons; Zionist bodies presented protests to the government; Jewish shopkeepers went on strike; youth organisations demonstrated in the cities.

It was December 12th 1941 when the *Struma*, a former cattle-boat of less than two hundred tons, steamed out of Constanza harbour with its cargo of seven hundred and fifty passengers including seventy children. For days, the Romanian customs officials — acting indirectly under the orders of the Germans — had refused permission for the ship to leave. At the last moment, they confiscated the food brought aboard by the refugees. So the ship sailed without provisions — with no drinking water, no lighting, no heat and no medical supplies. Day and night the passengers had to live crouched in cages slung along the ship's sides — five people to a cage one metre sixty wide and not more than sixty centimetres high. By the first night, many were sick with dysentery. Some became insane with thirst. The ship's engine failed and the vessel had to limp back to another Romanian port. No water was allowed to be taken aboard. Once again — after scant repair — the *Struma* put out to sea only to break down in the Bosphorus. The normal journey from Constanza to Stamboul is sixteen hours. It took the *Struma* four days.

But Stamboul had been reached, and the minarets of the Turkish city were the first symbols of freedom to the sick and starving aboard that ship. In Stamboul, there would be food, medicines, and permission to land.

The days dragged. Very slowly, the refugees realised that a permit to disembark might not be forthcoming. Five, six, seven, eight days... only then was food taken aboard, but without fuel so that nothing could be cooked. On the eighth day, the passengers were finally told that they could not land in order to travel to Palestine. The Turkish authorities ordered the ship's engine to be repaired and the vessel to return to Romania.

Engineers came aboard. After a few more days, the *Struma* set sail. Shortly after leaving Stamboul harbour the vessel blew up in the Black Sea — it is believed by the hand of one of the passengers themselves.[24]

A permit making it possible for the children on board to enter Palestine arrived at Stamboul two hours after the ship had sailed on its last journey.

The statement issued by the Executive of the Jewish Agency completes the story:

"The Jewish Agency has learned with grief and horror of the sinking in the Black Sea of the SS *Struma* with seven hundred and fifty Jewish men, women, and children aboard, refugees from Romania. The boat had been lying at Istanbul since December 15th , and the conditions as regards food and sanitation were described as "desperate'. Every effort was made by the Jewish Agency in Jerusalem to persuade the Palestine Administration to admit these victims of persecution. The Agency proposed that they should be put to the account of the immigration schedule which permits three thousand Jews to enter Palestine during the current six months. The matter was also taken up with the Colonial Office in London. The only concession obtained was in respect of children under sixteen who were to be allowed to enter Palestine. Two sets of arguments were put forward by the British authorities against granting the request of the Agency to make adult refugees on the *Struma* also eligible for certificates under the current schedule:

1. That these people had been under the Nazis and they might therefore include some enemy agents.
2. Shortage of supplies in Palestine.

As regards (1), the Agency has repeatedly urged that such refugees should be placed in internment camps and not released until and unless their characters were established to the full satisfaction of the Palestine Administration.

As regards (2), more than two-thirds of the *Struma* refugees were people fit and willing to work and to fight. To use the argument of short supplies against admitting some two hundred elderly people flying from torture and death reflects on the intelligence, as well as on the heart, of those who advise it. Moreover as these people would come under the schedule already granted, the problem of supplies did not arise..."

Chapter Three
July 1943

*Visit to the colonies — Children brought up to a pattern —
Parents and children separated — Jewish achievement in
the North — Farms in swamps and on rocks — Illegal
immigration — Cooperative living.*

The plums were ripening in the Sharon Plain; and from
early morning till dusk the colony workers were busy
gathering in the harvest.

At a settlement near Pardess Hanna where I helped
with the fruit picking, boys and girls who had been born
and brought up on the farm laboured tirelessly in the
orchards, packing the plums in great straw panniers and
loading them on carts or lorries for dispatch to Tel Aviv
and Haifa. In the shade of the trees, the July heat seemed
less oppressive than in Hadera. Had it not been for the
lizards that constantly darted over the sandy soil, I could
have imagined myself in an English orchard with a crowd
of schoolchildren helping to gather in the fruit.

Lizards... and the occasional giant hornet whirring
between the branches destroyed the illusion. This was
Palestine: red sandy soil, and above, blue sky with the
kites and hawks hovering in impatient hunger for scraps
from the colony kitchen.

But neither lizards nor hornets distracted the young
boys and girls from their work. They went on picking and
sorting in a mechanical way rather as if they were in a
classroom doing their lessons... a legacy I felt of their communal upbringing.

Although most of them spoke only Hebrew, those who
could manage to form a few sentences of English stumbled

along in the unfamiliar language telling me of their life in the colony, their pride in the increasingly good crops they harvested each year and their plans for ultimately marrying and raising families of their own. I wanted to believe what they told me... but the sentiments seemed too mature, too similar, to have come spontaneously from the lips of those children. As the day wore on, I had an opportunity of asking one of the older girls if she genuinely meant what she had been telling me in front of the others. We were in a part of the orchard that had been nearly stripped and she was searching for overlooked fruit, moving her ladder from tree to tree and answering my questions as she worked.

"Sometimes it's difficult to know exactly what we do mean," she said with a certain hesitation. "Some days I am happy here, with the sun and the warmth... I don't feel the heat as most do. As for the farm-work, it's hard but satisfying. Then at other times I feel that I am missing a great deal; when I see how much propaganda is made out of what we are doing on our farms, pictures of us colony girls working away smiling, as if we smile all the time... then I get mad, you would say..."

It was not difficult to understand her outlook. Zionist publicity photographs invariably showed the Jewish land-girls beneath a blaze of brilliant sunshine, laughing and waving, as they drove their carts along the highways or worked on the settlements.

"Some of them don't notice it like I do," she added with a little shrug as she moved her ladder to another tree and became momentarily lost in the branches. I held the pannier underneath as she threw the plums down. When she had climbed down again, she said: "I think the hardest thing about colony life is that no one is allowed to be an individual. We are all taught to think alike. We're brought up together in the colony schools, we sleep in the children's dormitories, we're trained to do farm work and taught to be proud of the produce we get from land which is ours after centuries of belonging to the Gentiles. We're told that our whole lives must be devoted to the cause of Eretz Israel, to the building of our National Home and to the rearing of families so that the Jewish population becomes a majority in Palestine instead of a minority. We're not given any time to think things out for ourselves or to dream about the Europe our parents came from. If we begin to talk of life in the cities of the West, in London perhaps or New York, then we're rebuked."

She picked up the ladder and a half-full pannier of fruit and we walked back towards the group of harvesters. "My parents brought me here when they came from Lithuania many years ago," she added. "I haven't known any other life. I don't suppose I ever shall." Later, when the mukhtar — the head of the colony — took me on a tour around the farm buildings, I found I could not forget the resignation in her voice. Her words imposed themselves on my mind and distracted me from what the man was explaining. When I was able to concentrate on what he was telling me, we had reached the dairy farm. I was shown the prize bull — a Frisian imported from Europe before the war, and the herd of cows, which gave rich milk and provided the colony in addition with butter and cheese. During the citrus season, the cows had eaten many tons of oranges and mandarines — fruit which would have been exported to England in peacetime. The mukhtar told me the colony had lost hundreds of pounds on citrus. "Most of our capital was sunk in the groves," he said, "but now exporting has ceased for the time being and we have turned to other things. Many of our farm workers have been forced to take jobs in the nearby villages. They travel in to Pardess Hanna and Hadera each day and return to sleep at the colony. Their earnings go into the communal coffer of course and are shared out equally amongst all the settlers."

Then I was taken through the great threshing sheds, past enormous barns, chicken-runs where fine white leghorns were scratching the red earth, trim patches of grass bordered with flowers and eventually to an oblong cement bungalow which was the nursery and kinder-garten.

Inside, behind windows half-shuttered against the heat, there were groups of toddlers sitting at small tables eating their midday meal. They were pattering away in Hebrew — a proof, said the mukhtar, that the language was truly being brought to life again. When I asked what other tongues they would be taught, he told me elementary English and Arabic, when the children reached their teens.

Then he explained the advantages of the children being brought up in the colony nursery and kindergarten, and did not, I think, entirely sympathise with my rather shocked surprise when I was told that the parents were allowed to play with their babies only once a week on the Sabbath. The older children were given permission to take their Sabbath midday meal with their parents in the colony dining-hall, when meat was served. On other days, the food consisted of vegetables, cheese and fruit.

Beyond the nursery living-room lay the dormitory. There I found younger babies leaning over the sides of their cots with a nurse in attendance. Their overwhelming delight at seeing a visitor, at being played with, was some-thing which tore at my emotions. Was it right to bring up children in this unnatural experimental way? Was it justi-fied to separate them from their parents and rear them in artificial surroundings? Here was a system of living in which the home as such had no place. The colony girls married, had children and farmed them out in the colony nursery very much as chickens in incubators.

Outside the nursery, I tackled the mukhtar again, asking if it was absolutely necessary for the successful running of the colony that the parents should be deprived of their children.

He was emphatic. "How could we possibly spare each mother the time to look after her own child?" he asked me. "No, they must all make their contribution towards the farm just as much as the other settlers. Eight hours or more a day on the soil, in the kitchen, in the dairy or the packing-sheds — one or the other, whichever they care to choose. Only those specially selected from among the colony women are allowed to look after the nursery. Usually they are qualified nurses, sometimes doctors. The children are brought up with the very best medical attention, and later the best educational facilities we can offer them. On the human side, yes, I suppose it is hard. It would be better if each family could be self-contained in its own little bungalow. But it would not be economic. The colony could not be self-supporting if we tried to run it that way."

Not one of the mothers I spoke to afterwards could properly answer my question as to whether they felt it worth while to have children who were in effect handed over to the colony within a few weeks of their birth. Those who had never known what it was like to bring up a child in their own homes did not see anything very strange in the system. Those who had already had children in Europe and had borne more sons and daughters on the colony were divided in their minds.

"At least they're free," they said to me. "They aren't living under the fear of persecution. They're not afraid that the footsteps outside the door at night are those of the Gestapo coming to take them away to prison."

A heavy price, I felt, to pay for the right to live in peace and freedom. Too heavy for many thousands of Jewish immigrants who had preferred to settle down in the crowded tenement blocks of Haifa, Tel Aviv and Jerusalem where they eked out a miserably poor existence yet preserved their family entities.

I asked one or two of the women if they would go to the cities to live were they given the choice over again. "Some have gone," they told me. "Those who found the colony work too hard — those whose husbands living in the easy freedom of colony life found affection for other women. But most have wanted to return. It's difficult when you've left to get taken back; but once you're really used to the life then you're not fitted for normal living."

At the midday meal, I was served by the kitchen girls in their speckless blue dresses with white kerchiefs over their heads. We had bowls of tomato and cucumber, haricot beans, stewed plums and dates, and cheese — all colony products, plain but nourishing. In fact, not one of the colonists that I met looked underfed. They were all healthy and strong, even those who had arrived in Palestine as thin emaciated escapees from German internment and labour camps.

Before I left, I talked with some of the middle-aged fathers about the processions I had seen on May Day. None would agree that their sons and daughters were being trained along lines which to outside people appeared fascist. "Uniforms don't mean fascism," they said. "What about the Boy Scouts and other similar organisations? The children of Palestine are being taught discipline and obedience in what we consider an ideal way; as for the accusation that they are being trained to become soldiers to fight the Arabs for the establishment of a Jewish state, it's lying propaganda, a fabrication by those who would like to see the Jews cleared out of the country, robbed of their inheritance."

I went away with a confused picture of men and women who had relinquished their individuality, their right to their own private lives, in order to play an integral part in the building of the Jewish National Home. Some I had seen had found contentment. There were others who, beneath brave words, had shown their disillusionment. But not one had been hopeless or bitter about the life they were now living.

As I went home in the colony truck with baskets of fruit and eggs which the mukhtar had given me, I tried to put myself in the place of one of those women who had come to that colony from Europe. I tried to picture the journey to Palestine aboard a ship under conditions at least half as bad as the *Struma*, the arrival at Haifa, being met by Zionist officials, given food and clothes and shelter and then the choice — of going on a colony or fending for

myself in one of the towns. What would have been my
choice? In my imagination, I was certain I should have
chosen to be my own master and to scratch an income in
Tel Aviv or some such place. But I could understand how
the simplicity of farm life, the certainty of somewhere to
sleep and eat would take away individual ambition. Easier
by far to be shepherded on to one of the colonies and to
settle down there to live and to die.

* * *

Jewish friends of mine in Hadera told me I should go to see
some of the colonies in the far north of Palestine, those
which had not been established many years and were not
as flourishing as the ones in the Pardess Hanna district.

"You will get a different picture, then," they said. "You
will see what it means to build a colony on mud or rocks,
to fight fevers and diseases, to weld people from all countries into big farm families."

There was no direct way to these colonies except by taxi.
I hired one and set off for the Huleh marshes. From
Hadera the road cut through the Mish-mish Wadi — the
Vale of Apricots — until we came out into the Plain of
Jezreel and reached Jenin. This Arab town during the
1936–1939 "troubles" was one of the main centres of terrorist activity. In the hills and wadis between Jenin and
Nablus, Arab gangs had their headquarters. Their arms
were concealed in caves and in isolated hamlets, and the
approach of police patrols was signalled by an elaborate
system of hill-watchers.

But that morning in July, Jenin was a town of sunlit
peace. Arab children played in the road; donkeys laden
with vegetables and fruit ambled through the streets; and
the village women, a few of them veiled, went about their
shopping as normally as the women of most countries.

Before noon we reached Tiberias — Tabariyah the
Arabs call it. To me the lake always looks like a sapphire
dropped in a saucer of sand. The stark mountains sweep

down to the water's edge in sharp brown folds; the lake itself, smooth or storm-tossed, is always blue.

The road curved around the lakeside, beneath spurs of arid cliff, past Arab villages and Jewish colonies, the turning to Capernaum, through the ancient city of Safed, until we came down into the fetid plain of the Huleh.

Then we reached the Tegart wall, the barbed-wire barrier built in an effort to control the frontier region.[25] The wall stretches from the Mediterranean coast near the borderpost of Ras El-Nakoura[26] inland to the Huleh. It is almost continuous the whole way. On the main roads where it breaks to allow traffic to pass there are police checkposts. The Tegart wall was at one time made a great deal of in the British press, but people in Palestine are inclined to laugh at it. It has not proved a great deterrent either to smugglers or to illegal immigrants. In the darkness, the wires can be cut and police patrols may not discover the point of entry for many hours.

Beyond the wall, we skirted the fringe of the Huleh, the most notorious malarial district in Palestine. Zionist health and reclamation experts have done a great deal to make the Huleh habitable. Swamps have been drained just as in Hadera. And the Palestine Government in its limited way has contributed towards the work. But despite all that has been done the incidence of fever and the mortality rate amongst settlers is higher in that region than in any other part of the country.

Beyond the tip of Lake Huleh, I came to the settlement I had been advised to see. This collection of dwellings had been started in 1938 on land thick with slime and mud and infested with the malarial mosquito. Colonists had come there, the mukhtar told me, from all countries in Europe. They had spoken varied languages and to begin with had been unable to talk to each other. Now they had all learned Hebrew and conversed fluently. Both the mukhtar and one of the colony girls gave a vivid picture of what life had been like when they began to build their first huts. Digging ditches to drain the soil had taken them many months of unforgettable toil. During that time, they had lived in wooden shacks erected on concrete piles driven deep into the soft ground. Yet even at the beginning, they had started to rear cattle and keep chickens. They had succeeded. They had defeated the worst conditions that Palestine could offer any immigrant from Europe. They had won through and proved, they said, that the Jews were pioneers and farmers as much as any other nationality in the world; that no matter how hard and difficult the task, the Jew could do it as well as another. But above and beyond that, they had proved that ground, out of which the government did not believe it was possible for anyone to make a living, could support people, if not in comfort, at least above the subsistence level.

Surely that had been proved already, in other colonies, I thought. Why should these refugees who had been through incredible torments in Europe have to endure the damp heat of the Huleh, to make homes in the middle of swamps, to live in fly-blown huts and toil from dawn till dusk in order to prove the contention of the Zionists that they could do it — and successfully.

When I hinted that there might be other reasons not entirely idealistic for establishing a colony near the Syrian border, the suggestion was met with a vigorous denial. Yet non-Zionist Jews assured me that colonies had been built in these inaccessible and unhealthy areas solely because of their strategic positions. At night, illegal immigrants could filter between the Syrian guard posts, reach such a colony close to the border and on payment of a sum of not more than ten pounds, so I was told, be given suitable clothing — farmers' boots, shorts and open-necked shirts — to pass themselves off as colony workers. In these clothes and with borrowed documents they were able to satisfy the police checks at the Tegart Line and so enter the country for which they had no immigration certificates.

Yet, if this is true, should the Zionists be censured for trying to help refugees from the terror of Europe? It is a question that becomes part of a much larger one — the whole Palestine problem. The authorities, however, are aware that the country has several thousand illegal immigrants — most of them Jews, but some Arabs, and that the bulk of them have crossed into Palestine from the north. Yet despite searches and check-ups, it is almost impossible to root out the illegal Jewish immigrants. They are sheltered and helped by those legally living in the country. And how hard it is to say that those who have found freedom after living under the Nazi heel should not help others less fortunate than themselves...

That day I drove from the Huleh along the border road to a second colony, perched on a rocky hilltop less than a stone's throw from the Syrian frontier. To reach this settlement my taxi passed through a special gap cut in the Tegart Line in order to allow the colony farm-cart to take produce into the nearest collecting centre. There was no police guard on the gap, and an illegal immigrant could have stepped into the freedom of Palestine as easily as one crosses a street.

But if that particular colony was an elaborate shield for illegal immigrants, then those who had worked the stony soil and built the wooden shacks must have been inspired with a love for the homes they were making as great as their sympathy for the Jews who found the doors of Palestine closed. Here were people existing among rocks and boulders on land, which, by the laws of nature, should have been incapable of producing food. Yet, scientifically, each slope had been terraced, rocks cleared, soil brought from the valley and fertilised. Crops were harvested; orchards planted; cows, goats, and chickens reared. And amidst it all there were youths and young girls from offices and shops in the cities of Europe now working with apparent enthusiasm to wrest even more out of the mountain-top.

The mukhtar led me to one of the terraces. "That's Syria," he said, pointing across the colony orchard to the flanks of a hill on the other side. "There's a guard-post just over there. At night we see the light shining."

I asked him about illegal immigrants. "Sometimes," he said. "In ones and twos they come, starving and sick. We put them in our little hospital."

He changed the subject, explaining to me the difficulties of growing apple-trees on the hillside and how, to begin with, they had feared that only the olive would flourish successfully in the gravel soil. Now they had apples and even plums. Next year they were going to try other fruits — guava and custard apple, mulberry and pear.

We went into the colony kitchen. Here, where the flies clung in black clusters to tables and plates, I sat down with the farm workers to a bowl of cream and cheese with fresh bread baked in the colony ovens. The kitchen was stark and plain with its wooden benches and cheap feeding utensils. But in another ten years, if the mukhtar's plans worked out as he intended, the mountain-top would be dotted with red-roofed chalets and the communal kitchen would be a great cool hall, floored with tiles and furnished with comfortable chairs, curtains and mats.

* * *

I visited one more colony before returning to Hadera — Nahalal, the first smallholders' cooperative settlement to be formed in Palestine. It was started in 1921, on the swamps and marshes of the Jezreel Valley that drain out into Haifa Bay, by a body of Jewish immigrants culled from all parts of Europe. The majority of them had not known persecution; they had come to Palestine as pioneers and as such, they were prepared to suffer and endure the long weary years of work needed to turn the swamps into fertile farmlands. First, money was borrowed from the Jewish National Fund and with this capital, the colonists bought pumping machinery to drain the soil and building materials to erect their first dwellings. Gradually the land was reclaimed, crops sown and stock bred. There were many setbacks. The first harvest was destroyed by field mice; the first herd of dairy cows died in a cattle plague.

But the colonists carried on. Today, Nahalal has paid back its loan from the National Fund and is a flourishing self-supporting settlement. The seventy-five families of pioneers who founded the colony — two hundred people in all — have preserved their family life. There are still seventy-five families in the settlement although the population is over eight hundred. Each family now owns nearly nineteen acres of grain land and seven of pasturage and eucalyptus grove.

I was told this by one of the colonists, Aaron Hasin, whose family had been one of the original seventy-five. "The cooperative life is very different to what you have been seeing in the other colonies," he said, "Here we don't give our children up to communal nurseries nor eat in the general dining-hall. Here, in one of the moshavim, as they are called, we do our buying and selling cooperatively, but our family life is preserved."

Hasin told me that one of the most important things they had all learned was how to help each other in times of need. "If one of the settlers falls ill, then his neighbours keep the farm going until he recovers. If a man dies, then his wife is given a permanent farm worker at the settlement's expense to see that she has sufficient to live on and keep her children."

"And now of course," said Hasin, "permanent workers are attached to those families whose sons have joined the army. This system of mutual self-help is one which has never failed us."

Hasin took me around the settlement, along the great circular road flanked with its neat tree-shaded villas and prim flowerbeds. There were children playing in their own gardens and women taking in clothes from the washing-lines. It was like a housing estate in England, a garden city on a miniature scale. Those Jews who have been fortunate enough to settle in Nahalal seemed to me to have achieved happiness perhaps greater than they would have known in Europe. Here was the contradiction to those who claimed that the colonies destroyed family life, moral codes, indi-

71

viduality and ambition. Here was proof that the Zionist experiment was not failing.

* * *

Back in Hadera, I talked to Zionists and non-Zionists about the places I had seen. The non-Zionists said: "Nahalal — ah, but that is one of the exceptions. It is the ordinary colonies — the *kibbutzim* — that we don't believe in. Places like the one you saw near Pardess Hanna and those beyond the Tegart Wall where the settlers are not paid for their work, where each is given food, clothes and housing — where each becomes a cipher in a political adventure."

The Zionists said, "Now you have seen a part of the tremendous effort being made by the sons and daughters of Zion in order to rebuild the Jewish State, you will no longer believe the accusations of those who are against Zionist ideals; nor will you listen to those who will tell you the colonies are shields for illegal immigration."

I answered them both as frankly as I could.

One girl, a new immigrant, staying with friends in Hadera said, "Go on a colony? Not until I've spent my last piastre. Be a piece of propaganda for the Zionists, so they can say, "Look there's one of our happy colony girls working away for Eretz Israel? No — not me!"

Viewpoints like these made me realise more acutely than anything else that the European Jews in Palestine, no matter what propaganda is circulated on the subject, are not coalescing into a nation, and have little likelihood of doing so under present conditions.

Chapter Four
July 1943

*Provocative stories in Jewish newspaper — Old Ma
Dubrowsky carried to her grave — Feasting at Irtah —
Hassan Abu Issa on Palestine's future — Pigeons and
flutes — Fatalism among the immigrants.*

Throughout that summer in the Hadera area there was a
minor crime wave indicative of the major unrest in the
country. It threatened to disrupt the peace of the village
and produced a tension akin to that which usually culmi-
nates in Palestine in a bomb outrage. The police worked
energetically to combat organised robberies and hold-ups
by both Arabs and Jews.

Kurt's friend, Eliahim, who kept a drapery shop in the
centre of Hadera, was robbed in daylight of one thousand
pounds' worth of stores by an Arab gang who escaped
before the alarm could be raised. Some of the goods were
later found in Tulkarm; most of them had trickled across
the eastern frontier into Transjordan.

Police dogs were employed night and day following trails
out of the Hadera area as each week yet another robbery
was carried out.

"It will get worse," said Kurt. "As the cost of living
increases, as everything becomes more and more scarce
except on the black market, there will be gangs of thieves
all over Palestine; in the cities, and the villages, everywhere."

The mounting tension throughout the country was not
relieved by the note of hopelessness in the Jewish newspapers. Side by side with stories of robbery, theft and
violence there was published news of post-war plans for

Palestine that held out no hope of settled peaceful living, but rather perpetual striving against great odds. The *Palestine Post*[27] re-printed one of the most challenging statements I had yet read. It was written by a Palestinian airman, Corporal L. Weissberger, in reply to the question "What I want after the War" and had found its way into the *Air Force News*, an RAF Middle East publication.

Here is Weissberger's reply: "The Palestinian airman gets back to Palestine to find agriculture and industry flourishing, security in villages and colonies, gaps between Jews and Arabs bridged — collaboration under a spirited government.

"His family from the battered Continent, having withstood the Nazi onslaught, preserved soul and body for the future — is now given the prayed-for rest.

"People freed from fear and suffering, building, ploughing, teaching and learning: Mount Scopus once again carrying the torch of civilization into lands of sand and rock; ships filling the harbours of Haifa and Tel Aviv; the air humming with the roar of giant passenger planes meeting on their way from East to West. And then the demobbed Palestinian airman will say to another Palestinian airman: "It was worth fighting for.'"[28]

But the question was "What I want after the war." not "What do I expect after the war?"

Such statements as this, touching on some of the most burning problems in Palestine — like the building of a harbour at Tel Aviv, which that would draw trade away from the adjoining Arab port of Jaffa — seemed unnecessarily provocative.

But those Jews who had joined the armed forces, of their own will or through persuasion from the Zionist trade union, the Histadrut, and other Jewish bodies, were being increasingly used as spokesmen.

Not only Palestine Jews were caught up in this political net. The Zionists casting near and far for proof that the Jews were a nation — that they should be given the right to have an army of their own to join in the

European crusade — brought in British subjects of the Jewish faith to underline their contentions. Flight Sergeant Sidney Cohen of the RAF, whom the British popular press styled the "King of Lampedusa" after the Italian unit stationed on the island had surrendered to him, was entangled in the net. English-born Sidney Cohen found himself inscribed in the *Golden Book of the Jewish National Fund* as a hero of the Jewish nation. *The Jewish National Fund* announced its intention of opening a special page in its Golden Book for Jewish men and women in the armed forces of the United Nations[29] who had distinguished themselves in action. I wondered what the reaction would be of those Jews living in Britain and America who had become assimilated into the nations in which they were born. Did they really want to be different from other communities, Methodists, Roman Catholics, who had also struggled long and hard for acceptance?[30] Did they really think of themselves as another race?" Above all, did they really feel the need for an army of Jews?

There was of course no non-Zionist newspaper in Palestine to give balance to the propaganda of the Hebrew press; and few Jews, who, except in private conversation, would dare to voice such sentiments.

Another unnecessarily provocative story was an appeal published that July in the Zionist newspapers, signed by various influential Palestine Jews and addressed not only to their brethren in the country but to Jews everywhere. The appeal asked for their support in setting up a temporary Jewish government in order to:

— intensify the war effort and ensure the status of an ally and fighting partner to the Jewish people.

— establish unity and peace within the Jewish camp.

— ensure the participation of the temporary Jewish government in the future peace conference.

— rescue the remnants of the Jewish people in the countries occupied by Israel's enemies.

— ensure the final solution of the Jewish problem, namely the redemption of Israel in its homeland.

The appeal ended by urging the Jewish Agency, the Vaad Leumi and other Jewish institutions to assist in realising the scheme.

Already the Arabs of Palestine were being unnecessarily provoked by the belief that the Zionists had in the country a shadow government ready to take over if and when the Jews should be given their state. A request for an open government, even though temporary, was bound to cause more unrest and bitterness.

A more forgivable piece of propaganda — this time with the legitimate excuse of being hard news — was the announcement in mid-July of the birth of one Imanuel Solnik, described as the first Pretender to the Jewish throne to be born in Palestine since the fall of Jerusalem and the destruction of the ancient Jewish kingdom. His birth was the occasion for a flood of congratulatory telegrams, among them official ones from Ben Gurion[31] of the Jewish Agency and Altman[32] of the New Zionist Organization [the Revisionists].

At the same time, the *Palestine Post* announced "that the Jewish birth rate in Palestine was higher in the decade from 1926 to 1935 than that of any European country except Romania,"[33] and "though it has fallen most recently it is surpassed now in Europe only by Romania and Portugal."[34]

This in itself was a straightforward statement but to those likely to be inflamed, provocative, because of its alignment of the Jewish community as a nation beside other nations in Europe.

* * *

How tired one grew of examining and dissecting apparently simple stories in the local press; of having pieces pointed out by one's friends, criticised and destroyed. Where was the coalescence of all Palestinian subjects into one peaceful community — the Jews and the Arabs — or the Jews alone? Was there an honest desire for peace anywhere, in the entire country?

I knew that if I was to answer those questions, I could not do so by staying in the seclusion of Hadera, where if I wanted I could shut myself away in my penthouse and be at peace with the sun or the stars. Yet it was difficult to wrest myself from the countryside, to say goodbye to Kurt, Old Ma Dubrowsky, and the many others whom I had grown to know intimately in the village.

When I hinted I must go they would not hear of it and as the summer moved on it was not I but Old Ma Dubrowsky who left us first.

She had been sickening for days, lying in her bedroom at the side of the hotel, unable to speak yet wanting to say so much to those around her. She died one night, a hot moonless night when the streets were breathless and no breeze stirred the leaves in the grove or the banana fronds. Pyedogs there were, moaning through the village, and down below, the sound of women sobbing.

I felt as if a voice of sanity had gone out of the village, as if I had lost the one person who amid the clamour of many tongues would speak to me with immense wisdom about the country. The next morning when I was awoken by the banging of metal tubs as the village undertakers arrived with their paraphernalia I wished that I had already left Hadera. Here was no dignified exit from the world, but only the ignominy of death. Zinc tubs, undertakers, and outside, surrounded by a little mob of village children, the wooden hearse ready to be drawn by its one emaciated nag. The sparrows flew down from the eucalyptus to perch on the oblong roof and to chirrup madly as they fluttered beneath into the open bier. Orthodox Jews had come as mourners. They stood around the hearse, one or two smoking as they waited for Old Ma Dubrowsky's body to be brought out.

The waiting seemed interminable. First, the undertakers came with their tubs that, which they stacked below in the hotel yard. Then a crowd of men and women, friends and distant relatives and Old Ma Dubrowsky herself loosely swathed in a black shroud, carried by the men. They moved down the outside staircase in a tight wedge out through the hotel entrance into the street. The rubbish-bin cats streaked across the yard; soldiers drinking beer outside the next-door café stood up, bewildered, as the body was borne past and laid on the bier. Then, as the rickety hearse moved off, the procession changed its mind. The bier was pulled away and Kurt and three others, slinging it on its wooden poles, set off down the village street. The undertakers turned the hearse around, stacked the zinc tubs inside and departed.

Up the hill in front of the hotel, I watched the procession growing smaller. The sun beat down furiously on the mourners. A camel ambled past, a bus; an army truck; in twos and threes, the children began to trickle away.

* * *

Before I left Hadera, I went to feast in the Arab village of Irtah.[35] I had been invited with a party of Jewish friends and we were met on the main road beyond Tulkarm by a village deputation. Two or three Arabs from the village who had worked on army installations and spoke English escorted us up the long winding lane towards the cluster of houses. The entire length of the lane had been covered with straw and chaff so that the visitors should not stumble on the stones or have to walk in the slush and dirt left there by the village cattle and goats. This thoughtfulness — I found it overwhelming — was but the beginning of a series of courtesies which made the evening one of the most delightful experiences I had.

First, we were led to the mukhtar's house and seated on red plush chairs specially set out in the open. The village men had gathered there to greet us. They stood around in a great semi-circle facing our seats of honour, and gravely listening to conversations they could not understand.

78

Then the mukhtar himself brought us coffee, sweet, thick and scalding hot. We sipped it ceremoniously, while through the side door of the house we could hear the clatter of dishes and women's voices as the meal was being prepared.

In that quiet dusk with the aromatic scent of dried dung blowing over the village and the sound of boy shepherds driving their flocks into safety for the night, I could have sat silent and imagined myself a hundred, two hundred years back. Irtah in the days of the Ottoman Empire had been I knew very much what it is today. Arab villages do not change. Western civilization may bring improvements, but the village as an entity remains. The houses of Irtah, square with flat roofs, clustered together in an indigestible mass, had looked to the Turkish tax collector two centuries ago exactly as they did to us that night.

But I was not to be left in peace. One of those who had met us, Hassan abu Issa, began to probe into my political views. "What did I think of Palestine?" he asked me quietly. "What did I think of the Arab–Jew problem?"

I told him that what I was witnessing that night — the easy mixing of members of both religions — gave me new hope after many weeks of gradual belief that the Palestine problem was insoluble.

"But this," said Hassan "is nothing to do with the politicians. This is the ordinary Jew and Arab getting together and being friendly. I believe that the ordinary people in Palestine want to mix with each other, and it isn't their fault that they don't. It is because they are not really allowed to. You see — the Arab political leaders wouldn't like the Jews to be accepted as Palestinians like ourselves. And the Zionists would find their political platform collapsing under their feet if there was no need for a Jewish state because the Arabs were prepared to welcome Jews into the country. The trouble is the ordinary Jews and Arabs never get a chance to say how they feel about things. The Husseinis and the Nashishibis — they speak for us —

and their immediate followers preach hatred against the Jews and incite us to violence..."

I found that Irtah had been regarded as one of the "good" villages during the pre-war troubles. The police in nearby Tulkarm had not raided Irtah or arrested any of the villagers. But this was an exception in an area infested with armed Arab bands and torn with political feeling. On hillsides around Irtah, isolated groups of mud houses and Bedouin tents had been centres of terrorist activity.

"And they will be again," said Hassan, "if the Jews should rise in revolt."

"Do you really believe they will?" I asked him.

"For us village Arabs — the *fellaheen* — it is difficult to know. We are told they are planning to seize the country by force, that they have secret arms dumps hidden in different parts of Palestine and that those who have joined the British forces have done so not so much to fight the Germans but to train themselves to fight us later. If it's true, then we shall fight back. But I don't believe it's true — not on such a vast scale as the Arab politicians make out. There are a few Jewish terrorists — just as there were Arab terrorists. But they don't represent the ordinary Jews in Palestine — the people in the colonies and villages who are just as much real people as we are, like the friends we have invited here tonight."

Hassan told me his father had been the imam of a mosque in the Hebron area and he had come into contact with many British people. "I suppose that's why I have a more moderate outlook than most of the Arabs," he said. "But even I would feel called upon to take up arms if there was civil war."

Darkness had fallen as we talked and through an open doorway we could see trays of food being carried from the kitchen into the room where we were to eat. When it was ready we were led inside by the mukhtar and seated at the table. The women who had prepared the meal did not appear. We were waited on by the mukhtar and the leading men of the village.

Arab meals are usually overwhelming. This lived up to Arab reputation. The table was laden with a variety of hot and cold dishes: roast pigeons stuffed with rice and nuts; chicken wings; liver fried with green peppers; kebabs — highly seasoned minced meat; kidneys swimming in *semna* (the Arab cooking fat made from sheep's tails, which in Palestine are the richest part of the animal) and served with pita, flat circles of bread warm from the oven.

We ate our fill, and had more loaded on our plates. Knives and forks had been provided out of deference to Western custom; but to our hosts' delight, we preferred to tear the pigeons apart with our fingers, not forgetting the suitable belches afterwards to show how much we appreciated the good cooking.

At last we had demolished the bulk of the dishes and the remains were taken away to be distributed amongst the villagers outside. Then we were served with great bowls of sugar and watermelon; sweet yellow and rose pink slices from the best of the crop grown on the village lands.

When our hosts ate we did not discover. Immediately after the meal, the table was cleared and chairs lined around the walls. Then selected representatives from the village came in to sit and entertain us.

What an entertainment was provided! Arab shepherd boys with their thin quavering flutes played the ancient melodies of the hillsides, while the men accompanied the tunes with the haunting half and quarter tone songs of the Arab world.

And as the evening wore on, and the music became faster, the village men in twos and threes danced on the carpet in front of us.

Later we moved outside. The moon was coming up over the minarets of Tulkarm and swathes of light picked out the rooftops of Irtah. In front of the chairs where we had sat ceremoniously, there was a patch of bright moonlight. Here the pièce de resistance of the evening was performed. A score of village men, linked in a chain made from their leather waist-belts, danced like a long sinuous snake to the weird music of the flutes and the quavering twangs of the one-stringed Arab violins.

Only then did the women of the village appear. In shy huddled groups, they came round the corner of the house where we had fed and seated themselves on the stone parapet in front. When I went over to talk to them they hid their faces behind their head wraps as they held out their babies for me to see. One boy, Hassan's son, ran to hide in the folds of his father's abba; he spoke a few halting words of English to me, then returned to the security of his mother's arms.

"You see," said Hassan, "Our children — they are like any other children. Jews and Arabs, English and other Europeans — there is no real difference. It is only the way we are brought up — the way we are taught — which turns us into peaceful citizens or criminals."

Later, in Jerusalem, when I saw Arab and Jewish children fighting each other, I was to remember Hassan's words, and to realise that it was not only the politicians and the press that were inflaming Palestine but the teachers in the schools who were preparing the soil for the seeds of strife.

We left Irtah at midnight. The moon had climbed overhead and a clean light illuminated the village and the straw-covered path. Hurricane lamps guided us over the worst stretches, and some of the children, overcoming their shyness, went with us as far as the main road.

We thanked our hosts. They drowned our thanks with cries of "Come again. Salaam — but come again. Always you are welcome here."

We drove off into the night, through the empty lanes and across open arid countryside where only the pye-dogs were howling and the Bedouin had long since drawn the outer flaps of their tents. Olive trees flew past the windscreen like gaunt ghosts. There was an air of unreality about everything, as if Irtah and what I had heard from Hassan had been only a wishful dream, a minority opinion that could neither influence others nor alter by one brick the crazy edifice that was Palestine.

* * *

August broke on Hadera like the angry breath from a kiln. The flowers had withered in the gardens and save for the dark splashes of cypress and palm the landscape was brown and dry. Trucks moving along the asphalt road left deep grooves in the sun-warmed surface. Women wheeled their prams wearily through the village; shopkeepers sat sweating behind their counters; the cafés were filled with soldiers drinking warm beer.

In the late afternoon when the sun was beginning to drop over the dunes I would go out on the roof to watch the passers-by and ask myself, now that I was leaving Hadera, how the European women could face living out their lives in the village. Heat, monotony, the growing fear of "troubles", the constant struggle against the rising cost of living, the scarcity of food, clothes, security. Was it possible that even those most violently anti-Zionist were at heart, in their sub-conscious, at sympathy with the main aims of Zionism? Or did they endure this alien climate simply because they had no other place to live? That was no reason for the settlement in the village of Jews from America and England, or from such places where there had been no persecution yet. Had they come to Palestine because they believed it would mean a happier, better life and now had neither the money nor the facilities to return?

"Kurt," I said, on my last night in Hadera. "If you could go back to Europe tomorrow, to a peaceful Europe with money to be earned and the home you used to have — would you go?"

Kurt shrugged his fat shoulders. "I can't," he said shortly, and added beneath his breath, "ein davar" (equivalent to the Russian *nitchevo* or "so what?").

We were drinking tea in the hotel kitchen while Ruth was busying herself over a stewpan, cooking *gefulte* fish — stuffed carp.[36]

"If you're honest," said Ruth, "you'll admit that you'd go back."

Kurt shook his head. "No. I'd want to — but I wouldn't. Palestine saps ones energies. We shouldn't have the courage to return. People who have lost as much as you and I grow fatalistic about it. We say "ein davar" and go on, knowing that we shall still be going on in the same way in ten or twenty years' time. We don't think beyond tomorrow. What's the good?"

Kurt flicked a cockroach off the kitchen table and filled my glass with old tea. "We're in Palestine and we've got to put up with it — and that's it. But the Zionists would have a mighty big shock if they knew what some of us really felt."

Kurt came up on the roof to help me with my bags. Malka, my Russian maid, had tears in her eyes. She could still speak no English but she bade me goodbye with a flood of soft Ukrainian dialect and an injunction that Kurt translated as meaning: "You will come back to Hadera because you will not be happy in Jerusalem. They are all strangers there. You must return."

I left her feeling saddened and uneasy at my change of home; yet determined that the sleepy monotony of the village should not claim me permanently.

Chapter Five
August 1943

Leaving Hadera for Jerusalem — Tel Aviv and its first air raid — Monastic interlude at Latrun — Jewish units in the desert — I quarrel with a Zionist publication.

The road to Tel Aviv stretched like a black ribbon between the sand dunes. On either side, lay clusters of Arab mud houses and square white Jewish villas built of reinforced concrete. Colony girls and Arab village women stood in little groups by the road, waiting for buses. Palestine Police tried to thumb lifts. Lorries filled with yellow melons rattled along, driven by Arabs in their white kaffiyehs and Jews in khaki drill caps.

We passed through belts of citrus groves where the pale green of the lemon trees contrasted softly with hedges of cypress, out into the open sand-wastes, then again into cultivated areas.

Tel Aviv has no grandiose approach. On the way into the city one drives through the slums of Petach Tikvah — a collection of tumble-down wooden and cement dwellings which is all that is left of what at one time was a flourishing Jewish settlement. Only the very poor now live there — the beggars from Tel Aviv; and those who are in hiding from the police, or trafficking in arms.

Beyond these slums, the skyline of Tel Aviv looks like a miniature Manhattan, an illusion that leads one to expect the buildings to be as solid as New York's skyscrapers, and as prosperous. But Tel Aviv is not prosperous. Its economy is as brittle as its tenements. Each lives off his neighbour. Those with capital have little in which to invest it except land. The price of land in the city area has rocketed to more than three hundred per cent its pre-war value. The main streets are lined with chromium-plated shops, expensively dressed windows, modern stores and cinemas. Behind, in the narrow ways leading down to the seafront or running inland towards the Sharon Plain there are cheap houses, cracked and crumbling; and slum blocks where garbage is thrown in the gutters and the people live in a physical misery made bearable only by the perpetual brightness and warmth of the sun.

I found the entire city full of such strange contrasts. Modern well-equipped hospitals, an enormous surplus of doctors — specialists in every branch of medical science and disease, model schools; and at the same time more beggars than I have seen in the poorest Arab city.

The last time I had been in Tel Aviv was in 1940, shortly after Italy came into the war. Italian nationals had been rounded up and placed in detention camps. There were already several hundred German detainees in the country — well-known Nazi sympathisers. The last Italian boat to leave Haifa, just before Italy attacked France, carried away Italian bankers and businessmen and the staff of Alla Littoria — the airways which serviced Haifa from Rome. Later, pilots of Alla Littoria were to return to Palestine to blast selected targets, which they knew as intimately as one knows one's home town. One day that summer Tel Aviv rocked to the explosion of its first and only bombs. The raid was well-timed; the streets of the city were crowded and the pilots unloaded their bombs down Ben Yehuda amid the traffic and the prams. There were the usual familiar scenes — ambulances with the red Shield of David, fire engines and police. One tenement block received a direct hit. Altogether more than fifty people lost their lives.[37]

As I passed through Tel Aviv again on my way to Jerusalem, I remembered the tremendous sympathy and practical help which had been extended to the people of the city at that time — sympathy which became alienated when the Zionists claimed that, since the Jews had been singled out for attack, they should have the right of retaliation as a nation. Certainly Tel Aviv had been raided because it was a Jewish city. There was no military target in Tel Aviv. It had been a Fascist propaganda raid — brutal but solitary. The people of the city had not had to endure successive days and nights of bombardment as in the cities of Poland and France. One felt there were stronger claims than the fact that Tel Aviv had been bombed to justify the Zionist demand that a separate Jewish Army should be formed immediately and that the Jews should be acknowledged by the Western Powers as one of the United Nations. Was not the death of thousands of Jews in German torture camps a stronger reason for the Jews wishing to fight the Wehrmacht and carry the Zionist flag across the battlefields of Europe?

Because of the Zionist demand immediately following the bombing, it was unfortunate that the people of Tel Aviv evacuated themselves in their hundreds into the Sharon Plain or up into the Judean Hills, taking with them exaggerated accounts of what had happened. I found few people at that time who were ready to give the evacuees sympathy when they realised they didn't intend to return to Tel Aviv for many months. Instead, I heard criticisms on all sides of Jewish lack of courage and such anti-Semitic sentiments as "Do them good to be properly bombed..." Yet the people who had fled out of the city in buses, taxis and carts had had their nerves shattered long before the war began with all its accumulated fury. They had known hell in the concentration camps of Germany. Was it right that the Jews as a body should be censored for the reactions of a minority who had been broken in spirit and health?

British soldiers who visited Tel Aviv that autumn were however bewildered to find that even those who had remained behind would not walk in Ben Yehuda Street or the other bombed areas at the time of day when the Italian planes had come over. Ben Yehuda Street, for several weeks after the raid, was a street of the dead.

The slogans chalked on the walls of the city after the 1940 raid were still blazoning their messages as I drove once again along the main streets three years later:

"WE WANT A JEWISH ARMY!"

"GIVE US THE RIGHT TO FIGHT"

"WE WANT PALESTINE"

The British authorities were more than willing for the refugee Jews to join British army and air force units, so why this insistence on the Jews being formed into a separate self-contained fighting force, especially when such action would of necessity provoke the Arabs?

* * *

On my way to Jerusalem, I went to visit the famous Trappist monastery at Latrun — a haven of peace in the midst of political and religious strife. The monastery is a large red and white building with fine columns and archways, surrounded by extensive vineyards and olive groves. Latrun is renowned for its wines and its fine Muscat grapes. The monks live on the income from their vineyards and spend the surplus on caring for the poor in the nearby Arab villages. Food, medicines and clothes are distributed free to those who come to the monastery, and a hostel kept open night and day for travellers who can rest there for a few piastres and feed off the best in the land.

When I drove up through the curved avenue leading to the monastery entrance, I saw the monks working in the grounds, their shaven heads gleaming in the sunlight, their backs bent as they stooped over the vines. Only one of the brothers is allowed to receive guests each day. He is chosen partly by ballot and partly in rotation. The rest of the brethren keep their vows of silence, while a few maintain perpetual vigil in the monastery chapel.

Because I was a woman, I was not allowed to tour the monastery. The white-robed monk who ushered me into the hall of the main building would only permit me to walk as far as the chapel. Here each Sunday the Christian Arab villagers, husbands, wives and children, come to pray and receive a blessing. Afterwards there are presents of fruit and eggs and even money, if needed.

Brother Augustus, the one who had greeted me, told me the stories of some of the Trappists who had found sanctuary there. Several had been refugees from Europe, Roman Catholics who had escaped through the Balkans to Palestine and had decided to dedicate their lives to prayer and work in the monastery. There was a Spaniard who had been blinded during the bombing of Barcelona. He had been brought to the monastery by a Jewish girl who had cared for him in Spain and given him food during their long wanderings through Europe. There was also, Brother Augustus told me, a plaque commemorating a British Army officer who at one time had been a novice at the monastery. He had returned to the forces at the outbreak of the war and was killed in action in Tunisia. Sometimes young members of the brotherhood found the rules of the order too severe. They left before they took their final vows. The majority stayed, including several Christian Arabs, converts from the nearby villages who were now fluent in French and Latin and were learning not only scientific farm-work but also the fine arts of the medieval monasteries such as illuminating parchments and bookbinding.

Before I left, Brother Augustus shared a bottle of red wine with me. Unlike the priests who attend the holy sites in Jerusalem, he was diffident about accepting a contribution towards the funds for the Arab poor. "We do not want charity," he said frankly, "By our own sweat and toil we earn enough to keep ourselves and our flock."

As my car drove away from the monastery, I was brought back with a jolt to the realities of the present. While the monastery was drawing its curtains to comply with the blackout, the floodlights of the Latrun detention camp, housing Italian prisoners, were — in accordance with the Geneva Convention — blazing across the valley. It seemed ironical that a house of peace should be in darkness while a camp of war was a beacon for the whole valley.

* * *

When I reached Jerusalem, I found the city shrouded in darkness. Stars shone bleakly out of a moonless sky. The Hebrew evening papers on sale in Zion Square proclaimed the latest sensational developments in the arms trial that had already been running for several days and was expected to last three weeks. People moved in dark masses through the blacked-out streets. The cafés were full, inside and out in the little gardens where one ate and drank blindly, groping for knife and fork and paying ten piastres for knocking a glass on the ground. Food was dear; taxis cheap. The atmosphere in the city was to me one of uneasy calm, ready to snap at a given signal and plunge the people into open strife.

I knew that in Jerusalem I was going to experience once again that feeling which dominates all Palestine — hopelessness.

* * *

That night, in the flat of some Viennese friends, I lay in bed turning over some Zionist publications given me in Hadera and which I had impatiently set aside. Perhaps, I thought, if I read some facts and figures about what was being achieved in the country, I should rid myself of the feeling that it was all to no avail, that the Jews would be better if they were left alone to muddle along in their own ways and not be forcibly "coalesced" into creating such artificial monstrosities as what is called New Jerusalem, the concrete blocks sprawling beyond the confines of the ancient city.

I looked at the August edition of *Life in Palestine*. On the first page there was an appreciation of the late Brigadier F.H. Kisch — a picture showing him examining a German "S" mine and a second picture of his grave in North Africa. The caption ran: "The Shield of David marks his resting place. Next to him lies a British Colonel, Jew and Gentile, comrades in arms, comrades in death."

Why underline the fact that a British Jew — Brigadier Kisch was born in London — was the comrade of a British Christian? Brigadier Kisch, himself an ardent Zionist and at one time political secretary to the Zionist Executive, would I think have been the first to quarrel with that caption.

On the next page of the magazine, I found the story of a hundred and thirty-eight Palestinian drivers — Jews — serving with the Royal Army Service Corps who had lost their lives in a naval action in the Mediterranean: first a review of how the company came into being and its life in the African desert, then this paragraph: "With all their strenuous military duties, the Jewish Transport units found time to think of their Jewish background. Their units were essentially Jewish units. Hebrew was the internal language."

If that company *was* at all representative of Palestine Jewry then the main internal language would have been Polish or German. But why should they give time to thinking of their Jewish background? Surely the Plymouth Brethren in the forces, the Indian Muslims, the Orthodox Greeks or the Irish Catholics didn't sit down in the middle of the desert to think of their religious backgrounds. When their padres conducted services, they attended. Doubtless, in the heat of battle they prayed to the God they had known since childhood. But why should it be necessary to insist that the Jewish units were different?

The article went on to describe the advance from El Alamein and how members of the company were the first to enter Benghazi and Tripoli. Then came a censored version of the action in the Mediterranean: rafts thrown overboard, men staying by their guns until the waters swept over.

"There are no words to describe the fine behaviour of the Jewish soldiers. They showed a high standard of self-control and readiness for sacrifice. A veteran British Officer present remarked to a Jewish officer that he had never seen such exemplary conduct. Men helped each other in the water and maintained calm throughout. They sang Hebrew songs whilst in the water. (Why not just "songs"?) They got the rafts together as well as they could and assisted those who were shouting for help. They clung to floating pieces of wood, rafts and an overturned boat.

"A destroyer passed close by a large group of swimmers but did not observe them owing to the darkness. The men remained in the water until nearly midnight (over three hours) when a minesweeper on the lookout for swimmers came near them. In order to attract attention the swimmers had organised themselves into a group which shouted in unison. Eventually the ship's searchlights picked out one group and the ship drew near. Ropes were thrown to the men in the water. They boarded the ship, which brought them to harbour the following day. Another boat picked up some survivors at another spot.

"One hundred and thirty eight lads did not reach safety. They found their death in the waves."

This was the first action story of a Jewish Transport Company, and so each tiny detail became of tremendous importance. But it was not allowed to stand alone as a straight, forceful story. The anticlimax of political comment was added. Here it is:

"This is the story of a gallant company, a story of continuous struggle against the enemy and unflinching faithfulness to the Jewish cause — ("Why not the Allied cause?" I wanted to ask) — a story of courage in life and in death which fills us with grief but also with pride and confidence. But the story is not ended. It will go on as long as the fight against the enemy and for the Jewish future continues."

There followed a description of the liberation of the first ghetto — in Tripoli, the production of margarine in Palestine, pictures of the Gertrud Kraus ballet and finally a description of the transformation of the sand dunes south of Jaffa into a flourishing settlement called the Holon quarter. I scanned it, but the first pages had made me want to tell Zionist acquaintances that far from achieving what I believed they honestly wanted, they were more likely to reinforce negative views about Jews among ordinary British people, including troops, many of whom had not before considered that Jews should not be regarded as one of them.

Chapter Six
September 1943

The illegal arms trial and its repercussions — Rachlin,
Sirkin, Rita Max — Arab reaction to Jewish arms running
— The late Fakhri Bey Nashishibi — Jamal Husseini,
great-nephew of the Mufti — Arab bitterness towards the
Jews — Viennese Jews awaiting return to a free Austria —
Haganah.

The Jerusalem arms trial will go down in legal history as
a case in which, although possession was not proven, two
Palestinian Jews were convicted of handling three hundred rifles and one hundred and five thousand rounds of
ammunition.

The trial, though rigid in procedure, was conducted in
the intimate atmosphere of a room that had once been the
salon of a private house. It lacked the detached dignity
required in a criminal case, but it made up for such short-
comings with an abundance of drama.

To reach the court one climbed a flight of outdoor steps,
submitted to searches by police officials in order to prove
that one carried no weapons, and then walked through the
witnesses' waiting-room into the court corridor. An Arab
tea-seller with his swinging brass tray sold refreshments to
counsel, witnesses and journalists alike. Journalists chatted
to witnesses, both before and after they had given evidence.
There was constant milling of military court officials, police
and journalists in the corridor flanking the courtroom.
Altogether, between thirty and forty special correspondents, representing the press of Britain and America, were
there to cover the case and once inside the small court there
was little space for members of the public.

In the well of the court sat the two defence counsel, Levitsky and Joseph. Leib Sirkin and Abraham Rachlin, the two accused, were seated with their backs to the windows, through which the Palestine sun burst in a monotonous glare. The prosecution, led by Irish Major Baxter, had to content itself with a small table squeezed between the two prisoners and their defending counsel. Of the few members of the public allowed to watch the proceedings, Yehaved Sirkin, wife of one of the accused, was the only privileged person. For her a chair was set aside by the ushers and there she sat through each hour of the drama, making tedious notes, and as each session ended, rushing to her husband with cigarettes.

One by one, a bewildering variety of people took the stand. Rita Max, the principal witness for the prosecution, was a Dutch Jewess who had come to Palestine with her husband and had lived for some time on a colony. Through her, the prosecution attempted to prove that Rachlin and Sirkin had been concerned in arms running on a great scale. But Rita Max's story served chiefly to detract from the moral characters of the two men. There were sharp questions about Room 13 in a Tel Aviv hotel where Rita Max had stayed with her child and been visited by both Rachlin and Sirkin. There were probings about taxi drives at night when Rita Max and the two men had kept rendezvous with alleged arms-runners. But for a witness who had turned state evidence, Rita's story was disappointing. Despite the help she gave the police she was detained in the women's prison at Bethlehem for more than a year after the end of the case and on release in November 1944 was only given sufficient money by the government to maintain herself and her child for a few months.

But Rita Max was only the first of a cavalcade of witnesses who in the course of their evidence touched on most of the intricate problems of Palestine, including the Haganah organisation, whose name ran monotonously through the case. Despite the laborious efforts of counsel for the defence to keep Haganah away from unnecessary publicity, the details of the defence organisation were freely given from the witness box. Haganah, which had previously been mentioned only in whispers, now became a commonplace subject for conversation in cafés and shops, in schools and in homes: Haganah — the right of the Jews to self-defence; Haganah — the organisation which armed the colonies to protect them against the depredations of the Arabs.

Politically powerful witnesses came to the box to deny allegations against their individual bodies. Mrs Goldie Myerson[38] of the Histadrut gave vehement evidence on behalf of her labour organisation. Ben Gurion, of the Jewish Agency, came to answer indirect allegations against that institution, and shortly afterwards resigned his post.

Throughout the intricate meanderings of prosecution and defence, and the impassioned declamations from the witness box, only two people in that courtroom, apart from the president, remained calm and controlled. And they were the two accused, who, nonchalantly dressed in shorts and open-neck shirts, sat as easily and inconsequentially on their chairs as they might have done in a cinema. In the box they were little different. Rachlin answered questions clearly and fearlessly. Sirkin stated without bitterness that he had been kept under arrest from June 3rd to July 17th without knowing the reason. Though it was not stated from the box, Yehaved Sirkin assured me later that the police had, in addition, not informed her of her husband's arrest. He had disappeared, and it was not for several weeks that she was able to gain any clue as to his whereabouts. When she discovered that he was held by the police and engaged a lawyer for him, the police informed the lawyer that a detention order for twelve months had been issued under the Defence Regulations.

That was the beginning. In the weeks that followed, the Palestine Police worked vigorously and tirelessly sifting evidence, finding witnesses, building up a case which was to uncover so much political slime.

The ordinary details of the proceedings, the final judgment and the dramatic farewell between Yehaved and Sirkin in that sun-spilt courtroom were given in the London press. The repercussions of the case on the situation in Palestine were not.

Leaving aside the turmoil it created amongst the different Jewish factions, the reactions among the Arabs were, to unbiased observers, as censurable as those amongst the most violently nationalistic Jews.

There never can be excuse for gloating; yet the Arabs disingenuously pointed the hand of scorn at the Jews yet again and said, "See who's causing the trouble now? Not us. We made a pact with the government and we're keeping it. Just look at the Jews and their Haganah — didn't we always say the Jews had more arms inside the country than we had? Aren't we right now? And look at what they said in the witness box about Eretz Israel and the National Home. Three hundred rifles! The Arabs have never run arms into the country on such a scale as that. Well, it's going to be easy now to convince Britain that the Jews should not have their National Home — let alone a Jewish state. They have been proved unworthy of it. They've deliberately flouted the government — at a critical time, while Britain is engaged in the greatest struggle of all history — and for that flouting they will pay. We, the Arabs, have proved ourselves to be reliable and to be steady friends of Britain in times of stress. The Jews have proved the opposite. They have been undermining British authority ever since the war began — and they'll go on doing it until there's a civil war or the Jews are sent out of Palestine."

And so on. I heard these sentiments from various Arab leaders, both moderate and right-wing Muslims. In the many conversations I had, there was not one word of sympathy for those Jews — the bulk — who were not concerned with either Hagannnah, the Jewish Agency, the Histadrut or militant Zionism. There was not one thought given to the ordinary Jews — the people of Hadera and the other villages — and to their right to live in contentment.

Often I was to remember that quiet evening in Irtah and the words Hassan had spoken to me about the ordinary people of the country as opposed to the political leaders. And I was to recall the sentiments of the late Fakhri Bey Nashishibi with whom I had several frank conversations a little time before his death.[39] Fakhri, one of the most amenable and free-thinking of the Arabs — he had himself married a Jewish woman — was not scornful of the Zionist effort in Palestine nor unsympathetic towards those Jews who without racial or political consciousness wanted to use the country as a refuge.

"Let the Jews who are already here stay," Fakhri would say. "Those who are here can be assimilated. I believe the White Paper has done more towards solving the Palestine problem than any other document the British Government has produced. Under the White Paper all Jewish immigration ceases after March 1944. And that's right. Otherwise, we shall have the anomaly of a Jewish majority in an Arab country. Ultimately, as things stand, we can be self-governing with a Jewish minority representation in whatever senate or parliament we have. We should be able to live peacefully under those conditions. But if the White Paper is not implemented — if more immigrants are allowed into Palestine — then I cannot be responsible for what the Arabs will do."

And another time he confessed that what the Arabs were relying on was the fact that many thousands of Jews from Europe would want to return at the end of the war to the countries of their birth. "Austrians, Poles, Czechs and even Germans — those are the ones whom we believe will prefer to go back to European civilisation. And that will help to reduce the proportion of Jews in the country and provide the Zionists with the biggest political headache they've ever had."

Fakhri would smile. He was westernised enough to be able to see both sides of a question and to have overcome the Arab tendency to indulge in such ingenuous feelings as plain hate or intolerance.

"But what if they don't want to go back?" I asked him one day. "What if they'd rather stay here, no matter how difficult it is?"

"In that case — we'll have to put up with them," was Fakhri's final answer.

When Arab circles were seething with the sensation of the arms trial, I wished many times that I could hear the diplomatic voice of Fakhri bringing wisdom into the conversation, and using his personal charm to calm and convince his more excitable countrymen.

In the world of the Palestine Muslim, there was no longer any Fakhri Bay. Those who were left to carry the political torch were violent when roused, intolerant and unpredictable.

* * *

Shortly after Rachlin and Sirkin began to serve their long sentences,[40] I met again one of the younger Muslims who had previously tried to convince me that the world would be a much better place if there were no longer any Jews in it. He was Jamal[41], a member of the Husseini family, a grandnephew of the notorious Mufti and distantly related to the Nashishibis. Jamal was as fiercely nationalist as any Zionist. He hated the Jews. In his short virile body he seemed to be all hate and no tolerance. Even so, he had a remarkable sense of humour but one which rarely got the better of him. He did, however, laugh at the antics of his granduncle and treated with contempt his escape from the Middle East to join hands with the Nazis. The Mufti was past politics, said Jamal. He had antagonised the British Government and done irreparable harm to the Arab cause. The Mufti had best be forgotten while the younger members of his family tried to present the Arab case in a different light, but a light none the less nationalistic and no dimmer. "Out with the Jews," said Jamal, and one knew he meant it.

In his lighter moments, he would recite a rhyme about Palestine, which began with Dr Weizmann[42] supposedly saying:

"Shalom, shalom, shalom,
The Mandate now is ours,
Shalom, shalom, shalom,
Thanks to the Allied Powers.

To which the Mufti replies:-

"Ma'alesh, ma'alesh, ma'alesh,[43]
We do not care a jot,
Ma'alesh, ma'alesh, ma'alesh,
We'll hang the bloody lot!"

Jamal's home was in the Greek Colony, a house surrounded with trees and furnished with Victorian settees and knick-knacks. Together with a British intelligence officer, I was invited there one evening. We sipped coffee, made in our honour by Jamal himself. And we talked, inevitably, of Palestine.

Jamal was in no mood for humour. He flung himself into the argument. He became excited, over-excited, as we presented moderate and tolerant viewpoints. He made violent anti-Jewish statements, and at the end of a long harangue, he dashed his coffee cup — from the best set in the house — on the tiled floor. The fragments of shell pink and gold china scattered towards the stairs as he began to apologise.

Beneath those impassive looks and despite his apparent self-control, Jamal cherished, like many Muslims, an uncontrollable temper, a side of the Arab character which English people find difficult to understand. When I next met him in Jerusalem, he was, I could see, no less violent beneath his impassive countenance. We talked in a café, and he expressed to me more rabid anti-Jewish sentiments, underlining them with quotations from the arms trial and gloating, not so much at the publicity given to Jewish arms running but at the fact that the splits between the different Jewish factions had become wider.

"We've had Arab quarrels before, long bitter quarrels between big families, but they are as nothing compared to what we shall see now between the Jews. There'll be the Jewish Agency self-righteously indignant that the youth of the country should be running in arms, and in reality sympathising with the arms-runners. There'll be the Orthodox Jews, those we have accepted in the country for many generations — centuries — protesting at the troubles which the Zionists have brought upon them. There'll be letters in the press, public meetings, demonstrations, and even strikes."

When I pointed out to Jamal that it was the Arabs who had first used the strike as a weapon of passive warfare against the government, he shrugged his shoulders and said: "Yes, we gave them the idea. It was a good one."

The reaction of the ordinary Jew to the arms trial was given me by my Viennese friends. We sat talking about it till the early hours round the old oak table which they had brought with them from their home in Austria. The living-room in their flat had a character which I shall never forget. Here, in mute eloquence, was the story of the family's tragic life, from the time when the old mother — then a young bride — had come from Frankfurt to marry, to the last days when the husband had died in a concentration camp and the two daughters had packed the family belongings, finally been granted immigration certificates and undertaken the difficult journey through the Nazi frontier posts into Switzerland and eventually, Palestine. The story was written around the room. There was the picture of the old mother's wedding, of Selina, the eldest daughter at the time she attended the Vienna Conservatoire, of Shoshannah, young and inexperienced — now a tired woman in her thirties, wearily working at her sewing-machine to help support the home. Selina, who shopped and cooked, was fair-haired with weak blue eyes.

There were premature lines on her face, a tiredness about her walk, for the responsibility of taking in paying guests and caring for her mother devolved on her. Selina had planned a musical career. It was several years since she had last touched her violin. The case was in the corner of the room. The carved dresser carried the pewter mugs which friends from Frankfurt had sent as a wedding present. Against the wall, there was the old tapestry-covered chair which Selina's father had used when he came home from his work at the bank. Each piece of furniture, each knick-knack was intimately associated with the family story and I could see that neither Selina nor Shoshannah — let alone the old mother — were living in the reality of the present. For all of them, their hearts were still in Vienna and Jerusalem might have not existed once the darkness had come down and they sat beneath the cut-glass chandelier.

"It isn't so much the fact that the Jews are running arms into the country that upsets us," said Selina. "It's because we know that sooner or later we're going to answer a knock on the door and find it's someone from one of the gangs, a member of the NMO or the Stern gang, or an official of Haganah, wanting money. They can't go on buying arms like this unless they're getting money from somewhere and it's ordinary Jews like us who are being forced to give it. What would you do in our place? How could we refuse to give what we had and report them to the police instead? The revenge would be terrible. I know what would happen. It would be our mother who would suffer, and that's what they'd threaten us with. If they come to our door, I shall give them whatever they want: antiques, money, anything — and who could blame me? It's all very well for the authorities to say we shouldn't help such people, but if we can't be sure they won't carry out their threats, what are we supposed to do? Palestine, after all, isn't our home. We're only here because we have to be. If I thought that I had to go on living here for the rest of my life, that I was going to settle down here, in this corner of Asia and never return to the land of my birth nor see Vienna again, I couldn't carry on. It's only because we've all made up our minds to save and prepare for the day when we can go back to a free Austria that I am able to go on. I don't feel Palestinian — if there is such a feeling. I'm an Austrian and I always shall be. And if I should ever marry now, and have children, then I want them to be Austrian too."

Selina spoke with all the fervour of a woman proud of her birthright, and I felt that here at least was one who should be given the choice to return. She told me she supposed it would take several years after the end of the war before immigrants were allowed to be repatriated. Her main concern was the fact that the Zionists would convince the British Government that those Jews already in Palestine had no desire to leave the country.

"If only people in England realised how we feel," she said. "If only they knew that to be uprooted from one's homeland and transported to a place which is really part of the East, then perhaps they'd begin to see a glimmer of light in the darkness of Palestine, the chance of a solution to the whole problem."

Selina, of course, did not believe that other Jewish families from Austria, particularly Vienna, could feel any different to the way she felt. Since leaving Vienna, she had I think over-idealised her life there, but even so, I did not doubt that Vienna was the place to which ultimately she should return to settle down.

How difficult it was to compare Kurt's rather sullen philosophy — his *ein davar* attitude of hopelessness — with Selina's outlook, to add up all that I had heard and decide which was a majority or minority opinion.

Even the Zionists themselves were not consistent in their attitude to the arms trial. Institutions like the Jewish National Council were of course indignant about the slanders which came from the witness box about the Zionists. But there were individual members of such institutions who welcomed the outbursts, who felt that it was

103

better for their enemies to come out into the open and to make accusations, which though they might shake the very foundations of Zionism, were no longer secret and so unanswerable.

A Polish doctor in economics and political science, prominent in moderate Zionist circles, expressed the view to me that it was far better for the name of Haganah to have been dragged through the mud of the trial than for it to remain an underground organisation which in people's imaginations equalled the Ku Klux Klan. Haganah was an unofficial body solely concerned with arming the defenceless colonies against unprovoked attack. That such colonies had suffered through being defenceless had been acknowledged many times by the Palestine Government itself, by the Palestine Police Force and by politicians in Britain and America. It was from sympathetic Jews in both these countries that the money had come to purchase the first arms for the Haganah organisation.

As for suggestions that the Jewish Agency was concerned in Haganah and arms running, it could be proved that it was not. Now that the Jewish Agency and the other Zionist institutions knew what their enemies were using as a case against them, they could deal with it.

"And from another point of view," said the doctor, "the accusations at the trial have done inestimable good in creating greater solidarity among the Jews themselves. Here in Palestine, within the loose framework of Jewry composed of people from many far-flung countries, the greatest stimulus to solidarity is broad accusations against 'the Jews'. Even anti-Zionists will stand by their Zionist brethren in times when the entire race is under a cloud of official displeasure."

Chapter Seven
September–October 1943

*The rains — Walk in the Old City — Unholy Sites —
Orthodox Jewish viewpoint — Criticism of Zionists —
Christian Arab minority problems — Beirut and its influ-
ence on the Arabs — Palestine as a crown colony?*

The autumn khamsins had begun. From the Mountains of
Moab the sand clouds moved across to blanket Jerusalem
in a pall of dust and make the last hot days of the year as
unbearable as the early spring. Unlike the gales and blizzards of northern climates, khamsins are not weather
vagaries to which people become hardened. Immigrants
from Europe find their resistance to these hot storms lessening with each successive year. Those who have lived in
Palestine since early childhood become acclimatised; but
for people from Central Europe in their twenties or thirties, khamsins, particularly at the end of the long summer,
are almost unendurable.

But there are compensations for the autumn khamsins.
The last storm invariably ends with the first rains. How
beautiful it is to see the dust being laid, to feel the air
blowing damply against one's skin. After the months of
dry heat, it feels as if the whole character of the country
had changed; as if, instead of being the land of desolate
mountain wastes and sun-bleached valleys, Palestine
really flowed with milk and honey. In staccato drizzles,
and in torrents, the rain pours down, beating the soil into
pock holes, turning the sun-cracked paths into lanes of
mud. Water rushes down the mountainsides, as if it had
been pent up there throughout the entire summer and had
finally burst its chains. The wadis are once again alive

with the sound of flowing water. And before November the first grass has begun to appear and the shoots of the narcissi and the scarlet anemone are showing on the hillsides.

In Jerusalem, beneath the Mameluke walls of the Old City, the slopes become an emerald green and down by Hezekiah's pool wild grasses begin to cover the baked soil. The pool itself, a slimy green throughout the summer, is blue with the floodwaters — like a miniature Lake Tiberias.

* * *

That autumn I went for many rambles around Jerusalem as I tried to sift all the conflicting views I had heard and to rid myself of the feeling that no matter how rationally one looked at it, there was no solution to Palestine, that the people were too complex, too twisted by political or religious feeling to be able to coalesce even into a crown colony.

The Mount of Olives provides the best panorama of the city. To reach it one takes the goat-path by the Garden of Gethsemane, the ancient way along which the disciples walked and which is now used mainly by the nuns of the Russian Convent who come down the Mount into the Old City to spend their few piastres on vegetables and fruit.

Up and up the path winds, steep and rutted, till one has passed the golden domes of the Russian Church, and is able to look back on the Mosque of Omar* and the minarets and towers of the Old City. It is, I think, easier to understand the fatalism of the Arabs, and the fatalism which some Jews are learning in Palestine, when one looks down on that ancient city and sees still standing centuries-old embattlements, the Golden Gate on which the priests of Solomon's temple trumpeted to the Children of Israel, and

*A common misnomer for the Dome of the Rock. The real Mosque of Omar is opposite the Church of the Holy Sepulchre, in the heart of the Old City.

the grilled windows of Solomon's stable overlooking the village of Siloam. To contemplate several thousand years in a minute reduces one to a greater feeling of passive hopelessness or fatalism, than anything else I have experienced. "Why rebuild the temple?" Ruth had said to me. And looking at the remnants of it I could say to myself, yes, why should this generation be concerned with rebuilding the glory of Solomon? The proof of his glory is still there. And in another century or so perhaps someone else will think about rebuilding it. Why should this generation trouble?

Walking home through the Old City in the rain-filled dusk I would see the ordinary people closing their shops for the night and the women, Muslim and Jewish, hurrying back with their purchases. The picture would seem so quiet and normal that it was difficult to reconcile it with what I knew was happening in the political underground. Sometimes I wanted to blind my eyes and close my ears to everything of real importance, and indulge in a simple tour of the holy sites where I should see only what the tourist sees and hear little but the detailed ancient history of Palestine. But there could be no satisfaction in visiting places which had been converted into religious pantomimes, sites without authenticity where robed monks and starched nuns hung baubles over altars and collected, from incredulous visitors, sums entirely out of proportion for their services. I did not want to see the gilt Madonna on one of the many sites of Calvary, nor slip silver into the hand of the White Father beside what is claimed to be the Pool of Bethsaida. Somewhere, in or near Jerusalem, there had been Calvary and Bethsaida, but I preferred to have them unspecified, and to imagine them as they were at the time of the New Testament.

The money which flows into Palestine from charitable institutions to support the Holy Sites is to me some of the worst-wasted money in the world. While millions of Europeans are suffering the worst imaginable privations, while even the poor in Palestine are sick and starving, there are those in Britain and America who willingly contribute towards the upkeep of such places as the Church of the Holy Sepulchre. That edifice, a living testimony to the bitterness between the different branches of Christendom (the Greek Orthodox, the Copts, the Armenians, each perpetually quarrelling with the other over his few metres of sacred ground) has been proved to have little justification for claiming to stand on the site of Christ's crucifixion. There are many other such buildings which have no real justification for sanctity. Yet it is over the preservation of these sites that some of the most violent religious clashes have occurred. Christians and Muslims accuse each other of polluting one another's domains. A dispute over a metre of stonework becomes as violent as a blood-feud.

Though I could find no pleasure but rather irritation in visiting such places, the lanes of the Old City itself were a constant panorama of interest. Here one saw the whole galaxy of nationalities that gives to Jerusalem its unique character: Muslim women with georgette handkerchiefs — token veils — hiding their shy brown faces; Indian soldiers on leave; Greek priests with flat-crowned mitres; Jewish colonists in their blue and khaki; desert Arabs in black abbas and flowing white kaffiyehs; a Bedouin sheikh with a dagger at his hip; an English schoolgirl in riding breeches; Jewish Settlement Police with the slouch-hats of the Australian bush; the Orthodox Jew in velvet and fur, and the Christian Arab woman from Bethlehem proudly wearing her white headdress draped over a miniature tarbush. The mosaic was constantly changing like the colours of a kaleidoscope, broken only by the flocks of emaciated goats and the sore-covered donkeys who threaded their way through the crowds.

Amid this spectacle, there were two minorities whose racial and political viewpoints I had not yet sought: the Orthodox Jews and the Christian Arabs.

In Hadera, the Orthodox Jews had seemed quaint relics of a bygone age; like old oil paintings come to life in the hot sun, bringing with them the archaic ritual and ancient dignity of medieval Jewry. Once I was able to forget the picture inside the synagogue of those same dignified figures rocking mechanically in their slipping shawls, the Orthodox Jew became to me a person who deserved respect for the tenacity with which he clung to the venerable laws of his religion.

Jerusalem tended to alter my outlook. Here, where the Orthodox Jews could be seen en masse, I grew to dislike the arrogant way in which they strode the streets of the city as if all other peoples and religions were of no account and they alone were the rightful inhabitants.

This was an impression shared by many other English people and one which I never wholly lost, although I grew to know an Orthodox Jew's family with great intimacy and gained the confidence of Mordechai, the eldest son, who had studied English and had a broader, less rigid outlook than the rest of the family. He spent many hours expounding to me the viewpoint of the Orthodox Jew. In the old family house near Herod's Gate, which one entered through a stone archway leading into a tiled courtyard, we would sit sipping home-made wine while Mordechai denounced those whom he claimed had brought trouble on the Orthodox Jews, and exhibited some of the fatalism which all those born in the Near East seem to possess. Mordechai's family, who traced their descent from King Solomon, had dwelt in Jerusalem since the seventeenth century. They looked upon all newcomers as foreigners and even usurpers of their own special privileges.

"The Jews from Europe are not real Jews," Mordechai said to me once, when I had been invited to his house for the brith milah of the latest grandson. "They have forgotten the main teachings of their religion. No longer are they practising members of the Faith, and that is the main reason why they have antagonised the Arabs. Though the Muslims may violently disagree with our religious beliefs, they have tolerated them. We, the Orthodox Jews, have dwelt in this land without let or hindrance for many centuries. We have faithfully abided by our customs, our traditions. We have prayed in our synagogues, observed our fasts and feasts, eaten kosher food and worn our traditional garments. We have been assimilated into Palestine and yet have retained our religious freedom. Under Ottoman rule, we suffered equally with the Muslims. And now..."

Mordechai would then begin a long and bitter denunciation of the Zionists, shaking his side-curls to and fro to add emphasis to his statements.

"Now," he'd say, "the Arabs are beginning to understand that we are brethren of those who come from Europe, that we have common forefathers with those who bring shame on the race by their behaviour in the towns and villages of Palestine. Zionism, what has Zionism done for us who have gone on patiently praying all these centuries and who now see irreligious groups of young people from Berlin and Vienna, Warsaw and the Balkans abusing our traditions? Admittedly, they have begun the building of a new Israel, and superficially it is a tremendous achievement, but I would rather there had not been one new stone laid and have prevented such shame as I have seen. And in what way has this building been started? By young women who walk without shame through the Arab villages in shorts, exposing their thighs, by unblessed unions in the colonies, by those who buy land from absentee Arab landlords, not caring whom they displace, by those who eat butter with meat... These are the Jews who in the very land where our religion found birth are irreligiously rebuilding Israel. And what have they built? There are more cinemas in the country than synagogues!"

It was difficult to sympathise with a viewpoint like this; to realise that it was meant in all sincerity and expressed the true feelings of a small but important section of Palestine's population. Here was an antique bitterness which I felt would never die. Rather would the rift grow wider as the Zionists brought more "evils" of western civilisation into the Holy Land.

Walking home from Mordechai's house along the

110

blacked-out alleys of the Old City, I felt more keenly than ever the tremendous hopelessness of Palestine. Here was no issue between two opposing sides but a problem with hundreds of ramifications, complicated by bigoted minorities, twisted and distorted until those outside the country could never hope to gain a clear true picture of what was happening.

The October moon, shining like yellow acid over the rooftops, seemed only to underline the darkness inside the homes of the city. At sunrise, the muezzin would call the faithful to prayer from the minaret near the police station, and while the Muslims went into the Temple area to wash their hands and enter the Mosque of Omar, the Orthodox Jews would walk down the twisty paths to the Wailing Wall to moan before the blocks of masonry which Solomon had placed there, to stuff prayers written on thin paper between the crevices. And their prayers would be for the rebuilding of the Temple, but not by the Zionists, who were bringing suffering and misery to the Orthodox Jews.

Therein, to me, lay the immeasurable tragedy.

* * *

The Christian Arab viewpoint I found more realistic. Here too was a minority sharply opposed to the outlook of the Muslim bulk of their people, the Muslims and, now that the Muslims were no longer actively opposing the government, fearless in their condemnation of the policies of the Husseinis and the Nashishibis. Since the outbreak of the European war these Christian Arabs — they number one hundred and thirty three thousand in Palestine but only the leading families are rich and politically conscious — had been able to live once again in comparative security, free from the menace of armed bandits invading their homes to demand money for the Muslim Arab cause. And in this forced lull the Christians found time to evolve their own policy with regard to the Mandate, Jewish immigration and the eventual fate of the country. The most outspoken amongst them were of course the students, young sons of wealthy families, the majority of whom were preparing to enter the law. At the YMCA, where I met many of these Christian Arabs, I found that they had all absorbed a certain freedom of outlook, a Western enlightenment which came from their impressionable years having been passed at Beirut University. This institution, run by Bayard Dodge, one of America's wealthiest men, has done incalculable work in educating Middle East Arabs. Dodge, who accepts no salary, has been a pioneer throughout the twenty years he has been on the job. Under his influence, co-education has been introduced into the university and together with the sons of Christian Arab and Muslim families from Kuweit to Akaba from the Hadrhamaut to Palmyra, there have studied the daughters who would formerly have been kept in seclusion. Dodge has done more than that. He has broken down many religious prejudices and induced students with varied religious beliefs to join in prayer together in the college chapel. In one year alone, out of five hundred and thirty-six Muslim students only seventeen attended their own religious services. The remainder joined the eight hundred and fifty-four Christians and the hundred and eighty-two Jews at communal prayers.

Yet once away from the influence of the University old prejudices regained strength. I found that the Christian Arab students had managed to acquire once again in Palestine their inherent hatred of the Muslim. Here at the YMCA, despite the worst autumn khamsin that Jerusalem could produce, these ex-Beirut students clung stubbornly to their European lounge suits. In their eyes, they told me, the casual open-necked shirt and shorts were identified with the Jews; and the alternative, native costume — the cool aba and kaffiyeh — might tend to confuse them with the Muslims.

Despite such inhibitions, I found most of the Christian Arab students broad in outlook, though disillusioned. One of the most sincere I met was George Boustani, son of a

112

Haifa lawyer whose family had moved southward from Syria several generations earlier. Boustani regretted the migration. To him, Syria, with its own important political problems, was still a happier land than Palestine, where he could look forward to no comfortable or peaceful future.[44]

"Palestine's quiet now," Boustani would say, in his faint American accent. "It has to be. Quarrels have been shelved while Britain gets on with the war. There's a truce — an uneasy one — between the Arabs and the Jews. There's an underground truce between the Muslims and the Christian Arabs. But we know what to expect when such truces end. If the strong arm of Britain is ever lifted from the country, we, the Christian Arab minority will lose our livelihood and suffer as other minorities have suffered in Europe. With a population of only one hundred and thirty three thousand, we can't expect to have much say in the government of the country, against over a million Muslims and half a million Jews. If a Jewish state is formed, where shall we be? If Palestine is partitioned and a Muslim ruler like the Emir Abdullah of Transjordan is asked to take charge of the Arab part of the country — our problem is if anything intensified. Either way we shall suffer from religious prejudice."

Boustani was ready to admit that the Christian Arabs held a disproportionate number of jobs in government departments; but this, he said, though it was a cause of dissension between them and Muslims, did not in any way affect the political picture of Palestine. The jobs were not executive ones which could influence the fate of the country. And the reason for their being held by the Christians was simply because proportionately the Christians were more highly educated than the Muslims.

When Boustani finally stated what he would offer as the best solution to the Palestine problem it was this: "Neither a Jewish state nor Jewish and Arab cantonments. So far as the Christian Arabs are concerned I think most of them would like Palestine to cease being a

113

Mandated territory and to become a British crown colony. This is partly selfish, because in a colony the Christian Arabs would be treated fairly; but also because we believe it's the only peaceful way of settling things. However, it would never please the majority of the people. Neither Muslim nor Jew would be satisfied with colonial rule."

Other Christian Arabs expressed to me viewpoints which coincided with Boustani's in the main outlines. There were some, however, who believed that if America took over the administration of Palestine under the League Mandate then there was greater hope of peace. This was suggested by those Christian Arabs who had migrated to America in their youth and returned to settle down in Palestine in middle age. There are several hundred families who have done this and have brought back with them some of the democratic tolerance of the American for other races and religions.

Chapter Eight
October 1943

Deserters hiding on colonies? — The Hulda raid and trial — Jewish right to self-defence — Freedom of the press in Palestine — Khasin's one-man newspaper — Jews boycott the Illustrated News *— Manchester Guardian on the White Paper — A plebiscite for Palestine Jews? — Arab fears — A temporary haven for refugees? — Visit to Maale Hahamish — Afforestation in Palestine.*

There had been rumours throughout the summer that the Jewish colonies were giving refuge to deserters from both Palestinian units in the British Army and from Allied forces. In Jerusalem, I heard these rumours insistently from non-Jews and from anti-Semitic English people. To the Muslims, of course, such rumours provided new fuel for the furnace of hate that was forever smouldering and ready to be enflamed. The colonies, said the Muslims, were not only shields for illegal immigrants, strategically placed near the frontiers or scattered in remote regions so as to make any partitioning scheme impractical — they were armed forts preparing for the day when the Jews would try to take over Palestine by force. As part of this preparation, these colonies were now harbouring deserters on a vast scale so that they would already have a nucleus of trained men later to be joined by those colonists demobilised at the end of the war.

The Palestine Police became more active in their patrolling of the settlements. There were surprise inspections made by mixed forces of police and military in the hope of arresting deserters and putting an end to yet another cause of bitterness in the country. In Jerusalem, I

115

met Zionists who sweepingly condemned such action by the authorities and maintained that no deserters were being given refuge, that the colonists would not deliberately flout the government at such a time and in such a way. There were non-Zionists who told me just as adamantly the opposite.

The Jewish man-in-the-street however, the city-dweller, did not concern himself with the truth or falsity of the rumours. He accepted them as yet another bone to be picked over between the government and the Zionists — yet another cause for disagreement with its train of misery and hopelessness.

* * *

It was at dawn on October 3rd 1943 that the authorities made their most dramatic raid, one which was to arouse the indignation of Zionist institutions in Britain and America and to provide justification for some of the Muslim accusations.

In southern Palestine one of the oldest, and perhaps bravest, of the Jewish settlements is Hulda. Its history has been tragic, but no more tragic than many other colonies. To Hulda have come refugee Jews from Europe, who though not all sharing the ardour of the Zionists, have worked consistently to turn the settlement into a flourishing farming community. They have succeeded.

At the end of September, information reached the military authorities that colonies such as Hulda were giving refuge to deserters from the Polish Army.[45] On October 3rd at 5am a combined detachment of police and military threw a cordon around the settlement. What happened is best told in the words of Brigadier A.J. Allen, the area commander for Lydda District who stated at the trial two months later that he arranged for a system of interrogation of the male settlers, who were brought to tables around which were Palestinian Police officers and Polish security officers. The women of the settlement were allowed to move freely and mixed with those who were already interrogated and those who had not yet been checked up. Everything went on calmly until 9.30 am, when the police discovered mortar bombs and ballistic cartridges hidden in a farm shed. When the arms were removed to open ground, the settlers became unruly. Police were assaulted. Brigadier Allen ordered the mukhtar to ask the crowd to disperse, but the mukhtar had no influence on the settlers. As Brigadier Allen considered the mukhtar responsible for the settlement, he ordered his arrest and also that of two others — Galatta and Sprijer — whom he had found to be inciting the crowd. During the fracas, the women settlers became more active while members of the Jewish Settlement Police maintained a hostile inactivity.

Altogether seven members of Hulda settlement were arrested and tried before the Jerusalem Military Court, charged with the illegal possession of seventy-eight mortar bombs and eighty-five ballistic cartridges. Five of the settlers pleaded not guilty, including the mukhtar, thirty-eight year old Israel Berenbaum. Galatta and one other pleaded guilty.

During the hearing, it was revealed that in the struggle with the settlers thirteen bombs disappeared and only sixty-five arrived at Ramleh police station. The British police driver who made the original discovery of the bombs maintained that it was incidental and that he did not search for them.

Brigadier Allen stated before leaving the witness box that he had received this letter from the Hulda settlement:

"We desire to express to you on behalf of our settlement our very deep regret at your having been personally molested in the heat of the excitement during the search at Hulda. It is because we appreciate the manner in which you and the soldiers under your command acted during those tense minutes that we are even more desirous to explain why we were so outraged at what happened in our settlement.

117

"Hulda has had a tragic history. It was utterly burned down by the Arabs during the 1929 disturbances. Three years later the present group restarted the settlement. It again suffered heavily in the 1936–1939 disturbances when seventeen of our people were killed. Nevertheless, the settlement has been successfully maintained and since the war twenty-two of our one hundred and twenty members have volunteered for military service.

"In the light of all this we trust that you will appreciate how pained and enraged our people were when they suddenly found themselves surrounded by hundreds of military and police as though they were a band of criminals. We beg you once more to accept our heartfelt apologies for the unseemly treatment to which you were subjected."

Brigadier Allen then stated that no Polish deserters had been discovered at the settlement.

After a two-day trial the military court found all seven settlers including the mukhtar, guilty on the charge of illegal possession of arms. Counsel for the defence in a plea for mercy claimed that the whole story of Hulda was in itself a factor of mitigation. Although many settlers had been killed in the Arab "troubles" and a considerable part of their property destroyed, Hulda had at no time retaliated or caused harm to its Arab neighbours. The colonists could be regarded as peaceful and decent workers. The men convicted were the eldest and most experienced men in the settlement to which they would be a serious loss.

The president of the court, Major W. Russell Lawrence, declared that the mukhtar ought to have put his foot down against illegal practices and that if he had educated his people properly this would not have happened. Moreover, nothing had transpired about the thirteen mortar-bombs taken from the police during the mêlée.

Counsel for the defence then pointed out that one of the convicted settlers was the chief poultry-keeper and his work was highly essential to the colony in these days of egg-shortage throughout Palestine. All the accused were

118

married and had children.

Counsel for Galatta declared that none of those who had murdered the seventeen settlers during the 1936 –1939 troubles or destroyed Hulda's property and put fire to their fields had been imprisoned, and it would be strange that these people who suffered so much should be imprisoned for providing for their defence whilst those who assaulted them were at large.

So ended the Hulda trial, with a statement from the president that the people of Palestine were expected to assist the authorities and that the production of mortar bombs must cease.

But the repercussions of the trial were many. To the slanders against the Zionists which had flown from the witness box at the trial of Rachlin and Sirkin were now added the condemnations of the military court against the arming of the colonies. The Hebrew press became outspoken in its criticism of the court's findings. Zionist youth organisations held meetings at which the rights of the colonies to defend themselves against unprovoked attack were upheld, despite the insistence of the government that these colonies would not illegally hide arms. The Arab papers, *Falastin*[46] in particular, slung mud and more mud at the Jews as a body, virtuously underlining the fact that it was now the Jews who were causing the trouble. The Arabs were quiescent and intended to remain so. It was easy for the government to see, they said, who was going to cause outbreaks in Palestine at the end of the war.

* * *

That autumn in Jerusalem, I had an insight into another side of life in Palestine — what is loosely called the freedom of the press. There was of course a strict censorship, both government and military, with a close liaison between the two. Opinion, so far as it did not actually inflame the population, was not censorable.

But freedom of the press in Palestine during the war

was restricted not so much by censorship as by lack of newsprint. Arab and Hebrew newspapers were given only limited supplies. The *Palestine Post*, Jewish-owned and controlled — the only English daily in the country — was no exception. It had to reduce itself to a single sheet. At such a time, a plan to start a daily in opposition to the Post seemed unfeasible. After many months of negotiations, however, a second English daily was put on the market. It was owned by a Russian Jew, Khasin, who was already printing a weekly English paper on the Sabbath when no *Palestine Post* appeared. Khasin, with a totally inadequate supply of newsprint, with only two Intertype machines and one Monotype, a couple of stone-hands and two reporters launched his new daily, The *Palestine Illustrated News*, amid a storm of opposition from official Jewish bodies who began a campaign against the paper, telling influential Jews in the cities of Jerusalem, Haifa, and Tel Aviv to boycott it and sending roundabout instructions to the Jewish newsboys to refuse to sell it on the streets. Into Khasin's possession there came a copy of a circular letter giving reasons why the paper should be boycotted. It stated that Khasin was not working in liaison with Jewish institutions, that his policy was his own, and that as the paper did not officially represent the Jewish outlook in the country, it was not suitable for a Jew to buy.

The first copies sold in Zion Square created a minor riot. Khasin had engaged special newsboys and the *Palestine Post* sellers began a free fight in an effort to drive the *Illustrated News* off the streets. But despite the underground and open war, the circulation increased. Under immense difficulties, the layout of the *News* — hampered by the inadequacies of staff and machines, both primitive — was gradually improved. Whereas the *Palestine Post* played up Zionist achievement, printed all Jewish news available, Khasin tried to devote equal space to both Jewish and Arab news.

Difficulties, however, were to increase. Khasin, who flouted Jewish religious practice by printing on the

Sabbath, wished to produce his paper on such fasts and holy days as the *Palestine Post* closed down. He received anonymous threatening letters, stating that time bombs would be laid in his offices and in the machine-room; that the compositors and stonehands working for him would be liable to personal attack if they consented to produce a paper on such days. But Khasin was not to be beaten. Already the Sabbath edition was being set and printed in an Arab workshop. There each Friday noon the *Palestine News* offices transported themselves — and under the direction of the two reporters, the Arab printers, who could read no English, set the paper by hand. They had learnt the letters of the English alphabet and could recognise them — but in reverse. Despite this, their galley-pulls were often cleaner than those of the European compositors working at their Intertypes. Throughout Friday night, when devout Jews had ceased work, the Arab flatbed press would be groaning at top speed spewing out copies of Khasin's *Illustrated News*. Within a few weeks of the launching of the paper the Arab press was also publishing the *News* on special Holy Days in addition to each Sabbath (though the latter was called simply "weekend" and undated).

English people who grew to know the opposition with which the paper had to contend bought it in preference to the *Post*, although its world news coverage was inadequate and much of its grammar quaint. Military camps placed large orders.

But the boycott, although it had not stopped the sale of the paper, had achieved something far more important. Only a few Jewish firms dared to advertise in it. The Arabs, of course, unless cinema proprietors or restaurateurs, did not normally advertise in a Jewish-owned paper. Khasin struggled on for many months, trying to defeat the unofficial boycott, but except for government advertisements, police notices and the like, the credit side of his accounts was bare. In the end, it was not lack of capital which closed down the *News* — but lack of newsprint

121

itself. Today there is still only the *Palestine Post* for English readers — and its selection of local news, although calculated to obtain sympathy from English people for the Jewish cause — achieves the opposite by a spate of persecution stories from Europe and of political wrangles between the Zionists and the Mandatory Power. For those who see anti-Semitism spreading swiftly and virulently among service people stationed in Palestine, and increasing amongst the English colony, the *Palestine Post* is a daily irritation and as great a boomerang on the Zionists, as are many of the dispatches sent to British newspapers by local correspondents in Jerusalem. Almost all the British national dailies are represented in Palestine by Jews; their cables naturally tend to whitewash Jewish culpability in the numerous incidents between the population and the authorities, and at the same time to play up Jewish achievement in the country with no leavening of criticism. Stories which consistently present the one viewpoint, omit unfavourable facts and give prominence to others, soon pall on the reading public. And so it is with dispatches from Palestine. If British — and American — newspapers could be represented by impartial observers, neither Jews nor Arabs, the people of the Western world would, I am sure, become more sympathetic towards the Palestine problem. There is little hope of this happening. A local correspondent — though permanent — cannot support himself solely on what he earns from overseas dispatches. His main source of income is derived from a salaried job with one of the local newspapers, either the *Palestine Post* or one of the Hebrew dailies. No Arab has yet proved himself an adequate representative of the British or American press. The Arab conception of a news story or a political survey is naïve, often ingenuously violent, and unacceptable to either a popular or more serious newspaper.

But though dispatches from Palestine tend to give a lopsided picture of what is happening in the country, there are certain British and American papers which do sift their stories before publishing them. One of the most scrupulous I have found to be the great Liberal paper, the *Manchester Guardian*. Although its editorial policy with regard to Palestine is pro-Zionist, it has never printed a doubtful agency or correspondent's story on the Arab-Jew question.

In the last months of 1943 as the question of the White Paper became increasingly urgent, the *Manchester Guardian* published several leaders on the Palestine problem. On October 27th, it devoted more than a column to "Palestine's Future", attempting to prove that only the establishment of a Palestine Jewish state could provide the necessary and the permanent remedy. It urged some definite action about the future of Palestine regardless of when the war should end. In May 1939, Britain had adopted the White Paper policy of Mr Neville Chamberlain's Government. The kernel of that policy was that Jewish immigration into Palestine was to be limited to a total of seventy-five thousand persons over the next five years; that "after the period of five years no further Jewish immigration will be permitted unless the Arabs of Palestine are prepared to acquiesce in it"; that the sales of land to Jews should be most severely restricted; and that within ten years an independent Palestinian State should be set up in which the Jews would be held down in a permanent minority. In the ordinary course of events, the *Manchester Guardian* went on, this policy would be imposed on Palestine in May 1944. At the same time, two other things are happening. Discussions are taking place among the Arabs, with the aim of constructing an Arab Federation with an independent Arab Palestine based on a permanent Jewish minority as one of its members. In Palestine itself the recent illegal arms trials are being used to create prejudice against the Jewish community and the Jewish cause.

After stating that it was inconceivable that the present government would petrify the National Home at a certain fixed figure of Jewish population and hand it over to the Arabs as an inferior permanent minority, the *Guardian* quoted Mr Churchill's declaration during the great debate of May 1939 that the White Paper was "another Munich":

Mr Churchill went on: "I could not stand by and see solemn engagements into which Britain had entered before the world set aside for reasons of administrative convenience... I should feel personally embarrassed in the most acute way if I lent myself by silence or inaction to what I must regard as an act of repudiation."

The *Guardian* then quoted Mr Herbert Morrison who warned: "The government must not expect that this policy is going to be automatically binding on their successors in office."

Finally, the *Guardian* itself said: "It is for the present government to say clearly that the sentence pronounced in 1939 on the promised National Home cannot and will not be fulfilled. The Jewish achievement in Palestine, the creation of a flourishing economy, the beginning of a political, social and spiritual centre for the dispersed Jewish race, is one of the indisputable results for good of the last war... There is no place except in Palestine nor can there be, where the wounds of the persecuted Jews can be effectually healed."

This was a fair summary of the Zionist outlook on Palestine. But for myself I wished to quarrel with the supposition that the Jews were a race and with the claim of a "flourishing economy" in a country where the economic structure was as brittle as a Japanese tea-set. That it plumped unreservedly for Palestine as the place — the only place — where the Jews could look forward to health if not happiness was understandable.

I knew that people like Selina and Kurt — although representative of the Austrian-Jewish outlook — were a minority and their desire to return to the land of their birth not shared by Jews from Poland and other countries where there had been anti-Semitism since the Middle Ages. Zionists who read the leader and discussed it with me said there was only one way to find out what the Jews of Palestine really felt about the White Paper, political re-birth, and the healing of their wounds in that little notch of Asia. That was a plebiscite amongst the Jews of Palestine; a free plebiscite in which neither the Zionist nor non-Zionist organisations would be allowed to bring pressure on the electorate and in which every Jewish man or woman could state fearlessly if he or she wanted to go on living in Palestine or to return to the European country of their birth.

The statements of both Mr Winston Churchill and Mr Herbert Morrison had of course been carefully docketed in the offices of the Zionists, ready to be produced at the end of the war when they hoped the Jews "as a nation" would be represented at the Peace Table. But did the Jews want to be represented "as a nation"? Did the assimilated Jews of Britain and America welcome such a policy, which would alienate them from the countries to which they belonged?

I heard many hard words spoken about Zionist aims and their backing by the *Guardian* from English people long resident in the Middle East. Bankers, oil experts and businessmen were losing all semblance of patience with the Jewish problem, as anti-Semitism rapidly increased amongst them.

An executive of the IPC[47] said to me one night: "What the Jews have got to decide is this. Are they a race or a religion? If they're a race then every Jew should be given a Palestinian passport. I cannot imagine Jewish members of the British Parliament willingly giving up their Foreign Office passports. Nor can I imagine any British or American Jew being prepared to relinquish his rights as a citizen of Britain or the United States so as to accept the nationality of an Asiatic country. No — look at it that way and you can see that the only thing binding the Jews together is a common religion — and the links of that bond would have been snapped long ago if it had not been for the Zionists."

Two days after its leader on "Palestine's Future" the *Manchester Guardian* published a letter from Dr Maude

Royden[48] suggesting that Britain should find settlement for the Jews in some Christian country since it was "not Muslims but Christians who had been chiefly responsible for the creation of the Jewish problem." Dr Royden recalled the Peel Commission report of 1937 which, she said, showed the enormous difficulties of creating a Jewish state in Palestine, and added: "Even if it were not so, there remains the question of our right to set up such a state; to cut a small notch out of an Arab country and give it to someone else. The rights of the Mandatory Power do not include the right to give away what does not belong to us."

Several Jerusalem Jews who read the letter agreed that it was more practical and more acceptable to think of settlement in a place other than Palestine. The prospect of emigrating to a Christian country — like Australia — where they would not be under the dominance of the Zionists and free to assimilate themselves into an established nation — gave them new hope.

The *Manchester Guardian* replied in an editorial agreeing with Dr Royden that the Christians owe a debt to the Jews, but added: "The answer is that though some Jews would find refuge in a Christian or any other country that would offer it, no country except Palestine satisfies or can satisfy the aspirations of a return to their own land. The greater part of the Arabs gained freedom only through the victory of the Allies. The Allies asked them to forego that small notch of Palestine for the Jewish National Home and if they are asked now still to forego that much for a Jewish state it should be added that even so the holy places would be entrusted to non-Jewish keeping and a way made easier for such Arabs as preferred it to transfer to any of the neighbouring Arab states."

Here was a gauntlet which the Arabs picked up and made much of. "Are we going to be dispossessed still further?" they asked. "Already absentee landlords in Syria and Transjordan have sold land over our heads to the Zionists. Now they are suggesting that we give up our right to what little land we have left — and become Iraqis or Syrians. Why should we be penalised in this way?"

* * *

In those tense months which preceded the stoppage of Jewish immigration, the ordinary people of Palestine grew weary of the political wrangling in the local and overseas press and increasingly afraid of how such inflammatory statements were going to affect their day-to-day lives. It was known that the Irgun Zvai Leumi — the illegal National Military Organisation — was speedily gathering its forces for what must be a last desperate attempt to stop the implementation of the White Paper. There were rumours of arms running on a great scale, of the arrests of members of the Stern gang as the police tried to combat the rising threat of terrorism, of secret arms dumps being discovered, and of an increasingly belligerent attitude on the part of the colonists themselves who, after the Hulda incident and trial, regarded themselves as victimised for exercising the right of self-defence.

Special guards were assigned to the families of police officials as threatening letters were received first by one high-placed police officer and then another. Opposite the house where I was living (I had moved to the German Colony, to the home of a Berlin Jewess) the branches of the cypress trees were hewn down so that the ghaffir could have a clear range for shooting raiders. Police officers in outlying forts kept their families indoors. Children began to be taken to school in armoured cars — as they had been taken in the pre-war troubles. There were odd shooting incidents; and a swift increase in tyre-jacking as the Irgun Zvai Leumi made itself mobile for the coming attacks.

There was, in fact, every indication that militant Jewish nationalism was going to strike thoroughly and effectively at those carrying out the policy of the Mandatory Power.

To me, and to many moderates I talked to, there seemed to be one obvious compromise which the government could offer, one which would at least allay open trouble in the country while Britain was actively engaged in the war against Germany. The whole question seemed not to be one of actual immigration, but of how far the British Government was prepared to go in making Palestine a temporary haven for European Jewish refugees. The figure of seventy-five thousand to be allowed in during the five years ending on March 31st 1945 was infinitesimal compared to the hundreds of thousands waiting piteously for the right to escape. "Surely," the ordinary middle-class Jews from Europe would say to me, "they can allow these refugees certificates to enter Palestine on the understanding that they are returned to Europe when the continent is liberated. Such a gesture by the government would pacify the militant elements of Jewry and should not arouse great antagonism from the Arabs. How could anyone, no matter what his race or religion, refuse succour to people who are daily facing death in the gas chambers or the concentration camps, or disablement by torture, or starvation and madness. Here in Palestine where the Zionists have hundreds of colonies on which such refugees could be lodged and fed, there is no excuse for refusing admittance. Let us even abandon the creation of a National Home — but let us try to save what we can of the remnants of European Jewry."

There seemed no reason — there had never seemed an adequate reason — why Jewish refugees from Europe, especially women and children — should not be brought to Palestine irrespective of their numbers and kept in specially guarded colony internment camps until the time came for them to be repatriated to Europe. One felt that if the Zionists were prepared to accept responsibility for clothing and feeding such refugees, then the British Government, White Paper or no White Paper, had no excuse for refusing to agree.

There was, however, one important excuse. I found — and it was not in a way unexpected — that the Muslims were bitterly opposed to Palestine becoming a temporary

128

refuge of any kind. "In theory it sounds feasible," they were ready to admit. "But once these refugees have arrived, once they are actually on Palestinian soil we know nothing will remove them. No guarantees, however sacred, would convince us that the Zionists would keep their word over such a matter. Already the Jews are trying to turn themselves into a majority in the country by the intensified rearing of large families, by making everything as simple as possible for unmarried mothers, and by encouraging births and more births naturally and artificially in their great pathological hospitals and laboratories. To allow thousands more to enter the country on the understanding that they will go back — we should never countenance it — nor accede to it. Not only would it undermine the entire plan of the White Paper — on which we stand. It would destroy the faith of the Arab world in the word of Great Britain."

This dramatic and violent reaction seemed to underline the fact that, as Dr Maude Royden had pointed out, it was better for the Jews to be offered settlement in some Christian country where they would at least be tolerated if not trusted.

Christian Arabs gave me a more moderate reaction. The fear of the Jews as temporary immigrants did not seem so potentially dangerous to them. Some of the Christian Arabs had been in Europe and seen the conditions in which the Jews had to live. They did not welcome the idea of temporary immigrants. They did not, on the other hand, discard it. But such a minority reaction could have little influence on government policy.

* * *

It seemed as if nothing could or would be done to avert the disaster then looming over the dying year. As more and more stories of horror came out of Europe — their Jewish angle stressed by the *Palestine Post* but basically true — as one heard of thousands more Jewish refugees swarming

129

into Romania and Bulgaria in the hope of being given certificates for Palestine — I felt as if the name of Holy Land was a mockery in the worst taste. Here, in Palestine, where Christian love had first found expression, where Jesus had been born, where Solomon had built his temple to Jehovah and the Mosque of Omar breathed the spirit of peace to the world of Islam, charity had been preached — and forgotten.

There was no satisfaction, only pain in seeing each day, as I walked through Jerusalem, the rain-washed slopes of the Mount of Olives, and being forcibly reminded that I was living in the City of Peace.

* * *

When I was invited one weekend to tour a forest area in the Judean Hills planted by Jewish settlers, I felt as if for a few hours I might escape from the oppression of the capital and return to Jerusalem with a refreshed outlook.

I went to Maale Hahamish, a comparatively recent collective settlement devoted to forestry. There were the usual familiar figures — refugees from Europe, former doctors, professors and office workers — now toiling to establish woodlands of cypress and casuarinas on the rocky slopes of the hills. There was a great tree nursery where thousands of boxes filled with cuttings were watered and tended by the womenfolk. There were mules hauling felled trees to the road to be sent down to the factories in the Tel Aviv area.

There were also several miles of virgin forest — cypress groves through which I was able to walk on ground made soft with the pine needles and in air that was fresh and scented. On that settlement, I talked to no one about Palestine. I gave myself up to the beauty of the forest and the alien sound of birds I could not identify. Through the thin branches I could catch glimpses of the rolling slopes of the hills, beaten into a jagged mass of copper and cream boulders by centuries of winter storms. And I let my mind wander back over the memories of several Arab towns I had lived in, to Ramleh where one of the things I most missed was the lack of shade out of doors. Amid the scrambled mass of dwellings, there was not one tree to keep off the burning heat. Cactus hedges there were, the frying-pan cactus which grows edible prickly pear, and orange groves and a few eucalyptuses near the cemetery. But the Arab-owned countryside around was bare of woodland, bleak and sun-scarred.

Arabs are not conscious of the need for the afforestation of Palestine, nor of the fact that hundreds of years ago the whole countryside was thickly covered with forests and vegetation. Of the many achievements, good and bad, of the Zionists in Palestine, to me the most admirable is the constant and painstaking work to reclothe Palestine's hills and plains. Over one hundred thousand trees a year are planted by the Jewish National Fund, mainly in the Judean Hills, Samaria and the Jezreel Valley. The King George V forest alone contains one hundred and forty-five thousand trees.[49]

Simultaneously with the individual efforts of Jewish organisations, the Palestine Government has devoted considerable sums to re-afforestation. Saplings and seeds are distributed by government officials free of charge and penalties enforced for allowing goats to devour young plantations. The Bedouin however can rarely be taught the importance of preventing their animals from making a good meal off juicy saplings and side by side with arduous and dangerous work, the Palestine Police have the tedious job of patrolling new forest zones. Despite all that is done, however, the actual area in Palestine under afforestation is still less that 0.2 per cent. Great Britain and Ireland have 4 per cent forest area and Greece, whose climatic and topographical conditions are similar to those of Palestine, has an afforested area of about sixteen per cent.

Chapter Nine
November 1943

Jewish strike — American statesmen oppose White Paper –The "Rape of Ramat Hakovesh" –Uncensored Jewish communiqué — Jewish newspapers suspended — Riots in Tel Aviv — Government offices set on fire — BBC increases tension — Ramat Hakovesh colonist dies of wounds — Shertok on the right of self-defence.

On Monday that first week of November 1943, I saw little knots of Jews gathering in Zion Square and King George Street. My few hours of respite among the trees of Maale Hahamish the day before were soon forgotten as I watched the police break up the gatherings and I knew then that the illegal arms trials were still having their repercussions on the political peace of the country.

The next morning the Jewish National Council called for a strike throughout Palestine as a protest against "the slanders of the Palestine Jews and their supreme institutions voiced in the recent arms trials in Jerusalem and the confirmation of the heavy sentences passed on the Jews."

That Tuesday there was not one Jewish shop open in the city. The stoppage of work was complete. Angry crowds moved through the streets; there were banners and slogans chalked on walls. Indignation meetings were held in various buildings. Even the Jewish schools interrupted their lessons and the children were told by their teachers that they were observing a day's mourning for Rachlin and Sirkin. So thoroughly was the strike carried out that the Hebrew papers which should have carried the instructions of the Jewish National Council failed to appear.

This then was what my Muslim friend, Jamal, had predicted. A strike — which the Arabs had first used as a weapon of passive warfare; but of greater importance than an Arab strike because it was taking place at one of the most critical moments in the history of the Mediterranean campaign, at a time when the 8th and 5th Armies were battling their way up the Italian peninsula, and all Palestine's effort was needed to supply those forces with essential goods. Anti-Semitic people pointed to this as a justification for their outlook. The Arabs sneered; the moderate non-Zionists deplored the action; and many of the little shopkeepers would have liked, but had not the courage, to ignore the order to close. However, a Jew who disobeys the orders of the National Council knows that they will be enforced unofficially. One or two Jewish shops who did attempt to keep open were picketed by Zionist youths and reluctantly closed their doors.

Such action as that ordered by the National Council unwittingly encouraged the more unruly elements among the Jews, and gave a roundabout blessing on the activities of militant organisations. Coming as it did at a time when American statesmen were voicing their opposition to the White Paper, it only increased the tension in the country and did nothing constructive towards gaining facilities for the entry of the refugees still waiting in Europe.

Wendell Wilkie,[50] in a message to a New York Zionist rally on the 26th anniversary of the issue of the Balfour Declaration, denounced the White Paper and called for its abrogation. "The extent of immigration into Palestine must be measured by the needs of the Jewish people," Mr Wilkie stated, "and by their ability to develop their homeland in accordance with the international covenant made with them."

Governor Dewey, in a message to the same meeting, said:

"Now even more than after the last war it is essential that a way be found to open the doors of Palestine. This will be

133

especially true if the doors elsewhere remain closed. Obviously, there is no easy solution. At the same time, if left unsolved, the spectre of hundreds of thousands of hopeless and wandering Jews will simply multiply the aspects of the problem throughout the world. No Jew would tolerate that, no Christian should."

The Zionists adopted a resolution appealing to President Roosevelt to take all appropriate action to open the gates of Palestine and set up a Jewish Commonwealth.

Messages like Dewey's and Wilkie's, sent with one eye on the coming presidential elections,[51] were not of great value. But they were made the most of in Palestine, both to encourage the Zionists in the country and to influence world opinion.

There was no need.

Before a week had passed, the Zionists were given a real hard news story through which they were able to achieve far more than either Dewey or Wilkie could ever hope to bring about. The "Rape of Ramat Hakovesh", as it was called, provided political food for all sides, pathos, tragedy, and opportunity for rousing speeches, demonstrations and more strikes.

The story began on November 16th, when a mixed force of police and military took part in another search of a Jewish settlement — Ramat Hakovesh. There were many versions of what actually took place, varying from the sober official communiqué to the highly-coloured uncensored account published by the Hebrew press. This account, which was not sent to the Public Information Office for approval, was printed simultaneously by all Hebrew papers, who at the same time carried identical leaders. The government immediately announced its intention of suspending these papers, two at a time, while the Hebrew afternoon publication *Yedioth Achronoth*[*52] was suspended until further notice together with the

*Spelling as in original manuscript

morning daily *Haboker*.[53] All nine Hebrew dailies however failed to appear the next day in an attempt to show solidarity with each other. The Public Information Office issued in their place the first number of a Hebrew bulletin, called the *Daily News*, containing telegrams and the official communiqué on the Ramat Hakovesh search, which stated:

"Highly tendentious accounts of the search which took place on the 16th November at Ramat Hakovesh have been given wide publicity, calculated to mislead and inflame public opinion. The actual facts are as follows:

"It was reliably reported to the security authorities that certain deserters from the Polish Army were harboured by Ramat Hakovesh and moreover that at this settlement was a training camp for a unit of an illegal armed organisation and that illegal arms were concealed in the settlement.

"Ramat Hakovesh was accordingly searched on the 16th November by a police unit acting in conjunction with Polish Provost personnel and Imperial military units.

"Certain military equipment was found in a camp within the perimeter of the settlement and the occupants were arrested. The mukhtar and members of the settlement refused to cooperate in the search for Polish deserters and by their attitude rendered it impossible for the Polish authorities or police to ascertain whether any deserters were present in the settlement.

"The settlers further endeavoured by acts of violence to prevent the police from carrying out their lawful duty and generally subjected them to extreme provocation. Notwithstanding the missiles and force to which they were subjected the police maintained the utmost restraint and carried their task to completion with a minimum use of force.

"No shots were fired until, on the withdrawal of the police party, the violence of the settlers reached a hysterical pitch and the officer commanding the party, who was

135

in charge of the rearguard, was obliged, in order to secure the personal safety of the rearguard, to fire two shots from his revolver at the feet of the aggressors, wounding one man but not seriously.

"Thirty-five persons were taken into custody."

This communiqué appeared on Friday. That weekend one of the settlers, Shmuel Woloneitz, died from injuries received during the search. The Jews of Palestine, inflamed by the uncensored account in the Hebrew press, organised violent demonstrations, mass meetings, and protests.

That account of what had happened read as follows:-

"WILD ATTACK ON JEWISH COMMUNITY POLICE FALL UPON RAMAT HAKOVESH"

"Ramat Hakovesh had the appearance on Tuesday of a field of battle. Blows, demolitions and violent assault occurred when hundreds of British police supported by Indian troops broke into the settlement in order to search for arms. The search immediately took the form of a violent attack, and many colonists, men and women, were beaten. Twenty-four were wounded and thirty-five arrested. At 9.45am a number of motor lorries, carrying hundreds of British police and Indian troops broke into the settlement. They were all armed and they placed the colony under siege.

"The attackers overwhelmed the colonists in numbers. The Indian troops hastily put up a wire enclosure and the British police went all over the colony where labourers were working and dragged every man they could get hold of into this enclosure. Even invalids were not spared. People were dragged from their beds. Telephone wires were cut and local police and watchmen overpowered and the arms in their possession seized. Blows were rained upon men and women indiscriminately. One hundred men were now enclosed and as they tried to escape they were beaten mercilessly. A second batch was put in custody separately and their efforts to break out were also unsuccessful.

"The officer in charge asked the mukhtar to help him in the search. The mukhtar replied that he was willing to cooperate if he were informed of the purpose of the search.

"A table was brought and a detective and a British constable who could speak Hebrew sat down. A Polish officer and two NCOs were fetched to assist in identifying Polish deserters. These Polish officers in private conversation expressed their disgust at being dragged into such an affair.

"After a thorough search, during which everything was turned upside down, walls broken up, tiles pulled up — nothing was found.

"When the men were segregated, the women of the colony resisted the police invasion. Blows were rained upon them and the cries of the children rent the air.

"The siege was complete. No one was allowed to enter or leave. A group of colonists was forcibly removed by lorry under pretext that they were responsible for the custody of secret arms. When they were being put into the lorries stones were thrown at the police. The interned colonists made an attempt to break out and some of them succeeded. The place was turned into a field of battle.

"At 3pm the mukhtar was called to the officer-in-charge and was told that dummy bombs had been found under the floor of a tent. He therefore proposed to arrest the twenty men who lived in that tent. The mukhtar replied that he was not present at the time of the search and there were no dummy bombs.

"The officer in charge, as he drove off, drew his revolver and fired. Two colonists were injured in the legs.

"Altogether fifteen men were wounded, five of whom needed medical treatment. When this became known the colonists from neighbouring places rushed to the assistance of Ramat Hakovesh.

"The colonists say that some of the police acted like human beings, but that most of them behaved with the greatest cruelty. People who were in German concentration camps say that their worst experience was to see British police behave in such a way.

"One can imagine the impression on the children of the colony. They will never forget the events of this day.

"During the riots before the war sixteen people lost their lives from Ramat Hakovesh. The number of volunteers from the settlement for the British Army is forty.

"Ramat Hakovesh, which for many years withstood attacks from wild and savage attackers has now had to withstand an attack from the authorities themselves who were unable all these years to protect the colony from people who uprooted their trees, who attacked them by ambush, who killed its men and women, who threw bombs and laid mines. Now these authorities have come and with truncheons and arms have shown the colonists that they must not protect themselves.

"The police who proved themselves impotent against wild destructive elements have now shown their strength against peace-loving constructive people.

"As conquering invaders with violence and cruelty the police attacked this tiny settlement which was suspected of a terrible crime.

"They may find amongst them hidden arms — arms kept for no other purpose than that of protecting innocent lives. Has the government succeeded in disarming the rebels, the breakers of the peace, the agents of the Nazi Government? Is the only danger to the country that of the suspicion of hidden arms in Ramat Hakovesh? Where does the government carry searches? Among those who rebel who destroy, who attack? Not at all. Only among the attacked and at a time when the colony has given many of its best sons and daughters to the army, and while they are away the government has thought fit to make an attack on their defenceless families.

"What was the high policy necessitating this search? To help the war effort? To increase war production? To shorten the war? Maybe it has been done to hasten peace and close the hands of the trouble makers.

"Such a hunt will have only one result, to strengthen the hands of the lawbreakers, to cause disorder and unrest in the country, to forfeit the confidence of law-abiding citizens.

"This attack on Ramat Hakovesh is really an open insult to the Jewish race."

So ended this account which was the main cause of the riots which broke out in Tel Aviv on the following Saturday when eleven British policemen and twenty-one Jews were injured in clashes. The demonstration lasted for several hours. Seven of the British police who were pelted with stones outside the government offices and eight civilians injured in the police baton charges were rushed to the

138

Jewish Hadassah Hospital and to the government Hospital in Jaffa. A fifteen-year-old boy was shot in the chest from a gun fired from a Tel Aviv rooftop. The police fired no shots. The ground floor of the District Administration offices was gutted by a fire started by the mob. The regular guard was barricaded in the building and even the Jewish Special Police on duty outside was stoned by the demonstrators. A flagpole with the Zionist colours — blue and white — was hung out of a window on an upper floor. Later, troops arrived and cordoned off the area. Police established operational HQ in a neighbouring shop and made arrests.

The same day there were also three protest meetings in Tel Aviv, at which a declaration by the Jewish Municipality was read, appealing for the release of the men arrested at Ramat Hakovesh, the lifting of the ban on the Hebrew press and the opening of a public inquiry. Speakers urged the public to keep the peace, but warned the government of the danger to public security involved in the Ramat Hakovesh incident. The Mayor of Tel Aviv and the editor of the Hebrew daily *Davar*[54] backed these meetings.

On Monday, the BBC Overseas Service unwittingly and carelessly added to the tension still prevailing in Tel Aviv when it blandly announced that an unruly mob in that city had stoned Jewish policemen during demonstrations in connexion with the developments in the Lebanon! (The Lebanese crisis was going full-blast at the time.) While English listeners saw the funny side of it, Jews in Tel Aviv and Haifa became enraged at what they considered was a British propaganda twist on what had happened.

The demonstrations in Tel Aviv were violent and prolonged; those in Haifa were orderly but no less intense. Nearly four thousand people crammed the amphitheatre on Thursday that week to hear a full account of the Ramat Hakovesh search. (The hall had a seating capacity of just over a thousand.) Malka Minkovsky, a girl from the settlement itself, was brought to tell the story from the platform. And at the end the massed crowds rose to sing the *Hatikvah* — the Jewish "national anthem". Several lorry-loads of British police stood by, but there were no incidents.

That weekend the authorities heaved justified sighs of relief. It seemed that the situation was quieting. Then came news of the death of Shmuel Wolineitz.

Jewish indignation soared to fever point. The official bodies of the Zionists set about organising the equivalent of a "state funeral." Shmuel Wolineitz became a Jewish martyr, killed on the altar of British incompetency and brutality. His body was placed in a coffin draped with the Zionist colours and brought to Jerusalem for a funeral service outside the offices of the Jewish Agency. Shertok,[55] head of the Agency's political department, delivered an impassioned address before the bier declaring that the Jews of Palestine were resolved not to give up the elementary right of self-defence and of possessing firearms for that purpose. But this public avowal of Zionist policy coming as it did from a man like Shertok — that little dynamo of Zionist ambition — did not create the furore it might have done from a politician less sincere. Shertok, though he may deliver inflammatory speeches and flout the government, has made himself, by his own personality, a well-loved enemy. Whereas Ben Gurion is despised and hated by the Arabs, Shertok is hated but admired.

Shertok began to speak at eleven o'clock. Around him were grouped thick crowds of mourners, including all the members of the Jewish Agency Executive, colonists from Ramat Hakovesh, and even schoolchildren who had been brought by their teachers. There was silence as the soft Hebrew words reached their ears. To me, who had to wait for the speech to be translated, it did not seem that the crowds were being inflamed. On the contrary, as I looked around at the sombre faces I felt that here were people ready to dedicate themselves soberly to whatever their leaders told them — that even the children would not act unless their teachers gave them deliberate instructions. In the coming months, when I saw processions of children demonstrating against British White Paper policy, I began to realise more acutely than ever that it was the Zionists themselves who by their fierce nationalism were causing the next Jewish generation in Palestine to be militant in the Zionist cause. Yet that morning, as the blue and white flag hung mutely over the settler's coffin, it did not seem as if there was a deep political purpose about the spectacle. One found it easy to believe that here was a tragic gathering paying its respects to the dead with simplicity and sincerity.

"When you came to settle in Ramat Hakovesh some years ago, you and your friends stood firm in the defence of your village," said Shertok. "Together with your comrades you made Ramat Hakovesh a symbol of high courage. Later, you went out to build up again what had been destroyed, to plant new trees in place of those torn up, to sow again the fields where crops had been burned, to fill up the craters left by the mines to which your friends had fallen victim.

"And now you have fallen, not in defending life and property, but in defending the right to self-defence. On this front, we all stand firm and united. We shall not flinch before any blind indifference, blundering or wickedness. We all stand here to strengthen the hands of your comrades at Ramat Hakovesh and say: Peace to your ashes."

So Shertok's words floated over the crowds. The cantor chanted the prayer for the dead and after the reciting of the doxology the coffin was borne by the dead man's fellow-settlers to the lorry which was to take it to Ramat Hakovesh. The mourners followed the cortege to Ben Yehuda Street, the children in trim columns flanked by the colonists and the Zionist officials.

A police armoured car and motorcycle outriders escorted the lorry to the settlement. At the hour of the burial all traffic in Tel Aviv stopped during the observance of a two-minute silence ordered by the municipal council. People in the streets of the city stood to attention. Black-draped

Zionist flags flew at half-mast from public buildings.

The next day, the *Palestine Post* began the report of the funeral with the sentence: "In the presence of thousands of mourners Shmuel Wolineitz was ...laid to rest in the Ramat Hakovesh Cemetery near the common grave of sixteen comrades killed during the 1936–39 disturbances..."[56] In Jerusalem, Shertok had an interview with the Acting Chief Secretary of the government. In Rishon-le-Zion there was a mass meeting. From the villages of Rehovoth and Affule came more protests about the "rape" of the settlement. Throughout Palestine, there were even exaggerated accounts of what Shertok had said — statements which people claimed had been cut out of the press reports by the government censor. Jewish schoolchildren in remote parts of the country were given vivid descriptions of the funeral by their teachers. All Jewish Palestine that was able to be organised devoted itself to keeping the memory of the attack on the settlement and the death of one of its defenders as alive as possible. "Remember Ramat Hakovesh" was chalked on the walls of government buildings by youths who evaded the police in the blackout. Illegal pamphlets were circulated, distributed often by young girls and boys. It seemed as if the whole of Jewish Palestine was being incited to harbour hate.

Chapter Ten
December 1943–February 1944

Feast of the Lights — Kurt writes from Hadera — Christmas at Bethlehem — The Irgun Zvai Leumi strikes — Repercussions from Sir Ronald Storr's Jerusalem dispatch — More bomb outrages — I go to Amman — Tewfik Pasha on the Palestine problem — The Arab Legion — Jewish immigration into Transjordan — Living conditions for the potash workers.

To the Jews, the Festival of Hanukkah that year was one of sorrow instead of happiness. The unbelievably moving Hanukkah song, broadcast each dusk by the Palestine Broadcasting Station, seemed like a lament for the sufferings not only of Europe's Jews, but of those who had believed they would find happiness in Palestine and were now wading through the slough of disillusionment. To hear that unaccompanied tenor voice singing the traditional Hebrew words with such clarity and beauty made me long to be irrational and become a turncoat to my convictions. How easy it would be to agree with all I was told, to convince myself that Zionism was the only possible salvation for the Jews — and that festivals such as Hanukkah celebrated in Palestine were many times more sacred and blessed than those observed by the Jews of the Diaspora.

Of the several homes I visited on Hanukkah evenings there was not one in which I did not feel the overpowering burden of sadness and the consciousness that this Hanukkah was different to all others — the last such festival before the doors of Palestine were finally closed to those in Europe. People who still awaited the arrival of relatives from the continent were now in despair. Three more months — and the curtains would be drawn on the tragedy while the militant organisations of Jewry in the Promised Land gathered their forces for an all-out bitter offensive against the authorities.

Each night the seven-stemmed candelabra shone brighter in Orthodox and non-Orthodox homes alike as one more candle was lit to celebrate the Feast of the Lights. Jewish restaurants had elaborate gilded candelabra. All Jerusalem seemed as conscious of Hanukkah as it was of Christmas which succeeded it. The shops were filled equally with coloured Hanukkah candles and glittering Christmas tree decorations. Paper chains could be bought at a price — ranging from four shillings upwards. Christmas cards covered with sprays of dried flowers claiming to have been picked in the Garden of Gethsemane or the Field of the Shepherds were sold to the troops at exorbitant profit. Christian Arabs prepared to keep Christmas in the traditional way. Yet over everything, there was that feeling of potential danger, of insecurity and fear. With dispassionate monotony, the local press each day recorded suicides.[57] People threw themselves from the rooftops of Tel Aviv's miniature skyscrapers after receiving last desperate letters pleading for admission to Palestine from relatives in Europe.

My old friend Kurt wrote to tell me that Hadera was no longer the seemingly peaceful village I had known. Although on the surface the people were going about their work as usual, the Ramat Hakovesh incident had aroused pacifist Zionists and there was now the constant threat of trouble. Kurt himself feared reprisals from some of the militant Zionist organisations for the pacifist views he had expressed in the village. He was anxious about his grove. "It is ironical," he wrote, "that before the war I was constantly fearful of the Arabs setting fire to my citrus trees — and now it is no longer the Arabs, but my own people, the members of the Irgun Zvai Leumi, who are terrorising us all. No matter how sincere they are in their beliefs — and I for one think of them as a set of gangsters and

144

nothing more — there is no justification for this underground mob rule of the country. Why doesn't the British army do something about it? Everyone knows how thoroughly the terrorists are prepared. One day my grove will be ablaze and time bombs will be set in the hotel. Is there no voice which will speak for the rights of us Jews who are not Zionists in the accepted sense?"

If the situation were capable of arousing a fatalist like Kurt, I could see that it indicated a growing consciousness of peril throughout Jewish Palestine. Was there ever going to be any solution to the country's problems? In those last days of the dying year, I did not meet one person who could face the future with any confidence. Christmas came and with it, the spectacle of Bethlehem — but Christmas that year seemed but a date in the calendar bringing with it no message of peace.

During a winter in Palestine before the war, I had gone to Bethlehem to attend the Christmas Night service.[58] Despite all the tinsel pomp of the ceremonies and the unruly fervour of the crowds, I had felt satisfaction in being in the Church of the Nativity as midnight struck and the Bambino was borne from the altar into the crypt. The many people who clamoured for admittance into the church had not then been controlled by scores of uniformed police. Those who had come to worship were allowed free access.

Christmas 1943 was different. Only those with official passes were able to attend the service. The Christian Arab women of Bethlehem with their picturesque white headdresses — as much a part of the church as its most treasured relics — were allowed to enter only in twos and threes. The majority were deprived of what is to them the most sacred blessing of the year. British police stood guard at the doors leading into the church. The Consular party from Jerusalem had reserved seats; government officials, service chiefs and other "entitled people" passed inside without hindrance; but the ordinary inhabitant of Palestine had as much chance of seeing the Star of Bethlehem lit over the altar at midnight as of escaping from the terrorism soon to burst on the country.

I wandered disconsolately around Bethlehem on Christmas night. For half-an-hour, I had been inside the church — allowed in unofficially by a police officer — and the High Pontifical Mass had seemed a travesty of what I remembered. There were more police than civilians. It was as if a service were being conducted in a prison chapel where convicts had to be carefully guarded. Outside, the atmosphere was less oppressive. Amid the swarming crowds, Arabs sold smoking-hot kebab roasted on skewers over flat charcoal fires. Overhead there were real stars — not the electric stars of the church. And through the village there blew a mountain wind, sharp and clean, whipping the dust from the alleyways and making the kerosene flares of the booths rampant tongues of light.

* * *

The old year passed uneasily into the new.

Elaborate precautions were taken by the police to avoid incidents. For the moment, it seemed as if the colonies were quiescent. Rumours of their harbouring deserters were not heard as frequently as hitherto; though there were constant tales of arms running, secret dumps and the training of illegal forces. At the same time too, there began to be whispers that the Arab fellaheen were collecting arms, though whether for attack or self-defence no one knew.

The first tense weeks of 1944, however, passed without major incident. In the Arab city of Jaffa, time bombs of Jewish manufacture exploded at a government transport agency's car park. There was an encounter between two armed Jews and an Arab taxi-driver in a remote part of Jerusalem near the entrance to St. Georges Cathedral. A police patrol gave chase. The Jews escaped after killing the Arab.

146

Not till the middle of February was the first important blow struck at the Palestine Government, the responsibility for which was openly admitted by the NMO (Irgun Zvai Leumi) in a letter to the Hebrew press. The blow was a dramatic and well-timed operation, which achieved its object without causing any loss of life.

At 9.40pm on Saturday, 12th February,[59] time bombs exploded in the Jerusalem Department of Migration. Before 11.30, seven separate explosions had smashed the walls of the offices and shattered the archives containing the carefully tabulated records of the quota of Jewish immigrants allowed into Palestine. The explosions in Jerusalem were not isolated. Simultaneous blows were struck at the Immigration Offices in Haifa and Tel Aviv. In Haifa shortly before eleven o'clock, the Migration Department offices were completely wrecked and nearby buildings damaged by bomb blasts. In Tel Aviv, four time bombs exploded a few minutes before eleven, extensively damaging the Migration Department. Three more unexploded bombs were found later.

In all three cities, police cordoned off the bombed areas and conducted nightlong searches in the hope of finding the perpetrators; but those who had planned and delivered the triple blow had made good their escape many hours before. The next day, when the acrid smell of explosive had gone from the streets of Palestine's main cities, and all that was left to remind people of the outrages were three shattered buildings and broken windows, there was an understandable feeling of relief. Some people I talked to shrugged and smiled. "We had thought it would be far more terrible than this," they would tell me, "If they are only going to blow up government offices, and at night when no one can be injured, then the Irgun Zvai Leumi is not the terrorist organisation we thought it was."

Even highly placed police officials were inclined to join in this feeling of relief, though they should have known that this was but the beginning of what the Irgun Zvai Leumi planned to do.

Zionist organisations followed up the bomb outrages with the issue of a memorandum deploring the incidents and calling on Jewish Palestine to fight the terrorists and to stand firm against extortions and threats.

In Britain and America the popular press — who now had their first hard story out of Palestine for many months — played up the outrages as incidents which would immeasurably affect the political picture of the country. So much so that the *Palestine Post*, normally conciliatory towards the London press, was goaded into protesting against the versions which appeared in certain British nationals.

"Here, during three years of daily provocation, despite heavy loss of life, the community consistently abstained from retaliatory action. [...]," said the *Post*. "The irresponsible acts of a few misguided youths who shoot at policemen or vent their exasperation at the world's inaction in the face of the Jewish tragedy by burning the files of the Immigration Department do not reflect upon the political claims of the community as a whole nor deflect it from its moral position. If they were presented in that way, as appears to have been done in a part of the London press, they have been very sadly and most harmfully misrepresented."[60]

No matter how one tired of the flood of protests and carefully inspired articles which appeared almost daily in the *Post*, one could not help but admire the smooth flowing phrases of its political leaders, nor deny that they always hit the Zionist nail on the head as truly as precision instruments. Gershon Agronsky,[61] the editor, for whom as an individual and a journalist most people have considerable regard, has unfortunately allowed himself to become a tool of politicians. His newspaper could have achieved so much in allaying anti-Semitism and in proving the claims of Zionism to be deserving of sympathy if he had not let political pressure override his good judgment.

Such pressure reached its peak at the end of February when the *Post* was induced to condemn the one-time

Governor of Jerusalem, Sir Ronald Storrs, for his out-spoken dispatch from the city on the Histadrut (the Federation of Jewish Labour) and Solel Boneh, the con-tracting and building company owned by Histadrut. Sir Ronald pointed out that when strikes were called throughout Palestine industry, significantly, strikes were not permitted in Solel Boneh. Firms financially ruined by these strikes were afterwards bought up by Solel Boneh, so that gradually Histadrut, through this company, was acquiring an important part of the coun-try's industry.

Sir Ronald's dispatch appeared in the *Sunday Times* of March 7th 1943. It shows something of the bitterness which such institutions can retain when one knows that Histadrut and Solel Boneh launched legal proceedings lasting for eleven months in an effort to make Sir Ronald retract. They were successful. The *Sunday Times* of February 27th 1944 had to express regret that the arti-cles had given offence to both organisations. "Sir Ronald assures us," said the newspaper, "that he had no inten-tion of reflecting on the great work done by these bodies in Palestine in developing the country's industrial and agricultural activities and in help given to the war effort. He has re-read the articles and agrees that they may be liable to the construction which was placed upon them."

The *Post*, however, not content with this, grudgingly admitted that "the ample apology offered by Sir Ronald Storrs and the editor of the *Sunday Times* to the Histadrut and Solel Boneh [...] should go some way to mitigate the hurt which they caused. It will be recalled that the one-time Governor of Jerusalem, on revisiting Palestine as a freelance journalist had accused the Labour Federation of promoting strikes often before a serious attempt at reconciliation had been made, of acting through Solel Boneh as a contracting, building and general employer, and of allowing the latter to reduce wages to an extent which it did not tolerate from private employers. It was thus able, Sir Ronald alleged, to deal heavy blows against its steadily diminishing rivals. Its collaboration with Arab workers he described as "phoney." These and other insinuations in that vein were not taken too seriously by the public, which has a way of correctly assessing the weight and value of itinerant writers but, perhaps not unnaturally, the charges were regarded by the attacked parties as libellous and made the subject of legal proceedings in London. The proceedings have now been dropped as a result of a full apology by the writer and editor, the former expressing regret at having misrepresented the activities of the two bodies owing to misinformation and withdrawing any suggestion that either of them have been guilty of conduct prejudicial to good order or obstructive to the war effort."[62]

This flogging of a dead horse seemed in the worst of taste and the epithets of "an itinerant writer" and "a freelance journalist" totally unnecessary.

* * *

Before February ended the terrorists struck again.

Extremists from the group known as the Stern gang carried out a series of attacks on individual police officers. In Haifa, a bomb buried under the runway outside the garage of the deputy superintendent of police exploded and wrecked his car. The superintendent escaped with injuries. A second bomb buried at the roadside and connected by wire to a press button several metres away detonated under a police traffic car containing two British inspectors and a British sergeant. Again the occupants escaped. Yet another bomb, unexploded, was found in a Haifa road.

While the Stern gang seemed to be concerning itself with personal attacks on marked individuals, the Irgun Zvai Leumi or NMO was going out for bigger game. The Migration Offices had been blown up; other government buildings were to follow.

On February 26th another triple blow was planned and put into execution. This time the attack was launched against the Income Tax Offices in Tel Aviv, Haifa and Jerusalem. At Tel Aviv, the offices were wrecked. At Haifa, there was only slight damage. The time bombs left in the Jerusalem Income Tax Offices failed to explode. The usual brown-paper parcels were found later by police investigators — with their alarm clocks, fuses and explosives.

How were the bombs planted? How was it possible, now that the blackout had been lifted, for these gangsters to enter government buildings carrying what must be conspicuous bundles or suitcases and distribute the contents at strategic points? In no case had the guards been overwhelmed or entry forced. It appeared that the bombs were laid during ordinary office hours. Were there secret members of the Irgun Zvai Leumi working as clerks in the Immigration or Income Tax Offices?

Many hundreds of Jews in different parts of Palestine were questioned by the police as a full scale comb-out was attempted of all doubtful characters. Police squads visited more colonies. The streets of the big cities were thoroughly patrolled at night. Around government buildings there were the uniformed shadows of British constables and sergeants with their machine-guns and revolvers ready for action. Police armoured cars with machine-guns mounted toured the streets of the cities or waited at strategic crossroads where they could command all lanes of escape. Even so, the Irgun Zvai Leumi and the Stern gang had the authorities on the run. Now that the first bombs had exploded and successfully wrecked several buildings, there were few who did not believe the paper notices pinned on doors at night which stated that bombs had been laid and warned passers-by to keep clear. Such hoaxes, attributed to the Irgun Zvai Leumi and the Stern gang, kept police investigators busy until the early hours. Even in the daytime ordinary office workers called the police when they saw suspicious-looking parcels. Usually they turned out to be someone's lunch packet. The object, however, of the gangsters was being achieved. The reign of terrorism — and some had smiled at the first blows — was now as complete as it could be, at least in the cities.

March 31st, the day on which immigration into Palestine was to cease, drew relentlessly nearer. While the Irgun Zvai Leumi perfected more plans, the Arabs sat back and waited calmly for the end. Muslims in Jerusalem were apparently appalled at the outrages but comfortably aware that no such blows struck at the British Government could achieve a change of policy nor keep open the closing doors of Palestine. Even in Transjordan, the Arabs were sitting back contentedly watching events from afar but not greatly concerned with them. The Jews could no longer buy land as they wished. No more Jews could enter Palestine. The Arabs had achieved almost more than they had dared to hope for — and now they could calmly appraise the situation.

* * *

At the end of February, I decided to visit Amman and renew some of my old friendships there. I wanted particularly to find out what the reaction of the Transjordan Arabs — the wealthy and influential Arabs — was to Jewish immigration into that country. The idea is not new — but the implementation of it would be. Before the war, when I had several conversations with His Highness the Emir Abdullah[63], I had found him not averse to the proposal that a limited number of Jews should be allowed to establish small colonies in certain districts of Transjordan. But since then the question of the Jews overflowing into yet another Arab country had been met with horror by many nationalist Muslims, especially those backing the plan for a grand Middle East Arab federation.

Driving from Jerusalem to Amman is arduous physically and mentally. In under an hour one drops from three thousand feet above sea level to more than fifteen hundred feet below. Ears go deaf as in an aeroplane. In the Jordan

Valley, the pressure on the eardrums is indescribable. Mentally, the journey is tiring through its immense contrasts — a concentrated panorama of desolation and gaunt beauty punctuated with the banana groves of Jericho and the amethyst flanks of Moab. On the road, winding down from Jerusalem the sun streams over the naked spurs of the hills burnishing the white and ochre boulders and penetrating into the wadis, where, in the early spring there are still faint trickles of water. Patches of grass, soon to disappear in the summer heat, are being eaten vociferously by the flocks of goats and sheep, which wander along the wadis tended by the Bedouin boys.

The car spins around precipice bends, passes the white notice board with its sign "SEA LEVEL" and emerges in the warm bowl of the Jordan Valley. Away to the south the wash of the Dead Sea is a flat glittering jewel. The Mountains of Moab running down sheer into the water form grotesque cataracts of bleak stone. Obscene patterns evolve out of the sloping sides of Transjordan's plateau. The factory buildings of the Palestine Potash Company seem an anachronism in the ancient picture.

Up the valley, lies Jericho with its clustered banana groves and miniature suq; and beyond, the Wilderness of Abraham where clay dunes sprawl in unending sequence northwards towards the middle reaches of the Jordan.

Down in the warm depth of the valley one feels physically exhausted and mentally overwhelmed. Here is nothing but desolation, land on which there is no live thing, no bush or shrub, no bird. Is this, one asks, the country where the Zionists say they can build farms? Are those desolate mountain slopes leading down from Jerusalem to the valley capable of cultivation? Can Palestine really support more population than it already has? Looking at the sepulchral slopes of the Wilderness of Abraham, one feels anew the tremendous hopelessness of Palestine — a feeling alleviated perhaps by the knowledge that there are Jewish colonies on the banks of the Jordan itself and the Wilderness is only one very small part of the country.

The Jordan itself, a disappointing muddy river, is no longer spanned by the rattling wooden bridge built by Allenby in the last war. Steel and concrete have replaced that historic monument to the British campaign against the Turks. On one side of the modern bridge, there is a Palestine Police post. On the other, the sharifian helmets of the Arab Legion mark the boundary of Transjordan as one's car halts by the Legion post and an entry visa takes up half a page of a passport.

Beyond the Jordan, the scenery changes as if one had moved from the deserts of India into fertile Kashmir. Here is the famous wadi,[64] which the Turks defended to the last when British troops launched an attack from Jericho. In that wadi, where water flows all the year round, there is always a fringe of vegetation. In early spring, the slopes are thick with flowers. On that day, I saw giant wild hollyhocks, blue lupins and marigolds rioting among the boulders and tipping the skyline with splashes of colour. Overhead, lone kites hovered, ready to dive on their prey. Further up the valley, near El Salt, a blue kingfisher sped out of the undergrowth and flashed deep sapphire in front of the windscreen.

Before, I had seen this same road whitened with snow-drifts and bounded by bare rock-slopes where the herds of sheep and goats moved perilously in search of fodder. The women of El Salt, in the bitter winter of the Transjordan uplands, had been weeping in the cold as they walked barefoot to the village well.[65]

In the summer, the scene would change again. The hill slopes would burnish into bleak brilliance beneath the uncharitable sun. Only in the brief spring was life pleasant and easy for the women of these desert villages.

The car sped on, deeper into Transjordan, curving around more precipice bends and emerging on the hill top from which one can see the first houses of Amman. Arab cities, no matter what alien culture may be imposed upon them, do not change. Other buildings, modern concrete edifices may grow up in their environs, but the city responsible for that growth retains its character, its flat dung-swept rooftops, its minarets and distinctive desert smells. Amman had not changed. Away on an eastern hill stood the palace of the Emir Abdullah; while in the town itself there were the Legion police and the crowded streets of the souk which gave Amman the unmistakable atmosphere of being on the edge of Arabia. Arabs in Bedouin clothes strode between the little booths; the red-and-white kaffiyeh of the desert-dweller fluttered brightly among the crowds; the shops had cartridge belts for sale. Men carried rifles openly, for in Transjordan it is not illegal to possess arms. Even the sounds of Amman had not changed. The stamping of fretful Arab horses with their flat saddles and woollen reins mingled with the clanging of the brass beaters and the blasts of klaxons on high-powered American cars.

Over all, there hung the soft dust of the desert covering man and beast alike with its grey film and respecting the gilded *aghal*[66] of the Bedouin sheikh no more than the rags of the beggar.

* * *

I had first met Tewfik Pasha[67], the prime minister of Transjordan, during the Palestine Round Table conference in London.[68] He greeted me in his Amman office with the sincerity of an old friend. There was coffee to drink — thick and scalding hot — and tales of prowess to relate to me about that romantic force the Arab Legion, of which Tewfik has always been especially proud. Sturdy sons of Bedouin sheikhs, hard horsemen and cameleers versed in the ways of the desert, the Arab Legionaries had already been sent by His Highness the Emir to become an integral part of Palestine's defences and so release British fighting units for their historic sweep through North Africa and the advance on Rome.

There are many stories of immense heroism in the Legion, of how Arab *jundis*, Legion privates, have died to save the lives of their English officers; how during the great Wahabi invasion of Transjordan men of the Legion on swift Arab steeds and in armoured cars swept east from Zizia and Amman to drive back the fanatical hordes. Hundreds of miles across the flint and stone desert the Wahabis were pursued — to the salt marshes of Kasr el-Azrak, the Blue Castle, and beyond to the Wadi Sirhan, the traditional raiding and grazing grounds of the Arabian Bedouin. Today on the tracks leading to the Blue Castle one can still see the bleached bones of the camels which bore that invading army and in the RAF station mess at Amman there is the faded green silk battle standard which the Legion seized in the midst of battle.[69]

The British commander of the Legion, Glubb Pasha[70], before the war did great work under Peake[71] recruiting Bedouin fighting men for the desert patrol section of the Legion. Mounted on camels, uniformed in scarlet and white robes, these desert-born warriors who had lived only by the rifle and sword learnt to police the tribes, to settle blood feuds and bring peace to the embattled edge of Arabia. Today Transjordan is able to set in motion the normal services of a civilised government largely because of Glubb's work — and the work of his legionaries.

Tewfik told me of important plans the government was making; education schemes for lowering the percentage of illiterates, welfare work among the tribes, free medical facilities and subsidised farming. Already the Beni Sakhr tribe, one of the most important and richest Bedouin con-federations in the country, possessed their first mechanical plough. They were now harvesting crops nearly ten times as quickly as they had done with the old wooden plough drawn by oxen, which did little but scratch the surface of the soil. Although most of the government schemes were still in their initial stages, Tewfik hoped in later years they would make the country prosperous and flourishing.

Talking about Transjordan, Tewfik's deep eyes and firm features seemed aglow with the pleasure of achievement in a country which at one time was as primitive as any part of Arabia. When I mentioned Palestine, his expression changed.

"The White Paper has settled the problem of Palestine," he said, briefly. "The Arabs approve of the White Paper and so far as we in Transjordan are concerned — Palestine is no longer the great problem it once was."

We discussed the plight of the Jews in Europe, for which Tewfik as a humanitarian had every sympathy. When I asked him how he would react to limited Jewish colonising in Transjordan, he agreed that it would help to open up the country, but he felt the political repercussions would be too varied and difficult to justify the experiment.

We talked for a long time about the possibilities, of how the fertile lands of Kerak could be developed by modern farming methods. But it seemed as if the Agricultural Department of the Transjordan Government had already conceived plans for opening up that rich and unexploited region. When I left Tewfik I felt as if I had been speaking to someone who, if he had not been an Arab, would have had active sympathy for the refugee Jews. As it was, Tewfik, not unnaturally, considered himself to be apart from the problem and to have neither right nor excuse for meddling in something which he felt the British Government had already settled.

Other government officials in Amman, Arabs who held minor posts in the educational and welfare branches, were more outspoken and ready to concern themselves with what was happening across the border. Most of them however held contradictory views.

The majority were nationalist and averse to Jewish immigration or to the suggestion that an Arab state should be formed composing Transjordan, a slice of eastern Palestine and a portion of southern Syria, with the central and coastal areas of Palestine left as a Jewish state. "This is Sharq el-Urdun — east of the Jordan," they said, "and east of that boundary we must remain if we are to make something of our country. Why should we get mixed up in the quarrels across the border? The Arabs of

Transjordan have little in common with the Arabs of Palestine — and even less with those of southern Syria where the Druze and the Ruwallah hold sway. In Transjordan, we have maintained our own traditions and in a way are truer Arabs than those more in touch with Western civilisation. We are proud of it and anxious to avoid entanglement in a political tussle about a land which, although a neighbour, is not a part of us."

Others thought the only solution to the problem was to make His Highness the Emir the grand ruler of an extended Transjordan. This would please many Muslims, they said, and also conciliate the Jews, if a state containing both Haifa and Tel Aviv was created for them. But as to the question of whether more Jews should be allowed into Palestine and the overflow absorbed into Transjordan, there was no definite reaction. Although the Bedouin and the semi-nomadic tribes might acquiesce, I had the impression that the townspeople of Transjordan would regard such colonisation as the thin end of a very wide wedge. Nor would they tolerate the idea of Transjordan being a temporary refuge from which European Jews would return to the countries of their birth after peace had been restored to the continent. The dominant idea seemed that of distrust: whereas the British Government implemented what it promised, the Jews, once granted concessions, exploited them and could not be trusted to fulfil their pledges if they went against their nationalistic beliefs.

Officers of the Arab Legion told me that so far as policing the country was concerned, the establishment of law and order would be far easier if Transjordan and Palestine were one. The long meandering boundary of the Jordan Valley was an invitation to border smuggling and arms-runners could feed that notorious centre of Arab brigandry, Beisan, with considerable ease because it lay in one of the most desolate frontier regions. Before the war, both Germany and Italy had been sending arms to the Arabs in that area and there was still a certain amount of such arms running.

It was particularly simple for the Transjordan Arab to indulge in this illicit traffic as there was no law against his being armed. In the days of the Ottoman Empire, of course, the Arabs of Palestine had also carried arms and there were many in Palestine who still did so, not because they were gangsters or brigands but as a means of self-defence.

I felt that the word self-defence had come to have a special meaning in Palestine. The right to self-defence was one of the main pleas of the Zionists. It could just as easily be a natural demand of the Arabs. Yet where did one draw the line between arming for self-defence and arming for attack?

I left Amman with mixed feelings. The Arabian sunrise was gilding the broken columns of the citadel as my car left the Philadelphia, flashed through the suq and started the climb into the upper heights of the plateau. Behind me lay the tiered amphitheatre of Graeco-Roman days, monument to the glories of a city that had once straddled one of the main trade routes from Baghdad to the Mediterranean. There, in its notch between the hills, lay the modern city with its minarets and square houses and desert dust. Was there any solution to Palestine beneath the rooftops of that city? In a few decades, how might the picture have changed? Great concrete cinemas, European cafés, produce from Jewish colonies arriving by lorries in a modern market square?

* * *

I had met and talked to Jewish colonists and city dwellers. I had lived in Hadera and made friends with the villagers. There was still one small section of the Jewish community in Palestine whom I had not contacted — and that was the men and women who had settled down near industrial installations in isolated parts of the country, like the potash works on the shores of the Dead Sea.

On my way back to Jerusalem, I went to visit some of these families. The works, like a grotesque mechanical monster, sprawl over many acres of barren soil on the edge of the Sea. Great salt-drying pans extend along the shores where the waters are evaporated, pumped from one pan to another and finally into the works where five hundred horsepower British Diesel engines provide the energy to convert the brine into potash.

The workers I found to be of all origins — German, Austrian, Czech, Polish and Russian. They were either refugees from Nazi oppression or emigrants from the Ukraine and the steppes of the Don. Engineers, chemists and technicians could afford to maintain their families in the civilised surroundings of Jerusalem. The majority of semi-skilled workers earned only sufficient to keep their wives and children in the tenement flats built by the potash company. The flats are small and, except for a brief hour at night when a breeze blows off the waters, hot and airless. Curtains are almost perpetually drawn against the glare of the Sea. The blaze of the sun is unending and scarcely endurable. Flies cover everything. Vegetables and salad have to be soaked in permanganate to kill the typhoid germs. Despite inoculations, the incidence of fever among the families is high. Life is hard — as hard as the old pioneer days of the Middle West.

The women I talked to in these tenement dwellings had however developed their own philosophy against the rigours of existence.

Pnina, who had come with her husband from Krakow in 1938 had known suffering and tragedy. Her first baby had died at the end of a nine-day khamsin. Her second had had malaria and sand fly fever, but had survived. A boy of three, he was now bronzed and strong, and enduring the climate far better than his mother.

"Our one consolation," said Pnina, "is that he's safe. No one can persecute him here. He won't have to grow up in the same furtive atmosphere in which I was reared. My family lived in Lublin and I know what ghetto life in Eastern Europe can do to warp one's outlook and give one that terrible feeling of being unwanted, hated. And I know

160

too what it's like here in the heat and the agony of this valley. I suppose if I'd realised what we should have had to endure I wouldn't have found the courage to come. But to Jewish people in Poland an immigration certificate to Palestine seemed like a passport to freedom — even before the Nazis came. I wouldn't go back to Poland now. I don't think we shall ever be really happy, here in Palestine, but at least we can walk out of doors knowing that people are not going to jeer or throw stones — and down here by the Dead Sea we shall not be involved in the troubles which the terrorists are making."

Pnina had once been youthful and pleasant to look at. I saw photographs. Now she was old before her years, worn with housework, sapped by the climate, but resigned. Both she and her husband lived only for their son, and for him they were making plans for emigration to America. They could see no prospects of a decent livelihood for him in Palestine. The country — or their part of it — was at the moment a safe resting-place until he grew older.

"We're trying to save," said Pnina, "so that we can send him away where he can become a normal person — where he can keep his religion yet be assimilated into a great nation. The last thing we want is for our son to have a Palestine passport."

Pnina, I knew, was not alone in her outlook. She was facing a personal problem confronting many thousands of families in Palestine — that of turning away from Zionist plans for building a nation and choosing a practical way of making their children normal healthy citizens of an established country. Yet, by a member of the Irgun Zvai Leumi or the Stern gang, Pnina would have been regarded as a traitor to her "race", a renegade who by her attitude undermined all that they were fighting for.

Chapter Eleven
March 1944

Jewish press condemns terrorism — Jews protest against police searches — The Palestine Resolution before Congress — Arab protests — Last days of the White Paper — Illegal pamphlets — Ramat Hakovesh memorial — Special day of prayer — Police HQ attacked — Six British police killed — Death penalty and curfew — Arab newspapers provocative statements — Iraq's statement on the Resolution.

After the peace of Amman and the quiet beauty of the Jordan Valley, Jerusalem seemed a city of noise and ugliness. Jewish newspapers were intensifying their editorial campaigns against the acts of the terrorists. More Arabs were being arrested for the possession of arms. At night the cafés were loud with bitter political argument.

At the beginning of March, all the Jewish dailies, with the exception of the Revisionist *Hamashkhif* (the newspaper most closely representing the views of militant Zionists), printed a joint statement declaring that the assaults and acts of sabotage committed recently in various parts of Palestine under the cloaks of high national slogans undermined the foundation of Jewish existence and endangered Jewish national and political efforts at a time when Israel's fate hung in the balance. "The entire Yishuv,[72]" it said, "which is ready to defend without fear and with all the means at its disposal its fundamental rights to immigration, construction and settlement, will find the proper methods of stopping the irresponsible acts of sabotage, the threats and extortions and so defend the honour of Jewish revival and Zionist enterprise..."

162

This assurance that the proper methods would be found to combat the terrorists was angrily recalled by the Arab press, when, before the end of March the Irgun Zvai Leumi delivered another blow at the authorities.

Before then the British Dominions under-secretary[73] had made a full statement on the February outrages in the House of Commons and people in Britain were becoming uncomfortably aware that a large standing garrison would have to be maintained in Palestine for many years to come if any form of security and order was to be kept in the country.

At this time, when the smallest spark was sufficient to enflame public opinion in Palestine, the Jewish Romanian Settlers Organisation chose to recall the unfortunate *Struma* disaster. At a memorial meeting in Haifa, crowds swarmed into the Hall of the Hebrew Technical Institute to hear once again how the seven hundred refugees had gone down in that fated boat and to listen to the cantor reciting the prayer for the dead.

No one wished to deny the Jews the right of mourning their lost brethren or of keeping alive their memory, but there seemed no reason for bringing the disaster before the public consciousness in those last four weeks before the expiry of the White Paper. The *Struma* had sunk in December 1941, and the anniversary of the sinking was surely the more natural occasion for a memorial service.

Such incidents, calculated or coincidental, happened side by side with the extensive investigations being carried out by the police. Special police parties with British personnel fluent in Hebrew as well as in German and Polish combed methodically through the residential quarters of Palestine's cities in an effort to dig out the terrorists before they could strike again. In Jerusalem, a grand-scale search was conducted on the Saturday following the joint statement in the Hebrew press. The search was not directed against the Jewish community as such; it was an honest if unpleasant attempt to bring law and order to the country. Yet the Jewish community council rose in protest because the searches had taken place on the Sabbath and had involved forcible measures to compel Orthodox Jews to enter police vehicles on that day. (No strictly observant Jew will travel in any vehicle on the Sabbath.) Six delegates from the community council called on the acting district commissioner of Jerusalem to convey their extreme disapproval of the police action and urged that, although supporting such security measures, they objected to the form in which they were carried out without regard for the dignity of religion and tradition. The regrets of the government at causing offence to innocent Jewish residents were expressed. It was pointed out that the prevention of disorders necessitated the police at times going beyond the ordinary dictates of etiquette.

The incident threw an important limelight on the lack of realism in the Jewish community and was taken by the Arabs as yet another example of the two-faced way in which the Jews were dealing with the terrorists. The Muslims pointed out that in reverse circumstances a police search conducted on a Friday would not have provoked an organised protest. The Jews, however, were not wholeheartedly behind the authorities. Unofficially, said the Arabs, they cherished a rather bewildered admiration for the fearlessness of the Irgun Zvai Leumi and so resented the thoroughness of the authorities in trying to stamp out the organisation.

Anti-Semitic English people regarded the reaction of the Jewish community as yet another example of the strange behaviour of "these aliens" — provocative and unnecessary.

* * *

March 1944 became a month of intense Zionist activity in the United States. Now that it was apparent that Britain intended to fulfil the pledges to the Arabs given in the White Paper, America seemed to hold out the only hope of

164

being powerful enough to influence Britain against such implementation.

Two prominent personalities of the Democratic and Republican Parties[74] were persuaded to introduce into both Houses of the American Congress what became known as the "Palestine Resolution." It called upon the United States to use its power for the continued construction of the National Home in Palestine and was referred to the Foreign Affairs Committee of the Senate which held a number of public hearings on the subject.

Suddenly the Middle East was aflame.

The Arab governments launched protests against the Resolution. Iraq asked that it should be completely withdrawn. His Highness the Emir Abdullah of Transjordan cabled the Arab kings and rulers appealing for a "united effort in defending Palestine." To the Iraqi Regent,[75] the Emir telegraphed: "I have cabled President Roosevelt on the painful results the Congress deliberations on Palestine have had in the East and indicated the tragedies which may result from any new turn in the discussions. The Congress no doubt lacks the facts about the realities of the situation." The Emir concluded by saying he had also cabled his views to King Farouk of Egypt, King Ibn Saud of Arabia and the Iman Yehia of the Yemen.

The Regent of Iraq replied that Iraq was ready to play her part should occasion arise.

The author of the Palestine Resolution, Senator Robert Wagner, sent an outspoken reply to Iraq, expressing resentment at foreign interference with the work of Congress.

A few days later it became known that further hearings were to be postponed, and discussions on the Resolution were suspended, though it was stated that "nothing will affect or postpone" consideration of the demand for Jewish immigration into Palestine which was then before both Houses of Congress.

The *New York Post* suggested a new Palestine Resolution demanding only the opening of Palestine for immigration, which it said could not justifiably be opposed by Britain. The *Herald Tribune* urged the State Department to make strong representations to Britain for a generous interpretation of the immigration provisions, pointing out that the White Paper was only a war measure and could not prejudice the future settlement of the Palestine issue. The *Palestine Post* pointed out that international issues like the Jewish and the Palestine problem could not be solved by fettering public discussion under the threat of power pressure: "The underlying conception of the Atlantic Charter [which Mr Churchill recently re-affirmed] is that the new international system is to be based on equity and inspired by creative justice [...]

Moreover, the reference of the Palestine issue to Congress was in line with the finest traditions of American democracy...."[76] The Egyptian paper *Bourse Egyptienne*[77] reported that Nahas Pasha, the Premier,[78] had sent General Smuts a message criticizing the South African Premier's support of the Zionist movement. The president of the Zionist Organisation of America, Dr I. Goldstein, repudiated the Iraqi protest that a Jewish state meant the elimination of Arabs in Palestine, and flatly contradicted allegations that Muslim and Christian holy places would be handed over to the Jews.

A flood of statements, protests and repudiations came from Zionist and Arab quarters. Finally, President Roosevelt himself was provoked into making a declaration on Palestine and Jewish immigration "designed to correct any misconception with regard to the attitude of the United States Government that appeared to have arisen following the temporary suspension of the hearings before the Senate committee on the Resolution." President Roosevelt reiterated the deep sympathy which the people of America and her government had always shown for the building of the Jewish National Home, a sympathy now all the greater because of the plight of European Jewry, and gave a pointed reminder that America had never given her approval to the Palestine White Paper.

So ended, momentarily, the storm over the Palestine Resolution.

* * *

It seemed that nothing concrete could be done to keep the closing doors of Palestine ajar. Even Zionists I spoke to in Jerusalem had grown fatalistic and could see no immediate hope of achieving any change of policy. The last days of the White Paper passed in a tense unreal procession.

Underground militant Zionism, however, had not relinquished hope in its own power of achieving a reversal of White Paper policy. The clandestine press of Tel Aviv and Haifa was working at full spate publishing a flood of illegal literature calculated to rouse the Jewish populace. Pamphlets and newspapers were being sold defiantly in the streets beneath the very noses of the British police, most of whom could not read the Hebrew characters and thought they were the normal daily papers allowed to be published. In Tel Aviv, several of these newspaper sellers were arrested and brought before magistrates. The majority were juveniles, boys and girls whose Jewish school education in Palestine had imbued in them a feverish sense of indignation against the government and an ardent belief in the ideals of Zionism. *Herut* — "Freedom" — the most widely circulated of the illegal newspapers was sold almost entirely by children. One fifteen-year-old girl was caught defiantly pasting copies of the paper on a Tel Aviv wall. There were other cases of children and youths being arrested for "being in possession" of illegal literature. And at the same time the clandestine radio, the "Voice of Israel", which had broadcast Hebrew programmes intermittently for several months, became stronger and was able to be picked up beyond the confines of Palestine.

In the middle of March, about a fortnight before the end of the White Paper, the Zionists forcibly recalled the incident of Ramat Hakovesh to Jewish Palestine. Workers, children and servicemen had been subscribing for some months to a fund for planting a Ramat Hakovesh Woodland in Minara, a new communal settlement near the Syrian frontier. Twenty thousand trees were bought with the six thousand pounds subscribed. The first sapling was planted by the widow of Shmuel Wolinietz, the colonist who had died after being wounded by the police. There was no doubt that the Zionists intended to preserve the memory of the settler as a martyr to their cause — a name to arouse the country in times of stress.

On 24 March, the eve of the Hebrew month of Nissan, the Chief Rabbi called for a day of fasting and special prayer for the rescue of the remnants of European Jewry. Many who did not normally attend synagogues joined in this special day of prayer. They included non-Zionists and even those actively opposing the building of the National Home. In Jerusalem, the great modern synagogue opposite the offices of the Jewish Agency overflowed with worshippers, and the sound of chanted prayers came through the perpendicular windows with an almost frightening intensity. At dusk when I passed the synagogue with its lights shining out on the main road and the crowds swarming along the pavements as they converged on the building, it seemed that this was one of the most perfect expressions of Jewish solidarity in Palestine that I had yet seen. Here were people I recognised — high Zionist officials, typists from government offices, liberal Jewish businessmen, Russians, Poles, Czechs, Germans — the tragic kaleidoscope contained every shade of the Hebrew faith and every nationality. I could see that the drama of the White Paper had imposed itself on everyone's consciousness irrespective of his political or religious convictions.

Would this solidarity last?

As I looked at the crowds in the growing darkness I felt that the concerted expression of faith was ephemeral — that the typists and the businessmen, the Czechs and the Russians, would return to their homes and offices feeling satisfied that they had obeyed the Chief Rabbi, but the thread which bound them together was as slender as Rahab's scarlet cord. On the night of prayer that cord was strong. By the morning it would have snapped.

The vibrant sound of the ram's horn, the shofar, heard that day by special permission of the Rabbinate, reminded me more of the *Last Post* than of a rousing call to action which could shatter the walls of the White Paper and allow the Jews free entry into the country. One wondered later how varied would have been the reaction of those worshippers had they known that, before midnight struck, the terrorists would have delivered one of their most ruthless attacks. But amid the murmur of footsteps outside the synagogue, in that atmosphere of dedication and unity, thoughts of terrorism seemed out of place. People came away from their prayers quietly and were absorbed into the floating crowds of the city. The night closed down as clear and cold as any normal March night. Over the Mount of Olives, the moon was a white lantern illuminating the domes and cupolas, throwing sharp shadows across the roads. Slowly the cafés closed their doors. Lights were flicked out in tenement flats as the people of Jerusalem, early sleepers, turned in for one of the few remaining nights before the White Paper expired.

* * *

The terrorists launched their attack before 11pm.

Walking boldly through the moonlit Russian Compound, disguised in British police uniform, a combined force of Irgun Zvai Laumi and Stern men reached CID headquarters, placed a ladder against the building and carried time bombs on to a first-floor balcony. The whole operation was conducted silently without disturbing the guards on the main doors or attracting attention from the nearby Jaffa Road. Only one police officer inside the building, Inspector John Scott of the CID, heard suspicious sounds. He paid with his life when he opened fire on the group of figures on the balcony.

169

The first bomb exploded as the gangsters were returning across the Russian Compound. The noise shook Jerusalem like an earthquake. In Darouti's Hotel, where I had dined that night, windows were blown across rooms as the blast swept through the building, bringing with it the acrid smell of gelignite and the cries of passers-by. Down Jaffa Road, near the Central Post Office, the pavements were as deep with splintered glass as a blitzed street in London.

The second bomb went off as I picked my way towards the CID billet. More glass rained down in jagged sheets on the road. A gust of air tore through the streets like a gale. Then, as the sounds died, the police began to swarm out of their shattered headquarters to take up the pursuit; armoured cars roared out of the police garages; shots sounded in the Russian Compound; ambulances from the government hospital whined their way towards the building. Police running down towards Mamillah Cemetery caught one Jewish youth carrying a bomb. Patrols spread out through the city, beyond the outskirts, along the main roads to Jaffa, Haifa and Hebron. Another Jew was arrested near Rachel's Tomb — in possession of a revolver and twenty-four rounds. Before dawn, there were many arrests; the entire police garrison in Jerusalem had been mobilised to hunt down the gangsters.

But it was too late.

Long before the second time bomb had exploded, the real instigators of the outrage, protected by their British police uniform, had passed swiftly across the Russian Compound and escaped in waiting cars. Not until the evening of the next day was the body of Asher Benjamin, one of the Stern gang, found in a sack in the Sukat Shalom quarter of the city. He had died shortly before midnight on the night of the outrage, shot, it is believed, by the one bullet that Inspector Scott fired before his death. Asher Benjamin was born in Jerusalem. He was the son of a well-respected family of watchmakers and had studied extensively and had been known in Jerusalem for the past two years as a successful businessman. He was the only member of the Stern gang to pay for his part in the assault.

In daylight, when the police could review the damage, the Russian Compound and Jaffa Road resembled the worst that a land mine could do. CID headquarters itself and the Wireless Signals Section had been virtually wrecked with most of the radio and telephone equipment destroyed. The ground and first floors in the south wing of the Russian Building were demolished. Many thousand pounds' worth of damage was done to the police HQ alone.

In the nearby ATS billet, British girls had been injured by flying glass. The billet was moved the next day. At the Russian church incalculable damage was done to ancient icons and relics. Stained-glass windows were destroyed. The law courts had to adjourn many hearings before their shattered interior could be restored sufficiently to enable the judges to carry on. Patients in the government Hospital across the Russian Compound were shaken by the blast. Shopkeepers in the Jaffa Road lost thousands of pounds' worth of stock first by blast and splinters, later by looting. In the Rex Cinema, a stampede was narrowly avoided as the audience, filing out in an orderly manner after the first explosion, broke and ran at the sound of the second.

While the fire engines and ambulances of Jerusalem were speeding through the night to the scene of the explosions, the cities of Haifa and Jaffa were rocking to the noise of other bombs. Once again the terrorists had struck a triple blow. People in Jerusalem, opening their morning papers to read the official police communiqué on the outrages, found that they had not been alone in their night of terror.

In Haifa, three British police officers were killed and three seriously wounded. Bombs demolished part of the District Investigation Branch HQ, wrecked all the offices and living quarters in the south-western wing and smashed in doors and windows in buildings within more

171

than a hundred and twenty yards' radius. Rescue work for those trapped under the debris went on all night. One of the police officers killed had been an intimate friend of the Jewish community, a sportsman apparently held in high esteem by Jewish youth organisations. Wreaths were sent to his funeral, and to that of the other two officers, by the Jewish community of Haifa. The chairman and vice-chairman of the Community Council called on the Haifa district commissioner to express their "profound sympathy for the victims and sternest condemnation of the act of violence."

In Jaffa, eighteen British policemen billeted on the top floor of their HQ escaped death by a few minutes. They evacuated the building after finding thirty sticks of gelignite and a bottle of acid concealed in police haversacks. The explosion rocked the street and sent great blocks of masonry tumbling on to the pavements. Suspects in the neighbourhood were fired at. There were no arrests.

In Tel Aviv, a British constable was shot dead in a main thoroughfare after leaving the central police station. Another British constable was wounded. The chief clerk at police HQ was fired at six times as he was leaving a house in one of Tel Aviv's principal streets. A passing Jewish labourer was wounded. Another policeman was attacked near Ben Zion Boulevard. The next day police raided one of Tel Aviv's largest cafés where the gangsters were reported to be hiding. Troops reinforced police patrols in the city. The municipal council issued a statement saying that the assassins lacked even one spark of humanity and Jewish conscience. Their act was a criminal challenge to the Jewish city and the Jewish community of Palestine.

"We declare that this insane act undermines our national effort," said the Council, "and we urge the people of this city to do everything possible to uphold the national institutions and the Tel Aviv municipality in their efforts to eradicate the evil which stains our life and work." The mayor and a delegation called on the district commissioner to express "their profound abhorrence at the dastardly crime."

On that Friday, the death penalty was reintroduced, for certain offences, in an Extraordinary Gazette hurriedly published by the government. The offences included the discharging of firearms at persons; the throwing or depositing of bombs, explosives and incendiary substances with intention to cause death or injury, or damage to property; the carrying of firearms, ammunition or bombs; interference with or damaging of transport services, or water, electricity or telephone services.

Jerusalem Radio shortly before sundown announced both this reintroduction of the death penalty and also the enforcing of a curfew on Jewish residential and business sections in Jerusalem, Tel Aviv and Haifa. In both Jerusalem and Haifa, the Jewish parts of the cities were carefully defined and the Arabs were left free to move about their own quarters, to keep their shops and cafés open and lead normal lives. The punishment, as it was called, of the Jewish city dwellers for the attacks of the irresponsible Stern gang created a storm of wild protests and complaints that ran concurrently with further official declarations condemning the attackers.

The Jewish Agency claimed that the deadly hand which directed the crimes was unwittingly or maliciously helping the enemies of the Jewish people; while the Jewish people themselves became un-cooperative under the rigid curfew restrictions imposed by the police. There were many stories of unnecessary arrests, of British police over-zealous in enforcing the curfew regulations. Women and children were taken out of the gardens of their houses to police HQ for questioning. The police were adamant. Between the curfew hours, no one resident in Tel Aviv or in the Jewish quarters of Haifa and Jerusalem must step outside their houses, even into their gardens. Only by ensuring that everyone was indoors could the police hope for any measure of success in house-to-house searches.

It was however a rather pitiful sight to see the streams of women and children and perambulators rushing home in the last half-hour before curfew while the Arab women walked in bland indifference of the regulations in their own quarters, often on the other side of the street.

Special passes were issued to entitled civilians in the curfew area. Those working for the War Office or government departments received their passes quickly after police and Special Investigation Branch check-ups. There were others less fortunate. The staff of the *Palestine Post*, most of whom lived in the official Jewish curfewed quarter, stayed until dawn at the newspaper offices to produce Sunday's edition. There seemed a great deal of unnecessary hardship and red tape until one realised that the police themselves had suffered in this latest terrorist attack, and that the bodies of John Scott and five other British police officers were still unavenged.

"The police," said the *Palestine Post*, "are at present facing a supreme moral test. To the forbearance they have in their vast majority shown, the police are now called upon to add stiff resistance to the worst of all temptations — the temptation to lump the innocent with the guilty, the peaceful citizen with the conscienceless terrorist. Understandable suspicion must not be permitted to become personal bitterness. Understandable personal bitterness, if it cannot be checked, must be kept from turning into vindictiveness, because vindictiveness can easily degenerate into revenge, and revenge is loathsome and costly. The guardians of the law should be the law's most scrupulous keepers. Let no man, civilian or policeman, take it into his own hands."[79]

This rebuke with all its implications served only to heighten the feelings of the British police and to create bitterness even where there was none. Arab politicians described the attitude of the Jews to the curfew and to the police activities following the outrages as impudent, provocative and deserving of permanent punishment. The curfew, however, did involve many innocent people whose only livelihoods were small businesses dependent on evening trade. Some were forced to become bankrupt and appeal to the Jewish community for help.

Others suffered, if not financial loss, great personal inconvenience; and many used to visiting sick or aged relatives in the evenings flouted the regulations and ran the gauntlet of the police checks. On the Saturday night following the outrages, eighty people were arrested in Jerusalem alone for breaking the curfew. On Sunday, one hundred and seventy two curfew breakers were arrested in Tel Aviv. They were not released till Monday afternoon after being fined by the magistrate who toured the lock-ups to deal with each case. Women had been taken into custody in nightgowns and bedroom slippers, arrested in the yards of their houses. Many men were in pyjamas. Some children were sent home without trial after being held all night.

On Monday, Tel Aviv suffered psychological reaction. Rumours that certain buildings had been mined sent a flood of evacuees pouring out of the city. The Pardess building, the Ashrai Bank, the government Income Tax Offices and the offices of the Jewish Agency were all evacuated. Police spent an abortive hour searching for mines and time bombs. The area remained cordoned off until curfew time. When at one o'clock in the afternoon a mine washed ashore at Bat Yam, further down the coast, was detonated by bomb disposal personnel, Tel Aviv seethed with a new Stern gang story. The mayor at a special meeting appealed to the people not to repeat wild and unfounded rumours. On Monday morning in Jerusalem, three hundred people were awaiting trial for curfew breaking. The atmosphere had become so tense and brittle that a woman office worker given an escort of three police to take her home through the curfew area became involved in a shooting affray when the party was challenged by another police patrol and shots were exchanged.

The Vaad Leumi and Jewish Agency executives announced the drawing up of "a plan of action to prevent acts of criminal hooliganism." While the Hebrew press once again jointly condemned the reign of terrorism.

175

Davar, deploring the outrages, said, "It is our misfortune that the youths engaged in these abominations appear to think that such is the new way of Jewish valour. The Jewish urban population has now been placed under curfew — but the punishment is not for anything which the Jewish community as such has done."[80]

Haaretz[81] asked: "On whose head will fall the blood that had been spilt?"[82]

Mishmar[83] pointed the hand of accusation at those Jews who deluded themselves that the bandits would repent and recoil from further violence, saying that the pause in the activities of the gangs had been used to intensify their preparations. "Its net is cast, and it will continue in its violence — unless we cut off its hand."

Meanwhile the six British policemen killed in the outrages had been given military funerals and to the hundreds of British police throughout Palestine the condemnations of the Hebrew press seemed only like one small raindrop on the bare Palestine soil. Words could do nothing against gangsters. Action was needed — action on a far bigger scale than the authorities had contemplated. Police to whom I talked wanted a vast combined police-military force to be set up to comb every metre of the country and finally rid it of bandits, gangsters and terrorists potential or established, Jew and Arab alike.

On the Sunday of that weekend[84] when tension seemed to be at breaking point, the Arab dailies took a hand in stirring the bubbling pot. *Ad Difa'a*,[85] in a sweeping attack on the Jews, said: "Some people think they can wash their hands of such crimes by raising a white flag with the left hand and shooting with the right, by calling for construction and assigning colossal budgets to it and spending the money on acts of destruction, declaring at the same time "We only wish to live in peace and security and to protect ourselves from the danger that surrounds us." Such contradiction is most bewildering. At one moment a group conspires to do evil while another group declares its blamelessness of it." *Falastin*, in a series of rhetorical

176

questions, linked the outrages with the August arms-smuggling trials and asked if the murder of young Englishmen was self-defence and whether the claim was true that the certain group responsible had no connexion with other organisations. *Falastin* went on to point out that the Jews were stabbing Britain in the back while she was engaged in combating Nazism.

It seemed irreconcilable that while the government censorship should carefully blue-pencil stories liable to incite the population, bitter and provocative opinion such as the Arab papers expressed should be unfettered. There were many in Jerusalem, who while only too ready to condemn the Jews as a community, felt that community was justified in protesting against these Arab comments. Even government officials told me they considered the Arabs had been given a little too much license this time; yet to bridle Arab opinion might have been even more provocative than allowing it free rein.

The Hebrew papers naturally retorted with outspoken leaders. *Davar*[86] asked who was responsible for the reckless incitement. "Is it only the writers of those insane articles? Not they alone. There are in this country press supervisors who always ensure that nothing is published which is not to their liking [...] We place the responsibility for this incitement at this time upon the authorities who permitted it."

Hazman[87] claimed that these efforts to profit by the tension caused by terrorist acts which had no connection with the Yishuv were not very original and bore the stamp of a "hidden hand working behind the scenes."

The Arab papers mercifully forgot to recall the printing by the Hebrew dailies of the Ramat Hakovesh story in its exaggerated and uncensored form. The slanging match died down, leaving only the tang of bitterness and statements carefully tabulated by both sides, ready to be produced at suitable moments in the future when either side acted in contradiction to their present avowed policies.

And as if, that weekend, the Palestine pot was not already sufficiently full, a politically powerful Arab country, Iraq, chose that moment to issue an official statement encouraging the Arabs and causing further dismay to the Jews. The Iraqi Government, dealing with the subject of Jewish immigration into Palestine, officially stated that they and other Arab-speaking peoples affirmed their belief that Britain was not able to repudiate the White Paper and that the Resolution before the United States Congress bound no one but the Zionist agents who were behind it. The Resolution was described as a tendentious piece of propaganda which had had a negative outcome as it had given the Arab governments an opportunity to interfere and put matters straight. The Iraqi statement ended with a comfortable assurance in the justness of the Arab Palestine cause and confidence that the rights of the Arabs, the rightful owners of the country, would be safeguarded.

Chapter Twelve
April 1944

Curfew nights — New police powers — Secret arms dump in Haifa — Reaction to the curfew lifting — Incidents in Tel Aviv — No cooperation from Jewish community — A German Jewess defends the colony women — Yavniel, an exception to prove the rule — Freud's pupil on the psychology of the Jews.

From my home in the German Colony, I was able to walk along St. Julian's Way and reach an Armenian restaurant in No Man's Land between the curfew area and the beginning of the Arab quarter. On the first nights of the curfew there were not more than half-a-dozen people who had risked coming out; but gradually the restaurant became a rendezvous for those now deprived of their normal places of amusement. British police, Christian and Muslim Arabs, English businessmen and Jews who lived in the Arab, Greek or German quarters would gather there to discuss the latest incidents. In the underground bar that ran from the restaurant beneath the Jaffa Road, intense political argument took place. George, the Armenian proprietor, ponderously intervened when emotions ran high. A representative of a very small Christian minority, George held himself apart from the racial controversies of Palestine and was content if he and his family were allowed to live in peace. Though the Christian Arabs might try to win the support of the Armenians to bolster their own minority cause, George was not to be tricked into meddling in politics. As an Armenian, he was a nationalist all on his own, and pictures of Russian Armenian generals such as Bagramyan, who was at that time driving the German armies west towards the Baltic, lined the stone walls of the bar and gave the place a flavour refreshingly un-Palestinian.

In that atmosphere, I made new friends and found different outlooks on the problems of the country. The British police, many of them high-ranking officers, had often come straight from arduous questioning of suspects supposedly connected with the Stern gang. They were unanimous about the uncooperative attitude of the Jewish community and ruthlessly determined to crush out gangsterism amongst Jews and Arabs alike.

Together with their intensive campaign against the Jewish community, they were conducting equally thorough comb-outs in Arab villages and well-known centres of Arab banditry before the war. Bedouin suspected of arms running across the borders were being brought in almost daily to the police posts. Even in their own midst the police were discovering potential bandits. An Arab constable was brought up before the Jerusalem military court two days before the White Paper ended for stealing a suitcase containing two hundred and thirty rounds of pistol ammunition. The suitcase was on its way to the Arab village of Attil. On the same day, seven other Arabs from the Gaza and Ramallah areas were also tried by the military court for possessing rifles and ammunition.

"But until we get more power," said my police acquaintances, "we can't hope to strike at the real criminals behind these small fry. Both the Jews and the Arabs have powerful extremist leaders organising their arms running, but so long as we have no right to arrest and detain without warrant these big shots slip through our fingers."

The government, however, was determined to give the police all possible legislation that could help in passively crushing the strength of the gangsters. The day before the White Paper expired a new defence regulation came into force authorising police constables and members of His Majesty's Forces to "arrest without warrant and detain pending inquiries while on duty any person who could not

180

provide good proof of his identity or good reason for being in the place where he was found." The time of detention was to be not longer than twenty-four hours except on a police inspector's authority. A police superintendent could extend the period to a week but had to report it immediately to the High Commissioner through the Inspector-General.

Armed with this privilege, the police swung into action on a big scale. There were many detentions without warrant but only for the minimum time. Lack of evidence forced the release of the majority of suspects. Unless actually caught in the possession of arms, the police had no legal case and were compelled to let their detainees go. Detectives trailed the suspects. They were invariably shaken off. Jews would disappear into the colony areas; Arabs would be swallowed up in the teeming quarters of the town or in the safe isolation of villages approachable only by mountain track.

"A punitive expedition is what we need," said a retired English police officer to me one night. "Tanks, troops and reconnaissance planes working in conjunction with the Tegart forts and police armoured cars. The whole corrupt country must be scoured from north to south before the government can sit back and go ahead with post-war plans for construction and trade. Yet Britain can't spare the strength and personnel involved in such an undertaking; and meanwhile the gangsters get stronger and more reckless, while public opinion becomes twisted and played-upon by unscrupulous political speakers and newspaper proprietors. Basically, Palestine, which should be the holiest of all countries, contains a greater concentration of wickedness to the square kilometre than any of the blood-torn Balkan states."

Arabs in George's restaurant, one a well-known lawyer, frankly admitted their hopes that the acts of terrorism would continue: "The British Government has officially forgotten what the Arabs did during the troubles. Now it is the Jews, and if only these outrages can be kept up in all their intensity and bloodiness, then any hope the Jews had of reversing that White Paper, or influencing America, is gone. There are even some who say that the Arabs are subsidising the Stern gang and the Irgun Zvai Leumi in a roundabout way to bring this about."

* * *

On 31st March, the streets of Jerusalem in both the curfewed and unrestricted areas were patrolled by powerful squads of police. People carrying parcels of any size or shape were stopped and questioned, their packages examined by police officers and their pockets searched for small arms. The day passed uneasily towards its ending — a day too obvious for the gangsters to risk striking again. While the cities of Palestine waited in tense expectation, the terrorists held their fire. Only small incidents occurred. In Tel Aviv, a seventeen-year-old girl was arrested for distributing Stern gang leaflets. Zionist youths in a too fervent outburst of nationalism rounded up Jewish girls known to be consorting with American soldiers and ceremoniously shaved their heads. In Haifa, the police continued their flat-by-flat search of the curfewed Hadar Hacarmel area, making many arrests after sundown and throughout the night into the morning of April 1st.

In Haifa, there occurred that day a series of incidents worthy of a Chicago gunman's life story. One of the Stern gang was accidentally wounded while cleaning his revolver. Three of his comrades set off to fetch a doctor. They held up a taxi, drove to the doctor's house, and brought him to the garage where they had left the wounded gunman. He was gone. They followed his trail to a nearby wadi where he had taken refuge in a house, forcing the owner to allow him entrance at the point of his revolver. The owner had already telephoned for the police. While the doctor was examining the wounded man, a British police inspector and a Jewish sergeant arrived. The three gangsters escaped by flinging themselves over the balcony. The wounded man drew out a hand-grenade and hurled it at the police. Both were injured. The Jewish sergeant died within an hour. The wounded gangster himself followed his comrades, escaping through the wadi and reaching the Hadassah Hospital where he died the next morning.

Meanwhile other police had arrived at the scene. The taxi-driver and the doctor took them back to the garage. There the police made one of their most spectacular hauls. Behind the seemingly innocent doors of the garage they found an armoury capable of providing the Stern gang or the Irgun Zvai Leumi with enough explosives to wreck all the essential government offices in the city. There were pistols, ammunition, switches used for setting off time bombs, cotton waste, gelignite, tools, electrical equipment and military uniforms for disguise. In addition, the police found a duplicator with ready-cut stencils used for rolling off inflammatory newssheets and pamphlets.

At last one of the caches of the gangsters had been discovered, one of many similar caches distributed in different parts of the country camouflaged as ordinary business premises, the true nature of which could easily have been exposed by neighbours who must have been aware of a certain oddness about the premises.

The next day the funeral of the Jewish sergeant was made an occasion for public demonstrations. Hundreds of mourners congregated along the streets of Hadar Hacarmel to see the coffin draped in its Zionist flag containing the body of a Jew killed by a Jew — of a citizen murdered by one of the gangsters who, as the politicians said, were driving a dagger into the heart of Zionism and were as much the enemies of the Jews themselves as of the British authorities.

The sergeant's widow followed the coffin; his thirteen-year-old son recited the doxology over the open grave. Shabbatai Levy, Mayor of Haifa, and other prominent Jewish officials attended the funeral.

The returning procession, ironically, became mixed up with loudspeaker police vans touring the streets of Hadar

Hacarmel to announce the official lifting of the curfew. Normal life — if there could be any normal life in a city ruled by gangsterdom — had returned.

* * *

The lifting of the curfew in all three cities of Palestine brought with it more than a natural easing of the tense atmosphere. People, now able to leave their homes freely and visit favourite cafés, cinemas and friends, forgot for a brief period political problems and became ordinary human beings intent on getting the best out of their difficult lives. Though official Zionist bodies immediately called for massed meetings in the principal cities, there were few who wished to listen to mournful orations about the expiry of the White Paper. Later it was to be a different story when political consciousness once again became uppermost. For the moment, Jewish Palestine forgot nationalism and even the sufferings of their brethren in Europe amid their restored freedom and the gentle slackening of police surveillance. The Hebrew press might try to rouse them from this contented lethargy. The Arab papers might attempt to goad them into demonstrating. But they were neither to be roused nor goaded.

The streets of Jerusalem swarmed with people from dusk to long after the cafés and cinemas had closed. The threat of the first spring khamsin was already warming the air sufficiently for people to sit out of doors. Even children roamed through the streets until after midnight, good-naturedly chased by British police and told to go home.

In Jerusalem, this free-and-easy atmosphere continued well into the month. In Tel Aviv — the city most truly representative of the Jewish outlook — the tension was restored more quickly. The first week of April saw another shooting incident. A Stern gang member was arrested in daylight after wounding a British police constable and a civilian. The gangster was carrying a matchbox bomb and hand grenades. Four days later two more British constables and a Jewish constable were wounded when gangsters fired shots outside the British police billet in Rehov Dizengoff. A time bomb exploded as the gunmen escaped towards the waterfront.

It was becoming obvious that neither the appeals of the municipal authorities, nor the pungent warnings of the Zionist executives, could give the people of the city sufficient courage to hand information to the police. CID personnel were powerless to deal with the terrorism without the co-operation of the local population. Yet no one took the risk of courting revenge from the gangs by aiding these officials. To look for a suspect amid the maze of flats, tenements and tumbledown villas of Tel Aviv is like chasing a criminal in Soho. Without information, it was practically hopeless. Certain active Zionist youth organisations, opposed to national militarism, began circulating pamphlets begging the citizens to expose who was being harboured, fed, clothed, given shelter and hidden from the police. Secret meetings were held in small private gardens and homes. Prominent Jews launched appeals. It was of no avail. The ordinary people of Tel Aviv were as frightened of giving away the gangsters as synagogue mice. Like my Viennese friends in Jerusalem, they preferred to hand over their money and valuables over to those who knocked on the door at night rather than provoke retribution on relatives or risk their children being kidnapped and held up to ransom.

"The vicious circle will go on spinning and spinning," said a government official to me, "unless the Jews discover some backbone in their race. Now's the time for them to prove their solidarity as a nation. If they have any legitimate claim to reversing that White Paper then they should attempt to prove that claim by action. It is impossible for the gangs to flourish without help from the local people. It is impossible for the police to crush the gangs until the people learn what co-operation means."

185

This was the official attitude. On the humane side, it was not so simple. Who was prepared to sacrifice his family in order to help the police end gangsterdom, and so influence the British Government to change its policy? The whole problem became too unwieldy. No one was prepared to take any risk. The Jewish man-in-the-street declared that the sooner the government acknowledged that fact and realised there could be no help or co-operation from the Jewish population, the better.

The Jewish Labour leader, Eliahu Golomb[88], in an attempt to stir the people of Tel Aviv to action, stated that the Jewish case was not parallel with that of the Irish, the Arabs or other people who gained political concessions through terrorism. The consequences of the mad recklessness of the Stern gang and the Irgun Zvai Leumi might be borne by the entire community; toleration by the public would be disastrous and could lead to fratricidal war. The public must not allow itself to be intimidated.

* * *

A Berlin Jewess whom I had known for some time in Jerusalem came to see me after spending a holiday that April on one of the colonies in the Sharon Plain. Lilly was neither pro- nor anti-Zionist. Her life had been as tragic as most and she was concerned only in living from day to day and avoiding facing the future. She had lost her family by deportation to Poland and her fiancée had been taken away to a labour camp in East Prussia. She had heard since of his death. In Palestine she had become engaged to an RAF officer whose CO did not approve of the union. The officer had been posted away and later lost his life on a bombing mission. Lilly had every excuse for being morbid and fatalistic. She was neither. Instead, she busied herself with the personal problems of other people and during her holiday she had heard much dangerous information which she was anxious yet afraid to share. The little she allowed herself to tell me revealed a very tragic and desperate state of affairs in the colonies. Side by side with the story of pioneer farmers peacefully tilling the soil, planting orchards, building dwellings and rearing families was the equally vivid tale of torn emotions and twisted loyalties.

"One way or another," said Lilly, "the women are indirectly mixed up with terrorism. Wives, sisters, daughters — they've got relatives or intimate friends who they know are involved in militant activities, yet they are all too afraid to do anything about it. One woman told me her husband had left the colony nine months ago taking a rifle and homemade hand-grenades. He had gone to join the Irgun Zvai Leumi. She had had two letters since — letters full of affection and longing, together with a fervour for the work to which he was now dedicated, that of forcing the government to change its policy. He stated that he would not return to the colony until the Irgun Zvai Leumi had achieved this aim. And meanwhile," said Lilly, "she is expected to go to the authorities and betray her husband. Or if not she herself, the other settlers are expected to give information to the police. It isn't natural. It isn't humane to expect people who have suffered in Europe and have found sanctuary in this country to expose their loved ones, no matter what they are doing, right or wrong. I wouldn't do it. If my husband had come to Palestine with me and had felt it right to join the gangs, I should have kept my peace, no matter how wrong I felt he was. And that's what the women of the colonies are doing. They are suffering as much as wives of soldiers — their husbands are away fighting. Must they ask themselves if the cause is right? Do the wives of British soldiers stop to ask themselves if their husbands are right in fighting? It's patriotism which stops them asking questions, and it's Jewish patriotism that's at the back of the colonists."

Lilly went on to tell me how she knew that the settlers had a secret armoury near where she was staying. In a disused citrus packing shed they hid weapons which Lilly was adamant were only for self-defence if the colony was attacked. "But self-defence has two meanings now. The government doesn't realise that on some colonies where they've never backed the gangs they are just as much afraid of attack from the gangs themselves as from the Arabs. If a colony does not surrender its quota of weapons to the gangsters on demand they are always liable to punishment, and the Stern and the Irgun Zvai Leumi know how to wreak vengeance."

This was something new, a pointer which followed only too swiftly on Golomb's warning of the dangers of fratricidal war — the possibility of large-scale fights between gangsters and besieged colonies, between militant Zionists and pacifist Zionist farmers. Were the ramifications of the problem never to end? Was there no simplicity in Palestine? "Differences amongst the Jews" was how these problems were mildly described. How fantastic that sounded in the light of these new facts. And how real Lilly's story became when later two of the Stern gang concerned in the Haifa outrages were chased to a colony on the southern shores of Lake Tiberias and killed in a successful police action. The colony, Yavniel, was violently opposed to gangsterism. Yet two of its members had joined the Stern group and were then dominating and terrorising the entire settlement. For the first time Jews aware of what was happening had the courage to go to the authorities. With hard information in their possession, the police were able to strike rapidly and effectively. A squad of British officers, NCOs and men, rushed to Yavniel and surrounded the villa where the gunmen had their hideout. The siege went on for several hours. Hand-grenades were thrown out by the gangsters and a time bomb which failed to explode. Rifles and revolvers spattered through the broken windows as the gangsters tried to hold off the police. At last, all shots ceased. When the police broke in they found both terrorists killed.

The colonists rallied round the police and demonstrated their thanks genuinely. The British police were overwhelmed. Yavniel seemed too good to be true — a model colony ready to co-operate and help the authorities. An exception to prove the rule.

* * *

Scarlet anemones[89] carpeted the hill slopes around Jerusalem in a last burst of colour before the spring sun scorched the land into barrenness. Arab women with flat basket-trays sold the flowers in Ben Yehuda Street, calling "geveirat"![90] after the Jewish women and making sufficient money to keep their families for many days. How beautiful it was to see the patches of crimson blossom along the dusty pavements — and the velvet-embroidered dresses of the women. Amid the drab browns and greys of the busy Jewish street it seemed as though the Arabs provided the only colourful note. But I have also seen great rivalry between children selling their piastre bunches in the streets. I have seen Arab flower-sellers beating up those Jewish boys and Orthodox Jewish children with their side-curls and velvet hats in a mad flurry of arms and petals as they pinned Arab opponents on the pavement. The hate between the children of both sides is I think more bitter than that between the adults. Children absorb propaganda easily. A child from the other side becomes an object of derision and rightful prey. To those who hope that the Palestine problem will eventually settle itself, the sight of such children fighting is an adequate answer. Few individual Jews or Arabs to whom I have talked wanted violence done to the other side. But in a body, agitated by their political spokesmen, urged by their nationalistic leaders, they were ready to flight and stake all to make Palestine a Jewish or an Arab state.

In Ben Yehuda Street that spring, I made friends with a former pupil of Freud, a Viennese doctor who had at one time taught at a Scottish university. After returning to Vienna, he had been forced to escape to Palestine. As a psychoanalyst he saw intimate facets of Jewish life in the country. The majority of his patients were Jews, most of

189

them refugees suffering mental torments and needing to be cured as much as physical sufferers. The little Viennese doctor rarely failed. He lived a strange life. A hermit who disliked having to go out of doors, he sat all day long in his consulting room above the noise of the traffic and clamour of the street and when not treating patients amused himself with childish games such as sticking different coloured papers around match boxes. Such relaxation, he claimed, kept him mentally alert. His greatest task, he told me, was to eradicate what he called the racial inferiority complex of the Jews. No one would know — no one could ever know — the mental anguish the Jews suffered from persecution. The physical torture of a Nazi concentration camp seemed to him more bearable than the anguish many endured at remembering the insults and the depredations they had suffered from former friends in Nazi-occupied countries. "The feeling of being unwanted — that is responsible for all that the Jews are doing," the doctor would tell me. "Even the gangsters have arisen, not because they were potential criminals, but because they too are suffering from inferiority complexes given them by the Nazis and before the Nazis by other political bodies in Eastern Europe who were as violently anti-Semitic as Hitler's gang. The so-called criminals of Palestine, the young men from the colonies and the cities who now spend their time making bombs and grenades to throw at the police have become exhibitionists in the worst sense. Exhibitionism is a swing against persecution, real or imagined. In Palestine, the children of parents who have known persecution have absorbed something of the attitude of their adults. It has found expression not in a furtive avoidance of trouble, but in gangsterism, exhibitionism, or whatever you wish to call it. In their own minds, their acts are rationalised by believing they are furthering the Jewish national cause. In their subconscious, they are performing these acts to prove that they are as much men as the soldiers fighting on the battlefronts of Europe. No psychoanalysis can be easy, but I should find it easier to psycho-analyse a member of the Stern gang than say a refugee straight from Europe."

Many nights I sat drinking coffee in the doctor's flat, talking about his past work in Vienna and of his hope that one day he could travel to London again to found a practice there. It was difficult to discover his attitude to Palestine. He held himself aloof from politics and was only concerned with how political questions affected people's private lives. I could always assume, however, that no matter what event took place in Palestine I should get a different angle on it from the Viennese doctor. At one time he wished to speak on Jerusalem Radio and tell some of the more dramatic and tragic of his case-stories to other suffering Jews in the country. He knew that many had neither the confidence nor the cash to consult a psychoanalyst but he believed he could give them comfort by trying to explain some of their "racial" reactions to daily events. The Palestine Broadcasting Society was not interested. The little doctor retired into the seclusion of his flat to mend more broken minds and bring peace to the suffering. Artists, musicians, writers, businessmen — all came to him with their problems. The results of his treatment were in many cases almost too successful. An artist I knew — on the verge of suicide, but producing canvases which showed great creative promise — came away from the little doctor after three months treatment contented and happy with her life, so contented that she no longer wished to endure the agony of creation. Today she is a waitress in a café, her career gone, her peace of mind assured.

Occasionally Arabs would come to the doctor; one Muslim, a wealthy member of a well-known family, wished to be cured of his infatuation for a Jewish girl. The little doctor, normally mild and gentle, refused to take him as a patient.

Sitting in his flat, watching him talking, I would often think how this pupil of Freud could utterly disrupt the political plane of Palestine if he were given free rein in

191

psychoanalysing the Zionist leaders, the Muslim politicians and the members of the government. If he could have been taken to the central prison or to one of the detention camps in the plains he would have cured those members of the Stern gang serving life sentences and turned them into potentially peaceful citizens.

"If only people would realise," he'd say, "that criminal impulses, the longing to kill or be killed cannot be cured by state punishment — that militant nationalism in itself is as much a fever as typhoid, needing skilled medical treatment, then the Palestine problem, in fact the whole world problem of nations and minorities and persecution could be solved."

In the quiet of the little doctor's room, it was tempting to sit back and forget realities; to believe that the cure for Palestine was a grand scale psychoanalysis of all its inhabitants. Amid ordinary people, in the cafés and streets, amid the arguments in George's restaurant and in conversation with friends like Lilly, the doctor's solution became an impractical dream.

For the present, there were bombs and revolvers, fierce hatreds and irrational passions; and only the strong arm of the government could hope to quieten the country.

Chapter Thirteen
May–June 1944

Palestine troops desert — Demand for a Jewish army — Important arms haul in Tel Aviv — Alleged torture of Jewish prisoner — Government price on heads of Stern gang —May Day in Jerusalem — Jews may not employ Arabs — Committee of National Liberation set up by Irgun Zvai Leumi.

The bomb outrages were followed by an increasing number of desertions of Palestinians from the armed forces. Those who had been persuaded into volunteering by both Jewish Labour and Zionist bodies were now restless at inaction in base depots, suffering from separation from their families and the growing feeling that their energies were being wasted in order that the Zionists could be proud of the several thousands of Palestine Jews who had offered their lives in the cause of the United Nations. The resentment which these soldiers had harboured at the treatment they received before joining up now turned into active antagonism against Jewish organisations. Many took the opportunity of a leave pass to Palestine to enable them to slip back to the colonies they had left and fail to return to duty. Police and military squads had to be deflected from the main task of rounding up the terrorists in order to chase these deserters. When caught they complained that they had joined because they had been threatened with loosing their jobs in Jewish industries in Palestine and in some cases had been beaten up in the streets of Haifa or Tel Aviv by Zionist recruiting gangs. They had been forced to go to the recruiting offices and sign in order to defend their livelihood and safeguard their families.

At the time of the great Zionist recruiting campaign in the summer of 1943, a crisis had taken place between the authorities and the Jewish Agency, and recruiting was temporarily suspended. The Hebrew press in repeated statements reiterated that recruiting must be started again and become "nationwide", although the objective conditions of Jewish recruitment were very difficult.

The bitterness which arose at the time had remained. Palestinian Jews serving in the Mediterranean theatre now wrote to the Hebrew papers and the *Palestine Post* deploring the recent outrages, which together with the aftermath of the recruiting crisis, was causing them to suffer from increasing anti-Semitism among the British forces. "Our British comrades," said one Jewish soldier, "are losing the precious little bit of sympathy they had for the Jewish people."[91]

Many felt that their rightful place was no longer with the armed forces but back in Palestine where by behaving as ordinary law-abiding citizens they could counteract the harm the terrorists were doing to the cause of Zion.

At the same time the Labour union, the Histadrut, at an important agricultural conference, allocated new cultivable areas for post-war colonies to be manned by demobilised Palestinian Jews, and the Jewish Agency set up a special department to deal with the rehabilitation of demobilised men.

Side by side with the desertions and the official Zionist plans for catering for demobilised soldiers, a campaign was started by influential Jewish politicians for the establishment of a Jewish army. Fifty-three members of the British Parliament tabled a motion stating:

"It is the opinion of this House that in addition to a million Jews already serving in the armed forces of the United Nations, facilities should be afforded for the formation of a Jewish army under British or United Nations command to fight on any required battlefield and composed of volunteers not presently liable to compulsory military service, stateless refugees and Palestinian Jews, together with volunteers of neutral countries and territories liberated by the enemy."

But the formation of a Jewish army necessitated the acknowledgement by Britain and the United Nations that the Jews were a nation. It involved indirectly all those assimilated British and American Jews who had volunteered for service with their own countries. It created a new awareness among Christian soldiers of the United Nations that the Jews were men apart. "To ask for a separate Jewish army is like asking for a Plymouth Brethren brigade or an Eastern Orthodox regiment," they said.

The campaign, however, was to become powerful and provocative, and to cause great misery to many western Jews as well as increasing tension in Palestine unnecessarily. Even Jewish women and girls who had joined ATS units[92] were to suffer from the belief amongst their Christian comrades that they wished to be alienated and to become part of a separate army. Although the British Ministry of Information was doing its best to see that no discrimination was made against Palestinian girls because they were Jewish, the Jewish newspapers themselves tried to stress the difference and create a barrier. It seemed irreconcilable that the Jews should be courting anti-Semitism; yet there was nothing more calculated to create it than such a report as this, which the *Palestine Post* printed in the middle of May. Datelined London, it began:

"Without mentioning that they are Jewesses, an official statement praising the Palestine ATS auxiliaries who are doing important and useful work including "hush-hush" jobs in Egypt, has been issued by the War Office through the Ministry of Information…"[93]

ATS girls from Palestine returning on leave became bewildered and disrupted by the spate of official ceremonies and Zionist eulogies on their work that constantly greeted them. The girls had not been forcibly induced to volunteer. Many I knew had joined because they felt it was their duty. Some wished to take a part in avenging the death of a relative or a loved one on the continent. The life

195

they chose was hard, far harder than that of any ATS girl in Britain. Driving three-ton lorries in the blazing heat of Egypt, working in the open in the desert, enduring camp life amid sand, heat and insects is a different matter to working in an army office and living in a billet in the British Isles. No one complained, except at the flood of propaganda that swirled around them when they came back to Palestine, at the publicity that discriminated between them and their fellow Christian ATS. Even from the beginning, when the first recruits had been absorbed into the British forces, prominent Jewish speakers had not made the lot of the girls easy, nor helped them to be assimilated. The Hon. Mrs Edwin Samuel, broadcasting over the Jerusalem Radio about her visit to a Palestinian ATS camp in the western Desert, was careful to stress that in the atmosphere created in that camp the Jewish note was predominant. "In the early morning the girl soldiers leave their places of work; some must drive there, others walk in groups with a Hebrew song on their lips — a moving sight that inspires the soldiers in the vicinity with enthusiasm. The soldiers know that these are the pioneer women from Eretz Israel."

But the songs to which the girls were accustomed were those sung by the British soldiers themselves — dance-tunes from America, BBC dance records; and not many were pioneer women. They were refugees who had lived in the cities of Palestine, not Zionists building up Eretz Israel.

There were also — although little publicity was given to it — a few Arab girls in the Palestinian ATS.

* * *

Rumours of more desertions of Palestine soldiers coincided with reports of successful police swoops on Stern and Irgun Zvai Leumi arms dumps. In Tel Aviv the largest arms haul yet made by the police took place in the Hatikva quarter. (Hatikva is the name of the Zionist national anthem.) A twenty-five-year-old girl was arrested; the three gangsters in charge of the dump escaped. Over a dozen bombs of different types, sacks of gelignite and gunpowder, fuse wire, detonators, small arms ammunition and many uniforms were found, as well as the usual illegal literature.

The police carried out their raid on the Sabbath. On the same night, Vichy Radio reported the story with details of the explosives seized. The official version had not then been released. The fact that an enemy country was supplied with news through underground channels from Palestine caused more consternation to the authorities and revealed the perfection with which the plans of the terrorists had been laid. Publicity was to them the bread of life. They had achieved it, even in war-torn Europe.

Arab banditry however was keeping stride with Jewish terrorism. In forty-eight hours alone, there were nine armed hold-ups on main roads in the neighbourhood of Arab villages. Near Haifa, Arab bandits disguised in British uniform carried out a raid on a Muslim's home. None of the attacks was directed against the authorities. They represented yet another of the outbursts of lawlessness in which the Arabs of Palestine have indulged for many decades, lawlessness stamped out with ruthless methods by the officers of the Ottoman regime when public hangings were a common custom and the Arabs lived in permanent fear of the ruling power.

Allegations that the British police were also ruthless in dealing with criminals were made at the trial of a Jew, Avtalion Iyov, charged with carrying arms and laying bombs in a Jaffa government car park. The trial created much bitterness in the country. Iyov's defending counsel, Mr Levitzki — who had also led the defence in the trials of Rachlin and Sirkin, said that the police had tortured and beaten Iyov in order to wring a confession from him. The British inspector present when Iyov gave his statement denied that there was a special room at the District

Investigation Branch at Jaffa in which prisoners were tortured. Iyov himself stated in the witness box that after his arrest he was taken to Jaffa police station where he was repeatedly questioned and allowed no sleep; he was placed on a bench, whipped and beaten with a stick and bastinadoed — in the traditional Ottoman fashion — on the soles of his feet. He was then pushed round the room by constables and fell several times. Later as a result of torture, hunger and fear he made a statement which he now declared was untrue.

Another Jew, who was with Iyov in the same lock-up cell, testified that Iyov could hardly stand on his feet. A Jewish advocate stated that he had not been allowed to see Iyov for three days after his arrest and then considered his appearance heartrending. He wrote to the Attorney-General requesting an inquiry. A British sergeant denied that Iyov had been beaten.

The next day the military court overruled the allegations of torture saying it was satisfied there was no truth in them.

Iyov in his statement described how he and two other men had pasted leaflets along Allenby Road in Tel Aviv. The trial lasted four days. Sentence of twelve years' imprisonment was passed and the court refused to recommend special treatment in view of the gravity of the offences.

* * *

And so another gangster was sent to the cells.

But the police did not rest. The leaders of the Stern group and the Irgun Zvai Leumi together with their trusted lieutenants were still at large, still planning to strike more blows against the government. Details about these men were carefully collected, sifted and filed. On May 8th, the Palestine Government printed in the press of the country the photographs of six of these gangster chiefs — all members of the Stern group, the "Fighters for the

Freedom of Israel," together with the offer of rewards for information leading directly to their capture. The names, nationalities and ages gave a more detailed picture of what type of men were really at the back of the terrorist activities. Five hundred pounds was offered for information about Jacob Levstein, a twenty-five-year-old Czech. Three Poles were valued at five hundred, three hundred and two hundred respectively. Another two hundred was offered for information about an Iraqi, Jacob Levi and two hundred for Yehoshua Cohen, age twenty-one, whose origin was Palestinian.

The photographs of the wanted men were displayed prominently outside police stations throughout Palestine. Everything possible was done to impose on the public consciousness the need for capturing these criminals. Yet no information was forthcoming. The Jewish community continued to shield the men from arrest and for many months, the photographs hung outside the stations without inducing anyone to enter and give information.

"Hiding on one of the colonies, disguised, given false papers…" said my police contacts. "It's like looking for needles in haystacks. Now they know they're wanted, they'll have altered their appearances. Maybe they're outside the country waiting for things to quieten before they come back and organise more arms dumps and explosions. If we could have another Yavniel, it would be a different story. Trouble is the Jews have no courage, no national courage. They don't deserve a national home let alone a Jewish state."

At moments like that I could not help but think of some of my trusted friends amongst the Jews, of people like Kurt and other friends I had made in Hadera; of Zionists with whom politically I might quarrel but whose beliefs I could not help but respect. The little understanding the Jews had achieved amongst British service personnel and civilians in Palestine was swiftly vanishing, and turning to contempt, as the whole community became blamed for the misdeeds of the criminal few, and when each day it became more and more obvious that only the Jews could be harbouring the criminals? At that time in Palestine, when police checks were kept on everyone, when all Palestinians had to possess identity cards and ration books, it was not an easy matter to be a fugitive from justice.

* * *

May Day that year, with its many processions through the streets of Jerusalem, brought back to me a vivid picture of Hadera, and its apparently contented inhabitants, now, like Kurt, emotionally torn by the conflict in the country, fearful of the future, and perhaps secretly dominated by Stern gangsterdom.

I remembered the scarlet and gold banners fluttering down the village street and the precision with which the children had marched. But here in Jerusalem the children's part in the celebrations was even more organised than in Hadera. In the afternoon toddlers from kindergartens and nursery crèches were paraded through the main streets of the city on their way to the Histadrut Hall. They carried flags, blue-and-white or plain red, and straggled along the streets in uneven and rather bewildered groups. Older children had been carefully drilled. I was struck more vividly than ever by the resemblance of these youthful marchers to those I had seen in Trieste. I also noticed a new facet to the May Day celebrations. In the previous twelve months, the Jewish Labour bodies had been working hard to achieve a semblance of Arab-Jew solidarity on labour. May Day became the platform on which they attempted to show how great this solidarity had become. Only by those who realised that the few Arabs who joined in the celebrations represented what was called "a renegade minority" by the Arab population could the picture be seen in its proper perspective. The Palestine Labour League — an Arab body with a small membership, fostered and encouraged by Jewish labour leaders, was given all possible publicity. In Jerusalem, the secretary of the Jerusalem Labour Council handed a red flag to the Arab secretary of the League, expressing the hope that the banner would symbolise the solidarity of Jewish and Arab workers. That this hope was neither sincere nor realisable could have been proved by many employers in Palestine. I myself knew of Jewish orange-grove owners who had attempted to employ Arabs alongside Jews, and had immediately been warned by the Zionist labour bodies that to use Arab labour was to undermine the foundations of the National Home. There had also been cases in which Jewish citrus cultivators had wished to employ skilled Arabs *instead* of unskilled Jews. Notwithstanding the relative workmanship of the men, the Jewish labour bodies ordered these cultivators to employ the unskilled Jews. The alternative was to be boycotted by the Jewish citrus export-marketing firms. Faced with the prospect of having to leave their crops to rot or deal themselves with the complicated business of transporting and shipping the fruit, the cultivators had to bind themselves not to employ Arabs.

The majority of Arab workers in Palestine, aware of such discriminations against them, avoid contact with the Histadrut or the Palestine Labour League; though on this particular May Day in Haifa, those Arabs who had been weaned over to the Histadrut went so far as to carry banners inscribed with both Hebrew and Arabic characters.

A more genuine and less political expression of May Day revealed itself among the farming colonies and settlements where the atmosphere was similar to that of a harvest festival. In the Valley of Jezreel, the flourishing colony of Merhavia was the pivot for the celebrations of that rich agricultural area. Three thousand workers from up and down the valley travelled on farm wagons gaily decorated with flowers and evergreens to gather in Merhavia's eucalyptus grove. Horses were gay with the last anemones; farm tools, picks and rakes were decked out with red streamers. Yet not even Merhavia could completely resist political pressure. Over the large colony courtyard there hung a banner demanding that the government should "Open the Gates of Palestine to the Victims of Fascism...."

Could there be no rest from political consciousness? No escape from the thought of how others were suffering in Europe? Could the Jews not allow themselves to indulge in one day's happiness without tempering it with sorrow? For the adults it was perhaps right that they should remember others less fortunate, those who could not wave flags or wear garlands in the comparative safety of a sunlit day in the Jezreel Valley. But for the children? Was it necessary that their young years should be so dominated by thoughts of anguish, by political yearnings involving a constant struggle against the Mandatory Power? "Open the Gates of Palestine." Yes, how right that demand seemed, yet how wrong the atmosphere of mourning, of hopelessness in which the children were being allowed to live.

"The Jews are methodically creating a generation which will potentially be of far more danger to the cause of Zion than the few hundreds of terrorists now attacking the authorities," said people in Jerusalem. "Can't they see that they are laying up for themselves exactly the sort of situation which they deplored in Europe? Constant dissatisfaction over the present regime, reiterated demands, and the ever-present picture of the unhappiness of their brethren — when children absorb this atmosphere, there is no one who can stay their hand as they become adults. If the Jews want a militant nation, then they are going the best way to make one."

A Jewish boy who came to stay at my house in the German Colony, a child of eleven, underlined the truth of this, when he talked to me one day about his plans. Israel as he was then called — his name in Germany had been Wilhelm — had been in Palestine four years. He had lived at first in Tel Aviv where he had attended a Jewish school and later on a colony near Ramat Gan. He was a sturdy child, intelligent and mentally developed beyond his years.

Israel gave me a glowing account of his life on the colony, how he rode the farm horses and helped with the harvesting.

He enjoyed all the simple pleasures natural to a boy of his age, but he enjoyed them in a spirit of defiance against those whom he believed wished to take such pleasures away from him. Israel had a younger sister, Hannah, and already he was taking upon himself the responsibility for seeing she was safe and happy as she grew up. His parents had been lost in a pogrom in eastern Germany and he considered himself an orphan. "When I'm old enough to fight," said Israel, "I'm going to learn to handle a rifle properly and make time bombs too. It isn't brave just to wait until the Arabs come along and attack our colony. Hannah's too young to know what it's all about — and I've got to be able to protect her. If I'm caught with a gun the police can only send me to a reformatory and I'm not afraid. All the men I know can shoot — and I want to shoot too. One day I shall be a grown-up member of our colony and I mean to be a good member, able to defend it...."

I suggested to Israel that it was wrong to learn to shoot and to make time bombs; that innocent lives were being lost because young Jews were throwing bombs at the police; and that he would be a better boy and a greater credit to the colony if he worked hard at his studies and learnt farming properly.

"What's wrong with shooting?" said Israel. "Everyone's shooting each other in Germany. The Gestapo used to shoot people and now it's the Arabs who are going to shoot us. It's our land — and they can't have it. And they're not going to hurt Hannah."

"Tell me about the farming," I said. "Don't talk about Germany."

Israel began a colourful description of his colony starting with the white leghorns and coming to the old milk cow, Ruth. "But you don't want to hear about shooting," he said. I told him to go on.

"Ruth's eight years old now. She's been on the colony a long time. But she's going blind. She was wounded in the head by an Arab bullet just before the war when they raided our groves.

Israel stopped. "You see," he said. "It is right for me to learn shooting. It would be wrong if I didn't. Somehow it's worse to think of the animals getting hurt than anything else and I'm not going to have the horses wounded. I've got three live bullets already that I got for eggs I sold to some men in uniform — and when I get older I'm going to get a rifle the same way, unless the Haganah give me one!"

Israel broke off to watch a gecko lizard dart up the garden wall and slither under the vine leaves. He was off and across the paths chasing the lizard before I could ask more questions or divert him into happier topics. For the moment, his childhood had won and the little soldier had become a potential biologist.

But what manner of man would Israel be when he grew to maturity? Ordinary boys all over the world dream of handling guns when they become old enough. By the age of eleven they have usually learnt that to be a soldier is the only way to shoot at people legally. Yet here was a boy fully determined to arm himself illegally and defend the colony and his sister to the death. Here was fervour pathetic in its sincerity. How much could that fervour achieve if it was directed into more constructive channels; if the teachers on Israel's colony could show him how to love his fellow men instead of nourishing him on fear and hatred?

* * *

The cool days of early spring were passing. In May, Jerusalem once again sweltered beneath recurrent sand storms and the political tension of the country kept parallel with the rising thermometer. The government introduced heavier penalties for the carrying of arms without achieving any appreciable difference in the numbers who were known to be organising the illegal traffic. The

204

Arabs viewed the possibility of the cells with their habitual fatalism. The Jewish terrorists regarded prison sentences as martyrdom — but a martyrdom to be avoided if possible. Even the fear of provoking fratricidal war was not sufficient to deter the Stern gang or the Irgun Zvai Leumi from shooting Jewish police when on the verge of capture. Already a Jewish sergeant had been killed by a Jew in Haifa. In Tel Aviv that May, a Jewish constable was shot and murdered in cold blood by four Stern assailants. The gangsters, covering their line of retreat as the Tel Aviv police swung into action, laid a bomb at the corner of Rehov Harak Kook which exploded among passers-by and drove people indoors in a panic.

At the same time, the forces of the NMO (Irgun Zvai Leumi) were gathering themselves for a major operation planned to arouse Jewish Palestine and lead it into open war against the authorities. The scheme was daring in scale, but careless in detail. It consisted of taking over by force the government radio station at Ramallah, a few miles outside Jerusalem, and broadcasting a call-to-arms to Jews throughout the country.

The NMO first captured three trucks from owners living in the slum suburb of Petach Tikvah. The vehicles were ordered for work outside the suburb. When the drivers pulled up at the appointed place, they were attacked, taken out of their trucks and left bound in a nearby wood. That evening, the trucks were loaded with bombs, rifles and grenades. NMO forces, men and women in khaki uniform, filled the vehicles and drove off along the main Tel Aviv-Jerusalem road to Ramallah. They passed through the empty streets of the village just before midnight. Near the transmitters, the convoy halted. Eight men of the party dismounted and slashed their way through the perimeter wire fence, overpowered the guard and reached the control room. The Jewish operator courageously refused to obey their orders to warm up the transmitters and put the station on the air. While one of the gang held him with a revolver, the others set about the task in their own way. Finding the electrical machinery too complicated, they changed their minds and began to lay bombs in order to blow up the station. At that moment, an explosion occurred outside. This was the pre-arranged signal to leave the building in case the police from the nearby Tegart fort should get wind of the attack. The gangsters fled. Outside, on the road skirting the station, the remainder of the gang had been hastily constructing barbed-wire roadblocks, mined, to prevent the police getting through. Ironically, one of these mines had been accidentally touched off.

The alarm however had been raised; and from the Tegart fort came the churning noise of police armoured cars starting up.

The trucks set off helter-skelter through Ramallah and down across country towards the main Tel-Aviv road. The police signals system hummed with messages. At Beit Nabala, an ambush was laid and the first truck halted, spattering machine-gun fire and rifle bullets. Under a heavy screen of covering fire the uniformed men and girls slipped out of the truck and fled into the darkness. The two remaining trucks, warned by the sounds of firing, pulled up some distance away and the occupants escaped. All three trucks had quantities of gelignite aboard.

The next day, a Tel Aviv doctor was arrested for refusing to give a satisfactory account of why and to whom he had prescribed morphine ampoules found in one of the trucks. The doctor held the key to one of the gangsters, but he refused to pass over the information.

Some months later, when I visited Ramallah, Arab labourers employed by the government were building concrete fortifications at the entrance to the radio station to guard it against further attack. The NMO had failed in its big plan, but it had maintained tension in the country and caused more diversion of labour at a time when it was urgently needed for work on war installations.

* * *

"Nothing but a gang of hooligans," said a retired English contractor to me in George's restaurant one night. "Boys and girls decking themselves up in uniforms, trying to capture a radio station. It's like a children's two penny weekly. It shouldn't be taken seriously. They didn't shoot or injure anyone. They had machine-guns and bombs admittedly — but the greatest mistake the authorities can make is to pander to the threats of the NMO. Ignore them, don't give them publicity in the papers, and the organisation won't be able to live. Publicity — like the Vichy Radio gave the Tel Aviv arms haul — encourages them, makes them think they're little heroes."

I felt there was an essence of truth in this; but not sufficient to justify the authorities in treating the gangsters of Palestine like naughty schoolchildren. The attacks were planned by adults, even if executed by adolescents. What was obvious was that none of these gangsters could carry on buying arms on the black market, feeding and clothing themselves and finding shelter, unless someone was financing them.

At that time, the theory became current that the gangsters were self-supporting, that they had taken over one of the colonies and, although apparently a farming community, were sufficient in a legal way to pay for their underground activities. This seemed far-fetched and was partially disproved when, at the end of May, a self-confessed member of the Stern gang was sentenced by the Jerusalem military court. The gangster, twenty-two year old Zvi Tabori, was arrested in the house of a Jew in Bat Yam where he had taken lodgings. He was paying a reasonable rent and never falling behind. Tabori would not disclose the source of his funds, but he made a statement in court reiterating the aims of the self-styled Fighters for the Freedom of Israel and claiming that his possession of a pistol was lawful as he had received permission to carry it from the only authority in Palestine that he recognised — the Stern gang.

On the same day as Tabori went down to the cells, and the Palestine Police congratulated themselves on raking in yet another gangster, the Vaad Leumi announced the holding of a further day of fast and prayer for the salvation of European Jewry. Jewish shops and businesses were ordered to go on strike after lunch-hour. All Jewish bus services had to be suspended. No cinemas were allowed to open. And mass meetings were to be held in the main cities in the afternoon and evening together with services in the synagogues and public sessions of local councils.

This half-day cessation of work, following so rapidly on the previous day of mourning for European Jewry, provoked outspoken comment from non-Jews and anti-Semitic people. "Must the Jews be so melodramatic?" they said. "Why all these mass meetings, shop strikes and organised lamenting? Isn't it enough that the politicians and the press are constantly driving it in on everyone that the Jews of Europe are suffering more than any other people have suffered throughout history? Isn't it enough that the Hebrew papers, when reporting mass hangings and shootings in Europe, play down the atrocities committed against non-Jews and stress only the sufferings of the Jews?"

There was of course truth in this. The Jews were suffering and no one could or wished to deny it; but the Christians were also suffering. In Holland where nearly a hundred Dutchmen had been martyred by the Gestapo on one particular occasion, less than twenty per cent had been members of the Hebrew faith. Yet the Jewish press of Palestine headlined the story:

"EIGHTEEN JEWS MURDERED IN HOLLAND."

* * *

Though the people of Palestine were more immediately concerned that spring with gangsterdom and days of mourning, the political activities of the Zionists abroad kept pace with the mounting tension inside the country. In Britain, the Labour Party declared that it was neither anti-Jewish nor anti-Arab but its intention was to establish a Jewish national home where the Jewish flag could be raised in the Jewish homeland. In America, it was stated that President Roosevelt had expressed strong opposition to the White Paper and that Mr Churchill was in accord with his views.

That May, Zionists throughout the world were shocked and bewildered by the formation of a so-called "Hebrew Committee of National Liberation" and the acquisition for its headquarters of the former sixty-three thousand dollar Iranian Embassy at Washington. "Hebrew and Jew are not synonymous terms," stated the Committee. "Religion and state are separate. The common adherence of members of the American nation and Hebrew nation to the Jewish religion is no different from the common adherence of the Americans and Germans to the Protestant religion. One of the first steps of the Committee will be to sell one million dollars worth of Free Palestine bonds to Americans."

The American Zionist Emergency Council immediately denounced the committee, and described the action of its leader Peter H. Bergson,[94] a former student at the Palestine Hebrew University, as "an attempt to perpetrate a colossal hoax on the Jewish people," and warned the public, press and officials, "not to be taken in by the brazen fraud of half-a-dozen adventurers of no standing and with no credentials and no mandate except from the pistol-packing Irgun."

Other members of the committee included Ben Eliezer,[95] a former member of the Revisionist party in Haifa, who at that moment was held by the Palestine Police in a detention camp.

The fact that the Irgun Zvai Leumi was attempting to set up a nucleus government in the shape of a committee of national liberation, ready to take over control in Palestine when the country was "liberated" did not strike non-Jews as "a colossal hoax" but rather as a frightening example of how powerful the gangs were becoming. At the same time, it helped to wipe away any suspicions that official Zionist bodies were behind the gangsters, which was what the Arabs maintained and were not afraid to state in their newspaper.

So the difficult months dragged on. Shootings, arrests, arms running, political conferences, demonstrations, quarrels between the Jews, political warfare amongst the Arabs — it seemed that there could be no ending to the grim procession, that the open wounds of Palestine would forever lie unhealed as more and more salt was agonisingly rubbed into them.

Chapter Fourteen
July 1944

Escape to Tiberias — Problem of the Yemenite Jews — Another Jerusalem bomb outrage — Attempted assassination of High Commissioner by Stern gang — More apologies and condemnations — Sir Harold MacMichael on the Jewish "impious will to power" — Partitioning scare — The Jerusalem mayoralty — Refusal of Jewish refugees to stay in Italy.

The interlude of a visit to Tiberias had for me more the effect of a sleeping drug than a stimulant. To leave the ancient walls of Jerusalem behind me, to be no longer a part of that unhappy city, made me realise how overbearing had been the burden of sorrow beneath which I lived, how enervating the personal and political passions. Away from Jerusalem, I could relax and speak freely, no longer afraid of provoking argument or making enemies of friends.

In Tiberias, I found new friends — a quaint gallery of people who, although a part of Palestine, seemed in the warm peace of the lakeside to be a community of their own. Though they might speak of urgent political questions, there was no urgency in their outlook. The gently lapping of the lake water, slim white sails skidding over the perpetual blue, the splash of a brown-skinned Arab boy diving for fish among the boulders — these seemed the only realities, and all that had happened through the stormy winter and spring a series of passionate facts which had been endured but were now set aside.

The lakeside at Tiberias, with its flame-trees and mulberries and its stone jetties for the fishing-boats, was built

211

by a German Christian immigrant, who named it the Lido. It is as remote from the normal conception of a lido as the Serpentine is from a snake. Arab waiters in white robes and red cummerbunds move silently between the trees bringing long iced drinks and pots of "English tea" — which for them is tea without sugar boiled with it. Sparrows, tame and ready to eat from the hand, flutter on to your shoulder. From before breakfast till dusk the place is virtually deserted, for in the intense heat of June and July few visitors come to Tiberias. For Palestine, it is a winter resort and even the overnight passengers from BOAC[96] no longer interrupt the lazy summer now that the flying boats use the Dead Sea as their "landing-ground."

No one came to disturb my peace. At night, from the little bungalow I had taken at the end of the Lido, I could hear only the cries of the fisher-boys and the impatient chugging of the police launch far out on the lake.

How lovely it was to sit there at night and watch the moon rising over the Mountains of Moab. It seemed no ordinary moon that cast a promise of its coming long before the first sliver of silver brightened the black slopes. I would watch the gradual lightening of the sky over the rim of Transjordan, a lifting of the darkness — but nothing that could be defined. Then slowly the light spread over the edge of the plateau and with dramatic suddenness the tip of the moon would become visible. It moved as one watched; climbing with easy speed into the black sky until the mountain-top had been cleared and the full rays flooded the slopes and turned them into gigantic shadowed monsters. The first rays to alight on the waters of Tiberias shot out across the lake like an electric flash, tipping the ripples with brightness and reaching to the nearest jetty. Down on the main quayside, where the Arabs sat through the evening sipping coffee, there would be great crowds standing silent and still, watching the moon's arrival as if it were the coming of a pagan god.

Around the edge of the Lido, the evening flowers gave off their sweet heavy fragrance until the air seemed filled with strange perfume and bathed with alien brilliance. In the cool aloneness of the night, it felt to me as if Tiberias was a fragile dream from which I would awake dissatisfied and dulled after experiencing the pleasures of unreality. Then the English voices rising from the police launch as it tied up in the Lido harbour would deny the illusion and force me to realise that even in Palestine there were really were havens away from the constant strife.

* * *

An English missionary who had worked among the Arabs and was now living out her last days in Tiberias would come to join me at night by the lakeside. Her mind was remote from political problems and concerned only with the intimate happenings in the Arab and Yemenite Jewish homes of the town. By both peoples, she was equally well-loved and trusted. Yet in her simple old way, she was sad at the influx into Tiberias of continental Jews. Once, the town had been a collection of old tumbledown houses clustered around the ancient walls and the waterfront. Now, on the hill slopes overlooking the lake, there were modern concrete villas, prim palm avenues and yet another of the great Tegart forts which one seemed to see at every turn as one travelled through Palestine.

"It is a pity," she would say, "that this modern architecture has to be imposed on a town which was just as much Arab as Jewish — in fact more Arab, for the Yemenites themselves are closely akin to the Arabs. The two peoples, until the continental Jews came here, lived in peace and happiness together…"

And another time she would regret the fact that the proportion of Christians living beside the holy lake was growing smaller and smaller as more Jews came to live in the town. Tiberias had always had a fairly large Christian Arab population, mostly Greek Orthodox, but now, she said, these Christians were being swamped and the little mission hall of the Presbyterian Church near the water's

213

edge was becoming increasingly empty as the Christians were forced to move to the cities in search of work from which they had been displaced.

"The Yemenites — they are good people," she would say. "They are really a little nation in themselves, distinctive in their dress, tall and strong. They have lived for so long among the Arabs that they have come to be regarded as rightful dwellers in the town; there has never been any discrimination against them. But now the European Jews are coming, I'm afraid... later, there is going to be trouble... a lot of trouble."

In the Tiberias suq, I would see the Yemenites doing their shopping side by side with the Muslim and Christian Arabs. I saw Arabs buying in Yemenite Jewish shops. The intermixing of the two religions seemed a natural occurrence in that quiet lakeside atmosphere. I wondered how long this peace would last, how right my English missionary friend was with her forebodings.

Youssef, a Christian Arab who took me rowing on the lake, was convinced that trouble would come, and not first from the Muslims. "The Yemenites themselves — the younger ones, who are being educated and understand what is happening, are allowing themselves to be influenced by the Zionists. And if they become nationalistic down here in Tiberias, then we'll have tension as great as in any other part of the country. And it won't be just the Arabs of Tiberias who will be aroused. Down at the end of the lake, in Semakh and other border villages, there are Muslims violently opposed to the Jews — as ready to attack and kill as they were during the earlier troubles when the colony of Degania suffered from raids. They will rise again... and this time it will be the Yemenites who will suffer."

Youssef had a small stone house built into the hillside where he was rearing his family and saving money to migrate to Haifa. His youngest son he had dedicated to the church and he intended him to study for the Orthodox priesthood. He hoped to send his eldest son to the

Palestine Arab College and if rich relatives in Syria would provide sufficient funds later to the Beirut University. Such bold plans for his children seemed out of proportion to Youssef's earnings as a boatman and fisherman. But inflation had put everything out of proportion and Youssef's nightly hauls of deepwater fish and his net-catches of *musht*[97] near the edge of the lake brought him in a comfortable forty pounds sterling a month.

Even in Tiberias, there was a growing awareness of what was happening and the feeling that plans should be made to overcome the hand of fate gradually enclosing everyone in its grasp. Many had died in Degania from fevers and Arab bullets. The colony had known perhaps greater suffering than any other in Palestine. Yet it was hard not to close one's eyes to this and enjoy the simple peace of the lake, cruising up to the inlet of the Jordan and south to where the Ruttenberg dam made the Jordan exit a beautiful still pool of green. Amid the tamarisk groves fringing the edge of the lake, naked Jewish children from Degania colony swam and darted among the reeds. Overhead blue kingfishers were as common as the sparrows on the lido-front.

I stayed in Tiberias through the first weeks of July while the thermometer hovered around ninety and silver waves of heat danced between the palms on the waterfront. The whole town, the lake and the shadowed Moab Mountains, seemed asleep in that soporific atmosphere. I could not, would not force myself to think of racial or religious passions. I did not even wish to believe the rumours which trickled through from Jerusalem of fresh outbursts of terrorism and strife.

* * *

But there was no permanent escape.

I returned to Jerusalem before the end of the month to find the CID billet at the foot of St. Julian's Way a blackened mass of girders and debris — dramatic testimony to

215

yet another blow by the Irgun Zvai Leumi. Barbed-wire barriers enclosed the building. A permanent police guard kept watch over the ruins and among the tombstones and shrubs of the adjoining Mamillah Cemetery where the gangsters had hidden before launching their attack under cover of machine-guns mounted on the cemetery walls.

Now, in the clean sunlight, the dust and fumes of the explosion had gone and the gaunt interior of the building was all that remained to show that the Irgun Zvai Leumi had successfully struck against the authorities. The shops and houses in the neighbourhood had new panes in their shattered windows; the smell of gelignite had been blown away in the sharp mountain air, and the ashes of documents and files were now being sifted by police officers who at the time of the attack had been trapped on the top floor of the building and were rescued by fire-ladder.

* * *

July had seen another bomb outrage but as the summer passed the policy of the terrorist gangs was to change. As it began to be borne in on the Stern gang and the Irgun Zvai Leumi that such attacks, although they might cause loss of life and do great damage, were not going to deflect the government from its avowed policy, a new form of terrorism was begun. This was the political assassination, beloved in the Balkans but as yet unknown in Palestine.

In order to achieve the widest publicity and to awaken Britain and America to the fact that the gangsters had to be acknowledged politically and their demands acceded to, there was only one figure at whom they could strike — and that was the High Commissioner himself. But the blow had to be dealt swiftly. Sir Harold MacMichael was relinquishing his appointment and was to be followed by Lord Gort. Unfortunately, timetables of Sir Harold's farewell tours were published in the newspapers.

On a hot August afternoon[98] His Excellency's car with aide de camp and police escort came up through the Bab

216

el-Wad from Jaffa on its way back to Government House. Sir Harold had been attending a farewell reception. His time of departure had been signalled to the gangsters and an ambush was waiting just outside Jerusalem.

The car drove into a trap.

Machine-guns spattered against the windscreen, injuring both the High Commissioner and his ADC. The escort, Police Constable Hills, attempted to chase the gangsters. He was later given the King's Police medal for gallantry. But the chase was slow. The Stern gang men escaped over the rocks and tracks, fled into a Jewish colony and were swallowed up from the police patrols.

That afternoon the news sped through Jerusalem like an angry flame. The offices of the Jewish Agency seethed with details of the disaster. No greater blow had been struck at the cause of Zion, no more irreparable harm done to the political aims of the builders of Eretz Israel than this calculated and criminal attack on the life of the High Commissioner. What sympathy would there be left in Britain or America for the Jews, if the gangsters of Jewry struck blows such as this?

A spate of official condemnations appeared. As usual.

Meanwhile the High Commissioner and his ADC were rushed to the government hospital and local newspaper correspondents filed cables at the Public Information Office for the British and American press. But out of the thirty or more cables sent by these journalists, not more than three gave the fact that the gangsters had found refuge, if only temporarily, in a Jewish colony. The implication running through the bulk of the stories was that the attackers were casual Arab bandits attempting a road hold-up.

The truth however became known. The Arab papers were justifiably outspoken. The Hebrew press unanimously condemned the outrage. In fact it seemed that everyone in Palestine was universal in condemning the attack on the High Commissioner.

How then had it been allowed to take place?

Sir Harold himself ignored the spate of public apologies and continued to drive around Jerusalem in his private car with no greater police escort than before. But the time for his departure was growing nearer, and the official Zionist bodies were feverishly trying to dispel the harm done to the Jewish cause before he returned to England.

The High Commissioner, however, was to make an outspoken speech about the situation in Palestine before taking his leave of the country, a broadcast message which was to provoke criticism from the Jews and appreciation from the Arabs because he dealt boldly and fearlessly with the subject of terrorism. The rebuke he delivered to those who believed in the law of force was complete. Coming from the lips of the one man who knew all the facts and figures, who was aware how great the tension had become, it created a tremendous consciousness throughout the country that something would and must be done to stop the reign of terrorism.

After speaking of the many dangers from within threatening the peace and welfare of Palestine, Sir Harold said, "The gravest of these is that political fanaticism which has been deliberately inculcated among the younger generation and regimented to ends which are the negation of all that is meant by democracy — that same impious will to power which reared its ugly head in Germany and brought to ruin the pleasant friendly world which many of us love to remember. Not all sympathise with it, thank God — far from it — and Palestine may yet be spared its natural consequences, but a great and urgent duty falls upon all who have wisdom enough to realise, and moral courage enough to combat, the danger to make their voice heard and their influence felt before it is too late. I can think of no greater tragedy than that the ending of a war waged to defend the cause of justice and freedom should be the signal for the outbreak of a futile struggle for political domination in the land that first heard the words "Peace on earth and goodwill towards man." Those are words not only of deep religious import. They enshrine the highest human wisdom, and the ailment of Palestine may be summed up in the words. "Too much cleverness: too little wisdom."[99]

Sir Harold's speech was quoted and re-quoted in the Palestine press. Arab papers such as *Ad-Difa'a* self-righteously pointed out that they were fully aware where that great cleverness and little wisdom were to be found, and went on to say that reports from abroad during the preceding months, particularly from America and Britain, had provided more examples of such cleverness and the Jewish love of domination and Jewish political fanaticism were constantly being manifested. *Falastin*[100] reiterated Sir Harold's references to political fanaticism and stressed his use of the word "deliberately" in his statement that such fanaticism was inculcated among the younger generation: "Will His Excellency's warning reach the hearts of those who are deliberately inculcating political fanaticism in the younger generation and will it be heard by every "interferer" in America who does harm to the peace of the Prince of Peace in the country where the words 'Peace on Earth, Goodwill to men' were uttered..."*

Thus the Muslim press reacted, praising every phrase of the High Commissioner's speech and deploring the way the Jews were training young boys and girls in the colonies and in the schools to become imbued with the same "impious will to power" as the Nazis themselves. Never before had the Arabs been so outspoken in their criticism of the Zionists' educational policy; never before had the blame for what was happening in the country been laid at the door of the Zionists themselves.

The Hebrew press tried valiantly to whitewash the official Jewish bodies and to undo the harm that they considered Sir Harold's speech had unnecessarily caused.

Mishmar asked:

"Apart from "political fanaticism" and "the impious will to power', could the High Commissioner after six years

Review of the Palestine Press, August 1944, published by the Public Information Office.

find nothing else worth mentioning at the moment of his departure? Does not a bleeding nation that is suffering as no other nation suffered deserve some more positive words of encouragement, consolation and appreciation? Was it only "political fanaticism" that was preached to our youths? Were not other doctrines preached to them? Doctrines which encourage our youths to reclaim swamp lands and revive the wilderness, to fulfil great human ideals and create economic, social and national assets of which any nation would be proud? Has all this been appreciated even once in a speech of the highest official in the country, who must understand and recognise comprehensively what is going on? There was little reason to expect that Sir Harold would find in Palestine the pleasant and friendly world for which he is longing so much — not because we do not know what friendliness is. Sir Harold was sent to this country on a most tragic mission — to put an end to all our hopes for national rebirth — and he was compelled to execute it in a period and under circumstances which turned an unjust and illegal policy into a cruel one [....] Unlike the initiator of the policy, the man on the spot has the opportunity to see for himself what measure of suffering and wrong that policy involved. However we did not find either understanding or appreciation..."*

And another Hebrew paper, *Yedioth Achronoth*, said that they too could not think of a "greater tragedy" than that the war waged for justice would end in unjust exertion of power. "The small nations cannot prevent the great from abusing their victory — for the purpose of political domination by force. We therefore hope the message of His Excellency will find attention in London."*

It was expected that Sir Harold's speech would be followed by another attempt on his life, and embittered anti-Zionists sarcastically wondered if the *Palestine Post* would select a more appropriate heading to the story than

*Review of the Palestine Press, August 1944

it had given on the day following the outrage: "Attempt on High Commissioner Fails."[101] Extreme precautions were taken by the police and security forces. On the night when Sir Harold attended a farewell dinner at Allenby Barracks, Jerusalem, the streets of the Holy City swarmed with armoured cars and mounted police. At that time, the Arabs were celebrating the month of Ramadan, a time when guns are fired at dusk to signal the end of each day's fasting and the right to taste food for the first time since sunrise. The guns of Ramadan fired their salvoes that night in the middle of Sir Harold's dinner speech. Sir Harold continued impassively. Outside Allenby barracks things were not so passive. Armoured cars, mounted police, foot police — everyone in uniform went into action. Arrests were made on the spot, strategic positions taken up by machine-gun units while police headquarters seethed with orders and reports. This time the Stern gang had the laugh on the police. That such a normal and expected occurrence as the guns of Ramadan could speed the police into action proved how thoroughly the gangsters had disrupted the country, creating taut nerves even amongst the guardians of law and order.

* * *

A few days later Sir Harold left Palestine. Until the arrival of Lord Gort in November, an Officer Administering the government became the chief power in the country. In matters of extreme political urgency, his decisions had to be approved by a higher personage and the most suitable at the time was the British Minister of State in the Middle East — Lord Moyne. This was to have a direct bearing on later events.

For the moment, Palestine without a High Commissioner went on in its normally tense and tragic way. The police carried out a few successful swoops on arms dumps, arrested a number of gunrunners and caught a few of the Jewish gangsters. But these successes were little when set against the vast and intricate mechanism of the forces of Stern and Irgun Zvai Leumi, whose ramifications were now known to be extending beyond the confines of Palestine and to be involving nationalistic Jewish youths in other countries of the Middle East as well as in the Western world.

At this time the well-worn question of partitioning came up again, started by rumours in the British press and increased by attacks in the Palestine Jewish papers, which declared that the rumours were circulated by government officials anxious to test the reaction of the Jewish public to this old and abandoned scheme. Partitioning has, however, been proved to be impractical. Cantonisation on the Swiss system is a dream of complacent theorists who mark lines on maps without understanding the intricate tapestry of Palestine. If there was to be any solution to Palestine, I knew that partitioning was certainly not it; nor were the suggestions put forward in September at the Arab conference in Alexandria of any practical value in solving the Palestine question. The idea of an Arab Federation had already died. No Middle East country was willing to give up its ideal of national independence. The scheme of a Greater Syria based on a union of Syria, Palestine and Transjordan under a Hashemite ruler such as His Highness the Emir Abdullah was foundering on the suspicion that it was a plan of Iraq, also under the Hashemite dynasty, to gain control of the Eastern Mediterranean seaboard. But on Palestine all the Arab nations showed a united and unshakable front, standing firmly by the White Paper and differing only in the form of Arab government which should rule the country.

While the Arabs of Palestine were expressing agreement with statements at the Alexandria conference, those in Jerusalem were more immediately concerned with the fate of the mayoralty. Mustapha Bey Khalidi,[102] already over seventy when he became mayor of the city, had died and left a vacancy that the Arabs were anxious to fill again. Although in Jerusalem the Arab population were in a minority, they maintained that an Arab personage should stand at the helm of the capital of a country that was Arab and not Jewish. The Jews insisted that, as sixty-five per cent of the people of the city were Jews and not Arab, and that as seventy-five per cent of the revenue of the Jerusalem municipality came from the Jewish sector, they never had and never would renounce their right to a Jewish mayor. They pointed out that they had decided to refrain from political action to bring this about during the period of mourning for the late Mustapha Bey, but that the Arabs had not shown such restraint. Therefore they were conducting a campaign which would place Daniel Auster, an old member of the municipal council[103], in the seat of the mayoralty.

The government was not long in making its decision. To the consternation of the Arabs, Auster was appointed acting mayor to succeed Khalidi — a decision of surprising courage and fairness.

For the Zionists, this news was to be followed by an event no less important — one that in its small way proved many of the Zionist contentions. It was the refusal of a hundred and fifty Jewish refugees in Italy to accept the proposal of the Italian Government in freed Italy to stay there and to abandon their plans of migrating to Palestine. One does not know what pressure, if any, was brought to bear on those refugees, but the reports of what happened give a simple straight story of a group of men and women refusing to contemplate life in a country where they had known religious discrimination and preferring the hardships of the Middle East. They stated that they wished to return to a country which, to them, had always represented home. One wondered if those refugees fully realised that they were exchanging one atmosphere of unhappiness for another potentially far more dangerous than an Italy controlled by the Allies and swinging towards liberal ideas under such tolerant thinkers as Benedetto Croce.[104] *Davar* made much of the incident and said the reaction of these refugees to the attempt at persuading them to stay in Italy was significant, above all, of the stubborn tendency of the rulers of the world to make a difference between the refugee and the Palestine problem on the one hand, and the firm determination of the Jewish refugees to frustrate this plot, on the other.

The Arabs, however, were not prepared to accept the story. Muslims in Jerusalem brushed aside the apparent facts and adamantly insisted that the Zionists had bribed the refugee families to refuse to stay in Italy. Had they accepted the proposal to settle down there, the Zionists would have suffered an irrevocable blow.

Amid this welter of crossed opinions and passionate attacks against the government and each other, Jews and Arabs moved in a rising crescendo of fear and hate. Allied successes in Europe, the advance of the Red Army, the prospect of coming victory served only to intensify feelings in Palestine. While other countries might, beyond the black clouds of the immediate future, glimpse a lightening of the sky, the heavens of Palestine were as thunderous as they had been on the day when the Rock was rent in twain.

Chapter Fifteen
September 1944

Jewish Brigade sanctioned — Irgun Zvai Leumi launches night attacks on Palestine Police forts — British police officer assassinated — A new curfew — "Illegal" sale of land to Zionists — Irgun Zvai Leumi loots government textile store — Official appeal to the Jewish community.

People passing through Palestine during those early autumn weeks were inclined to ridicule the atmosphere of fear in which they found the country living. English businessmen, oil company representatives and bankers touring the Middle East told me that Palestine was taking itself altogether too seriously, and that in Britain people were little interested in what was happening in that particular notch of Asia. They were wholly concerned with the immediate phases of the war and events in Europe. Palestine did not seem of great importance. A handful of gangsters run amok and groups of politicians of different religions striving for opposite aims — neither one nor the other was going to arouse the British public nor plunge Palestine into civil war.

I could not credit this lack of awareness. I felt that only a small section of British opinion could be ignorant of the repercussions that events in Palestine would have on the post-war world. To believe for one moment that people in Britain — closely bound by religious ties to the Holy Land, and through the Colonial Office deeply involved in the future status of the country — were not aware of the seriousness of what was happening took away the hope of any solution which might bring ultimate peace and happiness to both Jew and Arab. Yet I heard these assurances about the British outlook repeatedly as friends and acquaintances passed through Jerusalem in a procession of indifference to the realities of the situation. That this indifference was to be shaken, I was positive, without being able to supply proof.

* * *

The September days dragged on.

An isolated police raid on the Tel Aviv suburb of Petach Tikva ended with the arrest of a number of Jews alleged to be actively helping the gangs. They were placed in detention camps alongside other Jews who had been kept in custody for many months on the suspicion of terrorist activities.

But the arrests did not make big news. Palestine was more concerned with political whisperings about the imminent formation of a Jewish army. In the middle of September, the British Government pronounced its blessing on the setting up of a Jewish brigade. Although the news was welcomed by the Zionists, the welcome was not as wholehearted as the British Government had expected. All the Hebrew papers expressed regret that the matter had been delayed so long, and claimed that for nearly five years, since the beginning of the European war, the formation of a separate Jewish fighting force had been a very great and real necessity. This permission of the British Government was tardy — a gesture made at the eleventh hour, a half-hearted gesture because it allowed only the formation of a brigade and not of an army.[105] However, the implied recognition by Britain that the Jews were a nation with a right to their own fighting force was stressed by the Hebrew press.

"But the struggle of the Jewish people for full recognition has not yet come to an end," said *Hamashkif*, the Revisionist paper.[106] "The more persistent our demand will be, the greater are the prospects of its success. Our goal is the formation of a Jewish army." *Hamashkif* at the same time attacked the Jewish Agency. "What did cause surprise," said the paper, "is not the formation of the Jewish Brigade, but the statement by the Jewish Agency that this achievement was the result of their efforts." *Hamashkif*, speaking for militant Zionism, claimed that the British Government had agreed to the formation of the Brigade, not through efforts from the Jewish Agency, but because of Lord Strabolgi's activities in London. This intimate quarrel among the Jews themselves over who had won the prize seemed uncalled for and unwise — providing as it did yet another excuse for the Arabs to point their ever-ready hand of scorn.

The London *Times* was careful not to confuse the decision of the British Government with the acknowledgement that the Jews were a nation. The *Times* said that the agreement of the War Cabinet constituted an acknowledgement of the fine response of the Jews of Palestine to the call for volunteers.[107] "The *Yishuv* in this country is proud and glad that there is a reward for the volunteering of thirty thousand of its sons and daughters...."

But unfortunately the thirty thousand Jewish men and women from Palestine who had volunteered or been persuaded into volunteering was about the maximum number which could be squeezed out of the Jewish population without robbing the colonies of skeleton staffs or ruining Jewish industrial concerns for lack of labour. The new recruiting campaign which immediately opened for enlistment in the Jewish Brigade met with little response; and it was obvious that the Brigade would have to be formed mainly from the Jewish units already attached to the Allied forces but as yet not sent into any European fighting zone.

* * *

The political storm over the Brigade was at its height when the forces of Irgun Zvai Leumi (NMO), slashing across verbal argument, took matters into their own hands with a display of strength calculated to "frighten" the Mandatory Power into acceding to Zionist demands. This time it was no hit-and-run attack in which time bombs were laid and the gangsters fled before the alarm could be raised. The NMO forces had grown powerful enough to launch and continue attacks against defended buildings until they had achieved what they had set out to do. This new technique came into action on the night of September 27th 1944, when strong NMO forces deployed at strategic points throughout the country converged on four widely separated police strongholds and conducted battles that lasted in one or two cases until dawn. At the fort of Beit Dajan, near Jaffa, the police garrison had to withstand attack from shortly before midnight until early morning. A large NMO force launched an assault on Beit Dajan from four directions and smashed through the outer barbed-wire barricades. After two hours' intense firing from the police, the NMO unit was driven back beyond the defence perimeter. Other NMO forces brought up mobile floodlights, which they beamed on the walls of the fort. A second wave of NMO men again penetrated the defence area and threw bombs at the building. After concentrated and prolonged fire from the besieged, the NMO reluctantly gave up the struggle and retired in good order. They left behind them flags printed in Hebrew, Arabic and English — the three official languages of Palestine — warning those who might come to the rescue that each approach to the fort was strategically mined.

While Beit Dajan was under siege, a second NMO force, disguised in khaki uniform, was attacking the police fort of Kalkilya in the Arab district of Tulkarm. The NMO unit, armed with hand-grenades and bombs, made determined attempts to break into the building. But Kalkilya was well-defended. After several hours the attackers were forced to withdraw. On the roads and tracks leading to Kalkilya, red lamps in addition to flags were placed, giving warning of more mines.

The third police stronghold to be attacked that night was Katra, near Gedera. Here, the NMO force detailed for the assault succeeded in breaking through both the outer and inner defence lines. An Assyrian corporal[108] who tried to hold the main entrance was killed. The Orderly Room was set on fire, the flames sweeping beyond into the central part of the fort. Smashing the doors of the station armoury, the NMO force looted the police rifles and machine-guns and retired before any effective resistance could be put up. The Rehovoth Fire Brigade, summoned quickly to the scene, fought all night to extinguish the flames of the fort. Meanwhile, the NMO men, moving northwards across country came upon an army tender which had run on to a mine. Two Allied soldiers in charge of the vehicle were held up and ordered to hand over their arms. One resisted and paid with his life.

Beit Dajan, Kalkilya and Katra were country forts. The most audacious of the night's attacks was that delivered against the Eastern Police Station in Haifa. Here, in the midst of a thickly populated city, the NMO was able to execute a successful raid without either encountering police reinforcements from other parts of Haifa or suffering casualties. Armed with machine-guns, the gangsters launched their assault just before midnight. The protecting air-raid blast wall was wrecked with homemade bombs and the NMO force broke through into the building. Explosives with warning notices were placed on the surrounding roads, and after looting the NMO force retired with only two of its men slightly wounded.

This fourfold blow, though politically not as important as bomb outrages against the Immigration Offices and other government buildings housing valuable archives, revealed the fighting strength of the Irgun Zvai Leumi in a dramatic and startling way. Here was an organisation that on one single night, in scattered parts of the country, could detail more than one hundred and fifty men — the figure officially given later — to carry out armed action and evade capture. Here was proof that "a handful of gangsters run amok" were trying to impose their "impious will to power" on the government.

* * *

Zionists in Jerusalem deplored the outrages.

The Hebrew press appealed to the thinking public to regard the new terrorist acts as modelled on the gang warfare launched by such criminals as Al Capone against the forces of law and order. The NMO, the papers reiterated, was not acting within the framework of Zionist policy. It was out to create chaos.

But to the police the latest blows did not bear resemblance to the activities of Al Capone. The attacks on the four police forts had all had one purpose — not to seize the authorities, but to collect arms and ammunition in preparation for a countrywide rising.

On the day following the night battles, the police took up the chase throughout the country. Within twenty-four hours, they arrested two of the NMO gangsters in Tel Aviv carrying one hundred and fifty sticks of gelignite and more than four hundred and fifty cartridges. Scarcely forty-eight hours had passed since the attacks and the police were still scouring the cities for NMO members when the Stern gang struck again.

Jerusalem heard the news in a dramatic broadcast over the Palestine Broadcasting Service.[109] Assistant Superintendent P.J.Wilkin, walking in broad daylight through one of the city's main thoroughfares, had been assassinated. Two men, dressed in nondescript civilian clothes had fired eleven bullets into his body. They had escaped in a waiting taxi long before the alarm could be raised.

That afternoon the military commander of Jerusalem signed another curfew order prohibiting all movement in the Jewish quarter of the city after four o'clock. Jerusalem Radio broadcast the order at frequent intervals. Police armoured cars with loudspeakers toured the curfew area, warning the inhabitants not to leave their homes. Later, steel-helmeted police armed with tommy-guns, together with British troops, patrolled the streets of the Jewish quarter and kept guard along the boundaries of the forbidden area. Well over seventy-thousand Jews came under the restriction, cramped up in their flats and overcrowded villas awaiting the methodical street-by-street searches of the CID.

In the uncurfewed area, Jerusalem became a city of rumour and counter-rumour. Terrorism had struck on the capital in a new and more frightening form. A well-planned and neatly executed murder had taken place in daylight beneath the eyes of passers-by powerless to intervene. The lives of all police officials and public personages were now in jeopardy. No one who at any time had had anything to do with governing the country or imposing law and order was apparently safe from retribution. Wilkin had been instrumental in bringing many criminals to justice from the gangster-ridden suburbs of Tel Aviv. In January 1944, he was transferred to the Jewish Political Affairs Section at Jerusalem's CID Headquarters. Towards early summer, he had begun to receive threatening letters. The letters increased in violence and in number until the last letter before his assassination, which told him that he could no longer escape the sentence which the terrorists had passed on him. Wilkin, scorning the offer of a personal guard, had defied the threats. He paid with his life — and proved to the Stern gang that assassination was an easy and practical way in which to achieve their aims.

The curfew was continuous throughout that night and into the next morning, the Sabbath. Not till noon did Jerusalem Radio broadcast the announcement that the inhabitants of the Jewish quarter were free to leave their homes after 1 pm. They had, however, to be indoors again before six o'clock. The curfew hours were now fixed. From six in the evening till six the next morning — for an indefinite period.

Consternation among the Jewish public was immense. Once again, Jewish spokesmen asked why all should be

231

made to suffer for the misdeeds of the few; and again official Zionist condemnation of the murder was heard side by side with these unofficial complaints at the harshness of the authorities. There was still, however, no active cooperation forthcoming from the Jewish community. "And until there is," said police officers, "there will be no lessening of the restrictions. The Jews themselves must bring about their own salvation."

People's sympathies became torn and twisted in those difficult days of early October while the Jewish community lay boycotted from normal life, guarded and policed. It was ironical to see former members of the notorious Arab Higher Committee, the body responsible for the 1936–1939 "troubles" moving freely about their business. Had the Arab community been cordoned off and curfewed in those years one might have felt the present restrictions justified. But there had been no discrimination against the Arabs comparable to the stay-at-home order for the Jews. Nor had the Arab community been subjected to house-to-house searches.

During those curfew nights I talked to many British people known for their anti-Jewish feelings and while the majority maintained that the Jewish community deserved its punishment, there were a few who argued that the curfew was an admission of failure by the authorities. While maintaining their anti-Semitic outlook, they showed, perhaps for the first time, some understanding and sympathy for the ordinary Jewish people who were suffering for the deeds of the few. There were others who allowed their anti-Semitic feelings to rise to new heights of fury. "Attacks against the police, criminal acts against the government, shots at the High Commissioner, bland assurances from the Hebrew press that the gangsters represent only a small criminal minority, "the impious will to power" — that is Palestinian Jewry," they said to me.

I heard too regrets amongst government officials that Britain had seen fit to sanction the formation of the Jewish Brigade. And hopes that some voice would reveal to

Britain the true story of what was happening in the country — how the administration was being deliberately harassed and provoked both with political weapons and bombs.

* * *

One would have thought that during those tense months of 1944 the Zionists would have scrupulously avoided any activity calculated to inflame Arab opinion. With feelings strained to breaking point, and all that the Zionists had fought for at stake following the successive outbursts of terrorism, it seemed reasonable to expect them to be conciliatory over internal matters. But a bombshell was due to explode.

The Arab newspaper *Falastin* revealed the story. Under the White Paper, the sale of lands to people other than Palestinian Arabs had been prohibited. This prevented the Zionists acquiring farmlands on which to found new colonies. Yet one thousand dunams[110] of fertile land in Esdraelon owned by Arabs had however passed into Jewish hands. How had this transaction been possible? *Falastin* with a flourish described how a "renegade" Arab landowner had opened negotiations with prospective Jewish purchasers, obtained an advance sum, spent a few months in Egypt and returned to Palestine with an Egyptian passport. As The White Paper prohibited only Palestinian Arabs from selling land to Jews, the Land Registry sanctioned the transaction. "Thus a thousand dunams of our best lands have gone...," said *Falastin*." And a few days later the paper stated that in view of the many sales of Arab lands to Jews in prohibited areas "through the employment of cunning and crooked ways" the Palestine Arabs had decided to send a memorandum to the Colonial Office and the Officer Administering the government, protesting.

Backed by their newspapers, the Arab community sweepingly condemned the Zionists. The Zionists retorted that the Arabs had been only too willing to sell their lands at high prices and could the Jews be blamed for taking what was offered to them?

* * *

While Muslim nationalists fretted and fumed over the acquisition of more land by the Zionists, the police pursued their all-out drive to capture the terrorist gangsters. Settlements and colonies were subjected to surprise searches. CID officers accompanied by semi-military forces descended on the settlements before dawn, questioned the farm-workers and searched the buildings and villas. A clue to the murderers of Assistant Superintendent Wilkin led the police to the colony of Ataroth on the main Jerusalem-Ramallah road. But there was no information forthcoming.

Undisturbed by such police activities, the forces of Irgun Zvai Leumi continued to plan and deliver fresh blows. A bloodless outrage took place in Tel Aviv, where the terrorists carried out an audacious haul of textiles which subsequently found their way on to the black market. One October afternoon, an Irgun Zvai Leumi unit composed of about fifty armed men and boys, whose ages ranged from thirty-five down to fourteen, broke into the premises of the Controller of Light Industries. Some of the gangsters smashed their way in through the front door, overpowered the watchman and placed him, together with members of the staff, in the basement. Others, who arrived with trucks, entered through the adjoining garage, locking the garage employees and members of the public who came into the garage from time to time in a store room. The third platoon of the raiding party broke in through the roof. For three hours the Irgun Zvai Leumi worked undisturbed, loading rolls of cloth into their waiting lorries. The captives in the basement and the storeroom were warned they would be shot if they tried to raise the alarm. Not till the trucks had been driven safely away were they released.

And by that time the haul of cloth was on its way to a secret rendezvous.

That night eight drivers reported to Ramat Gan police station complaining that early in the day they had been approached by men who had chartered their trucks to collect fruit from Tel Litvinsky, a nearby citrus-producing centre. The drivers had been paid in advance and were taking their trucks to the colony when at a point near Merkaz Bala'ai Melachi they were stopped by armed men who forced them to leave their vehicles and robbed them of their licences. All the drivers were then placed in a nearby orange grove under guard and told that their trucks would be returned to them later. At about 5pm they were marched across country and released near the Petach Tikva road.

* * *

It was now obvious that something drastic would have to be done to restore law and order in Palestine. Armed attacks, kidnapping, murder, looting — there seemed no crime which the Irgun Zvai Leumi and the forces of Stern were not prepared to plan and commit. Although the police during those autumn months had been successful in rounding up several score of Jewish men alleged to be either criminals or associates of criminals, the masterminds behind the gangs were still at large. Who were these shadowy personages who flitted away from justice into the enveloping arms of the Jewish community? Were they to be found in Tel Aviv, apparently living normal lives as ordinary businessmen; or were they known by the Jews themselves and being given sanctuary on the colonies?

While the authorities concerned themselves with this imperative problem, the ordinary people of the country suffered and endured. The Jews suffered more keenly than others, especially those who came daily into contact with the English community either through employment or at social gatherings. They were now having to endure discrimination, and were becoming ostracised in a way they had never considered possible. In cafés and restaurants, Jewish people who understood English heard Allied servicemen denouncing them with unnecessary bitterness. A Viennese Jew, a former Russian born in Kiev, told me that he was leaving Jerusalem solely because of the change in the outlook of his English friends.

"Those who tolerated me," he said, "have now lost what little sympathy they had. Here, in Jerusalem, a Jew can no longer be happy among Western Christians. The gangsters have achieved something which was not one of their avowed aims — and that is the driving together of the Jewish community in Palestine. I have always considered myself a Russian who adopted Austrian nationality. But now I am being made aware that I am a Jew — no better than the other Jews who are as eloquent with political demands as with bombs and bullets."

A few days later he had gone. One by one, other Jewish friends of mine began to leave the capital. Most of them disappeared into the teeming residential districts of Tel Aviv. Some who had friends in farming villages like Hadera went to settle in the country and live on what little money they had saved.

"We had thought of Palestine as a haven — if only a temporary one," many of them told me. "But it has become a prison surrounded by the bars of racial hatred. Each new blow by the terrorists deepens that hatred. There is no hope left for any of us who contemplated peace and security in this country."

Some major step was awaited from the authorities.

It came on October 10th, when Jerusalem Radio broadcast an official communiqué in the names of the Officer Administering the Government and Commander-in-Chief Middle East Forces appealing to the Jewish Community to help the forces of law and order in stamping out terrorism. The communiqué was adamant and fearless:

"Palestine, through the exertions and sacrifices of His Majesty's Forces and the Forces of the Allies has enjoyed for five years virtual immunity from the horrors of war which have caused such unspeakable suffering elsewhere. Since early in the present year, Palestine has, however, been the scene of a series of outrageous crimes of violence by Jewish terrorists, acting with the deliberate intention of bringing about by force developments favourable to the realization of political aims.

"Officers and men of the security services have been murdered in cold blood and shot while doing their duty in the defence of life and property; innocent passers-by have been killed. Government buildings to the value of scores of thousands of pounds have been destroyed by explosives and fire. An attempt, providentially unsuccessful, was made to assassinate His Majesty's Representative in ambush.

"These events are proceeding side by side with the bitterest phase of the critical fight between the United Nations and Nazi Germany — the cruellest, most implacable and most ruthless persecutor that the long history of Jewry has ever known. The criminals in Palestine, with their active and passive sympathisers, are directly impeding the war effort of Great Britain, which is playing such a vital part in the struggle against Hitler. They are assisting the enemy.

"These facts will not be overlooked by public opinion throughout the civilised world.

"Every practicable measure is being taken by the Army and the Police in the difficult circumstances to prevent these crimes, to detect the authors of them and their accomplices and to bring them to justice. These measures will continue with all the resources, civil and military, available to the government and the Army.

"Mr Shaw, Officer Administering the Government of Palestine and General Sir Bernard Paget, Commander-in-Chief Middle East Forces call upon the Jewish community as a whole to do their utmost to assist the forces of law and order in eradicating this evil thing within their midst. Verbal condemnation of the outrages on the platform and

237

in the press may have its effect but is not in itself enough: what is required is actual collaboration with the forces of law and order — especially the giving of information leading to the apprehension of the assassins and their accomplices.

"Accordingly, His Excellency and the Commander-in-Chief now call upon the Jewish community in Palestine, their leaders and representative bodies to recognise and discharge their responsibilities and not to allow the good name of the Yishuv to be prejudiced by acts which can only bring shame and dishonour on the Jewish people as a whole."

While the ordinary people bowed their heads beneath the accusation of active and passive sympathy, the Zionist politicians and press vigorously denied that the community should be made to shoulder the blame for the criminal few. The *Palestine Post* regretted that the Authorities "had not found it necessary to give expression to some appreciation of the Jews' share in the war as firmly as to the condemnation and warning" …and went on to declare that the Yishuv would, while the situation lasted, "bear patiently with the inconvenience and the strain of searches…"[111] *Haboker* criticised the wording of the appeal, saying that people would draw the conclusion that the whole Yishuv was responsible "for this mad anti-British movement."*

But the reaction of the Arabs was no less intense than that of the Jews. The Muslim community in the capital pointed out that the government had misplaced its confidence in the Jews long enough. Now at last it was seen that the Jews had abused that confidence. They were fit neither to have a national home nor a state and certainly not a Jewish brigade.

Ad Difa'a quoted the old Arab proverb "To think well of another leads to trouble" and said the government was now faced with such trouble after thinking well of the

*12 October 1944

238

Jews despite the knowledge that Jews were smuggling arms in great quantities and had at the military court trials delivered many zealous speeches describing their nationalistic dreams and ambitions. The government had believed the many telegrams of condolences too long — so long that General Paget had to declare that the mere expression of disapproval from platforms and in the press was not sufficient. *Ad Difa'a* concluded by hoping that the government regretted having so misplaced its confidence.*

In the meantime, an account of the terrorist outrages was given in the House of Commons by Colonial Secretary Mr Oliver Stanley. He stated that there had been a recrudescence of Jewish terrorism, outlined the attacks on the police stations, recalled the murder of Assistant Superintendent Wilkin, and gave details about the robbery in Tel Aviv, when textiles valued at one hundred thousand pounds were removed. In answer to a question about how automatic weapons and ammunition were produced by the Jews, Mr Stanley pointed out that during the past five years there had been a great many troops moving about the Middle East and undoubtedly, a certain amount of arms had been stolen or in some cases sold by them.

Earl Winterton[112] asked if the Minister was aware that those in touch with people in Palestine were alarmed by the information that both sides were arming, preparatory for civil war after the European war.

Mr Stanley later reiterated that verbal denunciation by the Jewish community was not in itself enough. "What we want and hope to get," he said "is the active collaboration of the whole Jewish population of Palestine."

Review of the Palestine Press, October 1944.

Chapter Sixteen
Mid-October 1944

Return to Hadera — Zionist indignation over General Paget's appeal — Nazi agents chased and caught — Terrorists deported from Palestine — Zionists ask "Why no trial?" — Government explain how the Jews can cooperate — Roosevelt backs Jewish Commonwealth.

From where was this active collaboration coming? From the Jews in the cities? Or the farm-workers on the colonies? In Jerusalem, I could see no signs of the Jewish community actively cooperating with the authorities; and from what I had learned of the attitude of the men and women in the settlements there did not seem any hope of collaboration from that source. "What the government is doing is asking the Jews to betray their own brethren," I was told by Zionists and non-Zionists alike. "Does the government really expect us to reveal happenings we know of which might involuntarily lead to wrongful arrests?"

I felt there was only one type of Jewish community which might have a more realistic — a more fearless — outlook. Would not the Jewish villagers, men bred from early pioneer stock, be more willing to give practical help in tracking down the gangs?

The answer to that question lay in Hadera — the village which, amid all the political stress and strain of Palestine, clung ardently to its pioneer background. The village where Kurt and Ruth and other friends would tell me their attitude to the government request for cooperation.

* * *

I travelled down to Hadera in the middle of October.

The land lay parched and dull under the long summer heat; and the sand clouds moving overhead from the hilltops into the plain were as oppressive as only the last khamsin of the year can be. Hadera itself was labouring under the dust when, after the tedious ride through the Bab el-Wad and the bleached highway beyond Lydda, my car pulled up outside the hotel. The streets of the village were no longer as I had remembered them a year and a half before. Here were no streams of people, villagers, women shoppers, perambulators. Those whom I saw seemed furtive in their movements — afraid. It was not difficult to know why. The asphalt road, warmed by the sun, bore the deep imprint of police armoured cars. Police lorries were moving through the village. Road police on high-powered cycles swept by, apparently oblivious to pedestrians. The atmosphere was redolent of suppressed tension. As I stepped out of my car and looked up the hill past the smithy's shop, it seemed to me that the synagogue that day was no longer a symbol of the spirit of the early pioneers, but a mortuary containing the dead hopes of those who had fought so long and so courageously against the swamps and fevers of the Hadera area. What had those pioneers achieved, if fifty years later the people of the village were moving under a cloud of police displeasure, conscious that their hopes of ultimate happiness were vanishing as irrevocably as the torrent-filled wadis dried up in the spring?

When Kurt came down the steps to greet me, his smile was that of a tired old man. "I am glad you have come," he said with a heavy shake of his hand. "There has been so much... so many changes..." And his squat figure followed me up the stairs of the hotel into the old room where Ma Dubrowsky had spent her hours of anger as processions and demonstrations in the street below drove her indoors from the balcony.

There, in that room, with the blinds and shutters closed against the heat, we sat in half-gloom talking first of personal things — and then of the people I had known in the village. There was news of a certain Gavriel who had been arrested that summer, charged with keeping a revolver in his house. Gavriel pleaded that the revolver had belonged to his father who had served with a Saxon regiment on the Saar. The revolver had been a family possession since the end of the Great War. His plea was not sufficient to save him from a detention camp.

"It is the wrong ones they are getting, the wrong ones all the time, the innocent ones who have least to do with terrorism," said Kurt sadly. "Yet it isn't the fault of the police. No one can blame them for being ruthless — now. When no one is ready to give them information then they must arrest whom they can. There are many, many people in this village who know of strange happenings which they should tell the police, but there is fear, all the time there is fear, of retribution."

"Kurt," I said. "I can't believe that here in this village of families bred from pioneer stock there is no courage or foresight. Don't they realise that by holding back now they are laying up all the horrors and agony of civil war for their children. Can't they be made to understand that sacrifice now is as nothing compared to what they would have to sacrifice later?"

Kurt shook his head and went off to the kitchen to refill our glasses with tea. When he came back, he answered my question. "They don't look at it like that. They're all living in the present. They've always been forced to live in the present, persecuted and oppressed. But stronger than that is their loyalty even to those of their brothers and sisters who are committing crimes. Who knows? They may have friends, even relatives in the gangs. And directly or indirectly they are not going to be responsible for sending them to prison, sending them to serve the long sentences which the military courts impose."

We sipped our tea and he went on: "Besides that, people are afraid for themselves. If they go to the police, they may be found out over trivial offences they've committed

242

themselves. Living in Palestine in the fifth year of war is not easy for anyone law-abiding. You can't get enough to eat if you don't get the bulk of your food on the black market. People are always contravening. If a soldier gives a villager a tin of fruit from the NAAFI[113] then the villager has committed an offence in accepting it. It's all so diffi-cult. Even clothes have to be bought on the black market. I don't think there is one of us who could not be charged with some contravention. It seems wrong that such small matters should stand in the way of something national, but when you come down to the bottom of things it's how small matters affect people's lives that counts. And you won't get a grocer in the village telling the police he's over-heard two suspected terrorists talking about stealing a truck if that grocer has half a sack of sugar behind the counter to which he's not entitled."

"But you yourself, Kurt?" I asked.

"Me?" The squat shoulders heaved so that his head seemed to be sunk into his body. "Me?" he repeated. "Why should I be the one to move?"

And there I felt was the essence of the problem. Why me? Why not my neighbour? Why not anyone but me, an ordinary Jew, living in a modest way, not actively Zionist and not conscious enough of the trouble I am laying up for myself to risk retribution?

Later, when Ruth came in to join us I found her attitude was even firmer than Kurt's. We spoke only briefly of the months which had passed. Then I asked her what she felt about the government appeal for cooperation. "I look at it like this," she said. "It doesn't concern me. I've done my part towards the building of Eretz Israel — I've worked my fingers thick and sore toiling to make a living for myself. I'm an immigrant, a self-supporting member of the community. Why should I try to remember all I hear and risk being kidnapped or maimed — for giving information. Why can't the authorities deal with the terrorists them-selves instead of throwing the job on us?"

Ruth told me that her divorce was now legal. She was

hoping to marry again and become a citizen of another country. "That's what I want to do — get out," she said. "And if anyone's wise, that's what they'll do. What's the good of staying in Eretz Israel in the midst of bombs and bullets and appeals?"

* * *

I had come back to Hadera in the hope of finding the people more willing to cooperate than their fellow citizens in the towns and on the farms. Though this hope was not justified, the people of Hadera gave me new reasons for the lack of cooperation from the Jewish community, reasons which made the Jewish attitude more understandable.

A former doctor of law, a Czech Jew, living in the village, underlined for me the Jewish attitude. "It's the aftermath of Europe," he insisted. "When you've lived in perpetual terror of the Gestapo, no matter how just the British police may seem, you always retain fear of a police uniform. Those who have known loved ones taken away from them, who have themselves suffered, who have been afraid to walk down a street with a Gestapo officer at the other end, afraid to enter a shop in which they glimpsed a uniform — those are the people whom the authorities now ask to cooperate with them and censure them for not doing so. No — first we must educate the Palestine Jews to trust those who are ruling the country. And the spate of political protests from the Zionists, instead of helping, undermines what little trust these refugees have acquired."

When I left his house and walked home through the streets of the village the lights of the villas were shining defiantly through the palms and eucalyptus branches. The police patrols were no longer obvious. Those lights, glowing so comfortably on well-tended gardens, made a picture of contentment and security. If the terrorists were allowed to go on unchecked, unhindered, how long would it be before those lights began to flicker out? Did these people, living for the moment in uneasy peace, understand what civil war would mean? Families torn apart, rich farmlands laid waste, brother killing brother — the entire effort and the years of achievement of the Palestine Yishuv destroyed and its peoples decimated...

If there was to be any hope of quelling terrorism then that picture had to be brought forcibly before their minds. But there was only one body who could do this — the Zionists themselves.

* * *

When I returned to Jerusalem, however, I found the Zionists still concerning themselves with official indignation over the proclamation from the Officer Administering the government and General Paget. Even the Chief Rabbi of the British Empire, Dr Hertz, in a letter to the *Times*, pointed out that the wording of the warning had been most unfortunate:

"No responsible Jew anywhere endorses the senseless crimes of the terrorists, yet the Palestine authorities seem to hold every Jew — the humblest as well as the highest, inside and outside Palestine — as responsible for them. Moreover, they assert that these crimes bring dishonour upon the Jewish people as a whole. This is the first time to my knowledge that a British administration anywhere has condemned an entire people for the acts of a repudiated few."* Dr Hertz rightly recalled that the Mufti of Jerusalem had directed the Arab terrorist campaign in Palestine and was now collaborating with Hitler in Berlin, yet no official British representative ever declared that his misdeeds brought shame and dishonour on the Arab people as a whole.

At the same time, the Palestine Revisionists sent a strong protest to the Colonial Secretary against the allegation made

*13 October 1944.

by him in the House of Commons that there was any connection between their party and the Irgun.

Protests and indignation, though partially justified, still seemed out of place. The communiqué from the Officer Administering the government and General Paget might be considered ill-worded, published without due thought. But whatever criticism was made, it did not belie the fact that Jewish terrorism had neither lessened nor halted, and that it was taking place in the middle of the greatest struggle against the powers of evil in the history of Great Britain. It was detracting from that struggle.

* * *

No better illustration of the way these acts of terrorism were undermining Palestine's war effort could have been provided that October than the dramatic attempt by Germany to exploit the internal situation.

Gold coins flooding the countryside, sneak-aircraft flying over the Judean Hills to drop parachutists, Nazi spies at large in the mountains… this was the story which pointed a moral at the Jewish community, a story which could never have been brought to its proper conclusion without the "active cooperation" of the Arabs of Jericho and the semi-nomadic Bedouin of the hills between Jericho and Jerusalem.

The story began with five Arab shepherd boys who were tending their flocks a few kilometres east of Jericho. They watched an aeroplane flying northwards from the direction of the Dead Sea. The aircraft was losing height. It dived to treetop level and released a bag filled with gold coins. The shepherd boys made for the nearest wadi where they knew of a safe hiding-place for so much money; but the wadi was occupied by three strange men, one of whom, dressed in khaki uniform, ordered the boys in Arabic to run away as military operations were in progress.

The boys ran to their homes. Soon a group of Arabs was on its way to investigate. In the wadi, now deserted, they

246

found English sovereigns and other gold coins; paper money totalling about four hundred pounds, and quantities of ammunition. Pocketing the gold, the Arabs made off for Jericho where they hoped to change it in the suq for Palestinian currency. But the gold created a sensation. Law-abiding shopkeepers informed the police who sent a mounted squad to the wadi. They found what the Arabs had overlooked — a black German parachute and a metal container inside which were machine-guns, explosives and electrical, medical and other equipment in addition to German-Arabic dictionaries, documents and clothing.

So German spies had been parachuted into Palestine. German sneak-aircraft had attempted to supply them with money and arms. But the hunt was up. Jerusalem Radio broadcast details of the police find and appealed for the cooperation of the public. Arabs from the sparsely inhabited area between the capital and Jericho came to the police with stories of suspicious characters they had seen, tales of more gold coins and other information, which led to the police discovery of a radio-transmitting set buried in an olive grove as well as more arms and documents. Forty-eight hours later a Bedouin shepherd boy reported another find to the police — a second German parachute. Investigators sent to collect the parachute discovered still more arms and German sabotage equipment hidden in the ground.

Police squads took up the chase. Palestine Police, the Transjordan Frontier Force, and the Arab Legion combined in a full-scale search of the wadis and slopes. Arabs and Bedouin from the area cooperated. That same evening Faiz Bey Idressi, in charge of the police arrangements, found fourteen German maps of Palestine hidden in bushes near the site where the first parachute had been found. The next morning, Arabs came to the police with the news that three suspicious persons had been seen walking up through the Wadi Kelt, that gaunt ravine where the Greek Convent of St. Georges is built on precipice ledges. The three people had been wearing brand-new fellahin garments. They had been challenged by the convent watchman, but had failed to answer.

Police forces were sent to the wadi. A few days later, a British officer of the Transjordan Frontier Force with his patrol ran the German parachutists to ground in a cave between the Wadi Kelt and Bethany. All three were captured alive.

* * *

Neither the Arabic nor the Hebrew press had opportunity to make much of the story. The chase and arrest of three Nazi agents, however dramatic, was overshadowed by a happening of far-reaching importance — one which was later to be the indirect cause of the assassination of a British Minister.

On October 19th, the Palestine Government informed the country of action which had been taken to deal with terrorism. Forty-eight hours prior to the announcement, the police had carried out a surprise swoop on Tel Aviv and, in the course of extensive searches through the city between midnight and dawn, had arrested a number of alleged terrorists or associates of terrorists. Tel Aviv apartments were methodically searched, although many tenants at first refused to grant police entry. How many had been arrested? No one knew. In its statement, the Palestine Government recalled various police activities since the beginning of September and made the unexpected disclosure that within the past two months no fewer than one hundred and eighteen members of the Irgun Zvai Leumi had been caught. Prior to September, an additional one hundred and thirty-three terrorists had already been detained in the camps at Latrun and Acre.

The official statement went on:

"In the interests of public security and the safety of life and property in Palestine, two hundred and fifty-one persons who have been detained under the Emergency Regulations as terrorists or for complicity in terrorist activity have been transferred to military custody and removed to a place of detention outside Palestine."

Giving further details, the statement revealed that no fewer than forty-six arrests had been made during the police raid on Petach Tikvah at the beginning of September, when two hundred people were interrogated. Police had arrested another five men at Kfar Saba — men believed to have taken part in the attack on Kalkilya police fort. On October 10th, twenty-nine Irgun Zvai Leumi members were detained after the areas of Ramat Gan and Bnei Brac had been cordoned off and a curfew imposed. Three days later, two more terrorists were arrested when the colony of Tel Tzur was surrounded at dawn.

A second government statement, issued simultaneously, declared that air raid sirens would no longer be used to give warning of the approach of enemy aircraft. The "intermittent wails" would be used in cities and towns to warn the public of terrorist activity. All traffic would immediately come to a standstill and members of the public would be expected to cooperate with the police and give them information.

Zionist reaction was intense.

The authorities expected official Jewish bodies to applaud the government action in exiling those who were striking the deathblow at Jewish aspirations in Palestine — those who had displayed their "impious will to power" with bombs and bullets. They hoped that those bodies who had consistently deplored and condemned terrorist activity would now acknowledge the necessity of deporting those already caught while the main forces of the Irgun Zvai Leumi and Stern gang were still at large, planning new outrages.

But the pendulum of Zionist opinion swung violently in the opposite direction. The news, instead of being accepted as a ruthless but necessary measure, provoked the heaviest spate of protests yet to emanate from Zionist bodies. No matter how potentially dangerous the two hundred and fifty-one terrorists might be to the internal security of the country, the Zionists contended that their expulsion from the homeland, their exile without trial to another country was intolerable, unjustified and against the elementary rights of Palestine Jewry. "Who had assessed the guilt or innocence of the deportees?", they asked.

The two most representative newspapers, *Davar* and *Hamashkif* summed up Zionist attitude. *Davar*, under the heading "251 EXILES" wrote:

"Of the two hundred and fifty-one Jews accused of being members of the Irgun Zvai Leumi, or suspected of terrorist activities, who were exiled from the country for detainment elsewhere, a punishment has been inflicted with which public opinion of the Yishuv as a whole cannot put up. Our attitude towards acts of terrorism and their perpetrators is well-known. We have appealed to the Yishuv to give a helping hand in the mopping up of the destructive forces that undermine the last hope of the nation, and we shall continue to do so. We have welcomed the firm and energetic measures that were taken in order to trace the terrorists, and we did not deny the authorities the right to put the criminals on trial.

"However, never shall we put up with two kinds of punishment which in reality constitute one single punishment: the death penalty and the exile of Jews. Our opposition to these two penalties is deeply rooted and lies outside the ranges of topical disputes. It emanates from our recognition of the sanctity of life and from our recognition of the indisputable right of any Jew to live in Palestine, even in prison.

"In addition, we wish to be assured that all the two hundred and fifty-one exiles really did perpetrate acts of terrorism or were connected with the perpetrators and that the compilers of the lists who are responsible for the detainment and the banishment did not make mistakes. Yet even if all those two hundred and fifty-one people were found guilty after a thorough examination, the expulsion of Jews from their homeland, their last shelter, is intolerable..."[114]

Hamashkif, the Revisionist paper, was more downright:

"During the past six months the authorities have arrested hundreds of people following acts of violence committed in Palestine. The arrested people were not caught on the spot while committing the said acts. There is not sufficient evidence against them — or at least against most of them — and it may be there is no evidence at all that they have any connection with any illegal acts. They were arrested because they had been suspected of being members or sympathisers of an illegal group. Many were arrested only because of their political views. The Government has no right to ascribe guilt to persons who were not tried by a Court of Justice and whose guilt was not established. The administration is committing a mistake.

"The news of the transfer of the two hundred and fifty-one men from Palestine overwhelmed the whole Yishuv. Palestine citizens have an elementary right to remain in Palestine. They are entitled when they are under arrest to see from time to time members of their family, to receive parcels from their wives or parents, to read newspapers and enjoy all fundamental rights of prisoners recognised in all civilised countries.

"Why have the two hundred and fifty-one detainees, citizens of Palestine, been denied this elementary right? [...] No! Such measures cannot be considered part of the fight conducted against acts of violence. We protest against them, and we are sure that the whole Yishuv will rise and demand the return of the detainees to Palestine."*

The Hebrew paper *Haboker*, more moderate in its outlook, published one of the causes that the government considered made the removal of the detainees imperative:

"It is well known that attempts were made to set prisoners free by the use of force, and it may be that the government regards such attempts as justifying the deportations."

*19 October 1944

251

Haboker continued: "If that be the government's excuse we must say that it is inconceivable. The authorities have enough force to frustrate any attempt made in Palestine to release detainees."

The same paper also published a cartoon depicting an elderly Jew staring dumbfounded at the sky where a squadron of aircraft is seen passing. The old man mutters: "Strange world! To bring Jews to Palestine — they haven't got any ships; but to deport them — blest be God — they have even got aeroplanes."*

And is it truly a coincidence, asked the Zionists, that the aircraft used were Liberators?

When it became known later that the place of deportation was Eritrea, Zionist indignation grew deeper. By what right had Jewish "criminals" been exiled to a former Italian colony, without trial and with no hope of redress? How long was this intolerable exile to last?

* * *

The Zionist demand that Jewish terrorists had the right to be imprisoned in Palestine was taken by anti-Semitic people in Jerusalem as proof that the Zionists were unofficially backing the gangs. That October, the social atmosphere of the city changed. I found Britishers and Americans were binding themselves into tight little colonies and refusing to accept invitations to homes where they might meet members of the Jewish community. Even those who had no anti-Semitic disease refrained from visiting their Jewish friends. It was as if a social curfew had been placed on the Jews. This, together with the cloud of official disapproval under which the Jews moved, drove them deeper into the privacy of their own quarters. Only a few became outspoken. The majority proudly refused to explain their point of view to those anxious to help them.

*29 October 1944, under the headline "Teko" (stalemate).

As further raids were carried out by police forces, the tension mounted. Before the month ended Petach Tikva was again surrounded and searched. Police flying squads arrested fourteen more Irgun Zvai Leumi members. Another twenty-two arrests were made when nine hundred people were interrogated in the little coastal resort of Nathanya, north of Tel Aviv.

But arrests no longer provided reassuring news for the Jewish community. Thirty-six more men in custody: was their fate to be similar to that of their brethren in Eritrea? Were they to be detained without trial indefinitely?

Meanwhile the parents of those men already deported had organised a demonstration against the government's action. They met outside the Municipal Offices in Tel Aviv to protest against their sons being sent out of the country. At the same time, in Tel Aviv and in the farming-colonies up and down the valley, meetings were held where the attitude to the government's policy was defined in increasingly bitter terms: "We are asked to cooperate with the police — to give information which will lead to the arrest of alleged terrorists," they said. "How is it possible for us to betray our fellow men like this when we know that their guilt will not be proved and that they will be detained on suspicion and flown away into a land of exile?"

* * *

At the end of October, the government issued an official explanation of the form it considered cooperation from the public should take. Pointing out that every citizen had the right to arrest without warrant and hand over to the authorities any person who had committed a crime or escaped from custody, it insisted that help must also be given the police in effecting arrests or preventing escapes. It also stated that information about suspicious activities must be passed promptly to the nearest police station. The official explanation ended with a criticism of certain newspaper reports, which it said had given a misleading picture of the kind of cooperation the government expected. The public was not supposed to investigate terrorism on its own or to attempt to counter lawlessness with lawlessness.

While the Jewish community received the statement with a heavy heart, President Roosevelt in America, on the eve of the election, declared that if he were returned for a fourth term he would back the policy of establishing a Jewish Commonwealth in Palestine. Zionist rejoicing over Roosevelt's support was, however, tempered by the violent reaction of the Arabs. Muslim opinion heaped derision on Roosevelt's declaration, claiming that it had been made solely as a bid for the votes of the several million Jews in America. Roosevelt, said the Arabs, had no intention of implementing his promise. But, at the same time, in case any future president of the United States might consider fulfilling the promise, the Arabs of Palestine wished to show their intense opposition in a concrete way. They were therefore issuing a rousing challenge to the Arab population of the country to boycott all American goods and thus, in the words of *Falastin*, strike against the murder of justice and honour.

* * *

Challenges and protests, demonstrations and arrests followed each other in a chaotic procession. Jerusalem, the capital, laboured amid the unrest like a tired old woman, impotent to deliver the country from its mental and physical agony. No more adequate expression of the emotions of the people could have been delivered by the most eloquent Arab and Jewish newspapers than the storms which at that time broke thunderously over the Judean Hills. Under granite skies, punctuated by sheet lightning, the Holy City — the city of Christ and chromium as it had been described — seemed a sodden graveyard of rich hopes and high endeavour.

Chapter Seventeen
November 1944

New High Commissioner arrives — Arab strike — British Minister assassinated — Eden's statement — Jeers in the House of Commons — Churchill's rebuke — Another illegal arms trial — The right of self-defence — Arab bandits attested.

Lord Gort's arrival in that supercharged atmosphere produced an instantaneous reaction. Both Jews and Arabs welcomed him in the role of a deliverer — a man who would rule the country with wisdom and justice. "Now the policy of the White Paper will be abandoned," said the Jews. With equal conviction, the Arabs declared that there would no longer be any talk of reversing the White Paper.

All the colourful and impressive ceremony which Palestine could muster greeted Lord Gort's arrival in the country. The Dakota transport which flew him from Gibraltar landed amid cheering crowds of Arabs, Jews and British officials at Lydda airport. Groups of Arab villagers and Jewish colonists who had walked many kilometres to catch their first glimpse of the man who had come to save their country waited by the roadside between Ramleh and Jerusalem. In the city, police flying squads and armoured cars with machine guns patrolled the streets. Incidents were expected. There were none. Lord Gort's car moved smoothly through the capital, escorted by the white and grey chargers of the Transjordan Frontier Force and greeted by the pipers of the Arab Legion. The only hitch in the official programme was the absence of Acting Mayor Daniel Auster, over whose appointment the Arabs had protested so bitterly. No transport had been authorised to bring Daniel Auster through the police barricades.

In the ballroom of Government House, the great colonial-style mansion which dominates Jerusalem from a peak of the Judean Hills, the swearing-in ceremony was carried out with simple dignity beneath the draped Royal Standard and Union Jack. Every facet of Palestine was represented in the gathering — the Chief Justice in scarlet robe and wig; the Latin Patriarch in brilliant crimson; the Chief Rabbis in their traditional black; Muslims with red tarbushes bound with white kaffiyehs; Palestine Police in navy and silver. Amid this splendour Lord Gort's service dress struck a note of pleasing simplicity. And it seemed right and fitting that Lord Gort should listen to the welcome of the Chief Justice who declared with realism that he could not offer the new High Commissioner the whole-hearted cooperation of the people of Palestine which the urgency of the hour demanded. Lord Gort replied by quoting from the *Book of Proverbs*: "Where there is no vision, the people perish."

* * *

Neither Arabs nor Jews gave Lord Gort time to accustom himself to the peculiarities of the country and the stress and strain of the internal situation. On the morning after his arrival, the *Palestine Post* made a new appeal for the return of the deportees. The paper underlined that Lord Gort's arrival coincided with a time when the British, the Jews and the Arabs were confused, distressed and disquieted; and stated that if bringing the deported suspects home could contribute to restoring peace to the country, neither pride nor prestige should be allowed to stand in the way. It expressed the hope that Lord Gort might prove equal to the challenge. The revisionist paper *Hamashkif* pointed out that Lord Gort was the young general "whom Mr Hore-Belisha, the Jewish Minister of War, discovered and promoted to the rank of Chief of the British Imperial Staff."*

*3 November 1944

256

Lord Gort had been scarcely forty-eight hours in the country when the Arabs carried out an organised strike in protest against the Balfour Declaration, the anniversary of which falls on November 2nd. Throughout Arab Palestine — in Jaffa, Gaza, Nablus, Acre, Lydda and Nazareth — and even in the Lebanese city of Beirut, protest meetings were held at which appeals were made to the Arab countries of the Middle East to save the lands which were threatened with being bought by the Jews.

The Arab press chose that moment to recall that there were still numbers of Arab political prisoners interned or exiled during the 1936–1939 troubles who should now be allowed to return to their families in Palestine. The Jewish paper *Hed Yerushalaim* appealed to Lord Gort to release the prisoners from the colonies of Hulda and Ramat Hakovesh, and from the Emek and Tel Aviv in order to let them join the Jewish Brigade.

The anniversary of the Balfour Declaration passed with uneasy tension as both Jews and Arabs organised demonstrations and public protests. The Jews were no less bitter than the Arabs. The Balfour Declaration, or the Mandate, which Dr Weizmann had dramatically declared before the Royal Commission to be the Bible of the Jews — had promised the setting up of the Jewish National Home. While the Arab newspapers printed extracts from the Declaration within heavy black frames, the Jewish papers stated that the National Home that Balfour visualised had now been changed into the White Paper Ghetto. If Britain were to implement her promise, the Balfour Declaration could become what had been intended — a Jewish Charter of Freedom.

The welter of appeals and requests which poured into Government House at the beginning of November had scarcely been sorted and laid on Lord Gort's desk when news came from Egypt which was to shake the political structure of Palestine to its foundations — news of the murder of the British Minister of State Resident in the Middle East, Lord Moyne, at the hands of Jewish terrorists.[115]

* * *

The gangsters had struck again.

They had carried out the most calculated and cold-blooded crime of their black record, a crime which was to provoke anti-Semitism from British members of Parliament and induce Mr Churchill to deliver a rebuke to Jewish national aspirations.

Splashed and bannered by world press and radio, Lord Moyne's death was as dramatic and brutal a story as the murder of King Alexandria of Yugoslavia amid the splendour of Marseilles' Canebière. The full details of the assassination were given world prominence. In America, in Britain, throughout the melting pot of the Middle East, the newspapers headlined the fact that the assassins had been Jews — although for forty-eight hours after the first news-flash of Lord Moyne's death there was no official confirmation of either the nationality or religion of his murderers. Even when the Egyptian Government announced that the two men who had been caught after attempting to escape from the scene of their crime would speak only Hebrew it was still not officially confirmed that they were Jews. Mr Churchill, when he rose in Parliament to pay tribute to Lord Moyne on the day following his death stated only that he had "died at the hands of foul assassins" and that no official information had been received which fixed the authorship of the crime or gave a clue to its motive. Mr Churchill's restraint was unfortunately not remembered when his later rebuke to the Jewish community was received with indignation and sorrow. General Sir Bernard Paget, Commander in Chief. Middle East, had already described the two assassins as Jews and the Jewish Agency itself seemed in no doubt about their identity, expressing horror at the "revolting crime" which raised anew the growing danger of the continued existence of the terrorists. "The Yishuv is called upon to cast out the members of this destructive band," said the Agency, "to deprive them of all refuge and shelter,

258

to resist their threats, and to render all necessary assistance to the authorities in the prevention of terrorist acts and in the eradication of the terrorist organisation. Our very existence is here at stake."

The *Palestine Post* very naturally refrained from identifying the men as Jews until it was officially confirmed. No truer words were ever written by the paper when it said: "If, as appears likely from the reports, the murderers of Lord Moyne are Jews, then, however deep the sympathy for Britain in its loss and for Egypt in its difficulty, even deeper sympathy must go out to the Jewish people themselves. The shots fired at Lord Moyne were aimed at them."

Two days later Mr Eden rose in the House of Commons to give an account of the assassination. "The two prisoners," said Mr Eden, "have made the following confession: 'We are members of the Fighters for the Freedom of Israel organisation and what we have done was done on instructions from this organisation.'" Mr Eden stated that the organisation was that known as the Stern group. The prisoners had admitted that they were sent down to Egypt for the express purpose of murdering Lord Moyne. "The reason they had given," said Mr Eden, "was that Lord Moyne was head of the Political Department of the British Government in the Middle East and was carrying out a policy which was against that of Jewish nationalists. The Stern group therefore decided to kill him."

Mr Eden then described how the actual assassination had taken place when Lord Moyne's car came to a standstill at the beginning of the drive leading to his house. "At one time," said Mr Eden, "Lord Moyne was regularly escorted by Egyptian police in a car which accompanied his own and a police guard was stationed at his house by day and night. Some months ago, however, the police escort car and the day guard at the house were dispensed with on Lord Moyne's direct instructions."

Certain members of the House of Commons jeered when Mr Eden announced that the assassins were Jews. Earl

Winterton asked if Mr Eden would consider publishing a White Paper on the full extent of terrorism in Palestine, especially in view of the malicious rumours that the Government hesitated to publish such a paper for fear of creating anti-Semitism in Britain. Eleanor Rathbone wanted an assurance that full publicity would be given to the fact that not only the Jewish Agency but all responsible Zionist and Jewish bodies throughout the world deplored deeply the terrorist activities of the Stern Group. Mr Eden replied that he had no doubt such statements would be fully published but felt he should add that what the government hoped for from these organisations "who have such sentiments at heart" was "not only statements but active cooperation..."

Lord Samuel, in the House of Lords, was overcome with emotion when he rose to pay tribute to Lord Moyne. "The House will understand," he said, "the distress I feel, having devoted years of my life as High Commissioner for Palestine to the building of a new State there, to aiding a movement inspired by intense idealism ... to think that it may be possible that these murderers come from the Jewish population of Palestine."

* * *

While Egyptian and Palestine police prepared their case against the two Stern men awaiting trial in a Cairo prison, world condemnation of the crime provoked a new outburst of anti-Semitic feeling. Among Britishers and Americans in the Middle East, the entire Jewish community seemed to be held responsible for the assassination. Though Jewish official spokesmen might deplore the crime and the government attitude in the House of Commons be one of scrupulous fairness, people refused to accept either one or the other. Letters from England told me that Lord Moyne's death was regarded as justification for anti-Semitic behaviour towards even British Jews. "British Jews are being increasingly regarded as foreigners — as having no more right to British nationality than the refugees from Europe," one correspondent told me. "The Zionists have unwittingly encouraged anti-Semitism in Britain by their nationalist ideals, by stressing that the Jews should be regarded as rightful citizens of Palestine. The terrorists have completed what the Zionists began."

Such disturbing news from England coincided with public statements underlining the gravity of British reaction to the assassination. Victor Gollancz, referring to jeering from certain benches when Mr Eden announced that the terrorists were Jews, stated that this kind of opinion sprang from hostility for the Jewish people as a whole. Hitler's propaganda had been so successful that when a Jewish terrorist committed an abominable act it was at once in the minds of a great many people a bad mark against the Jews as a whole.

On November 17th, Mr Churchill delivered his famous rebuke in the House of Commons. He called on the Jews — every man, woman and child of the Jewish community — to help bring terrorism to a speedy end.

"This shameful crime has shocked the world. It has affected none more strongly than those like myself, who in the past have been the consistent friends of the Jews and the constant architects of their future. If our dreams of Zionism are to end in the smoke of the assassins' pistols and our labours for its future to produce a new set of gangsters worthy of Nazi Germany, many like myself will have to reconsider the position we have maintained so consistently and so long in the past."

Palestine Jewry received his statement with a heavy heart, trying to alleviate the stern words of the rebuke by declaring they were in the nature of a family scolding. They were the words of a friend of Zionism, said the Zionists, and as such must be acted upon by all who had the future of the National Home at heart.

The *Palestine Post* quoted *Proverbs* to illustrate its viewpoint. "Faithful are the wounds of a friend...",* and

*19 November 1944

went on to ask how the Yishuv, who had been told by General Sir Bernard Paget, Commander in Chief Middle East, that it must not counter lawlessness with lawlessness, could now implement Mr Churchill's appeal for action against the forces of terrorism.

Amid the wider problems that the assassination had aroused — the future of the Jews in Palestine, the attitude of the British Government, and the new outburst of anti-Semitism — Muslim reaction became stifled. What the Arabs said about Jewish terrorism and its latest expression in the Cairo murder did not seem of imminent importance. The focus was on the Jews. Even the details which began to trickle through to Jerusalem, of how the Stern gang had plotted the murder of Lord Moyne, did not cause such emotion in Jewish circles as the fact that the first official interview of Jewish Agency representatives with the new High Commissioner began with an expression of grief over that crime. From the beginning of Lord Gort's tenure of office, the Jewish community had been placed under a cloud.

In Jerusalem, that black November seemed to be one of long unending grief. To go about amongst the people, amongst the Jewish community, and see the suffering of the ordinary families made one feel desperate to help, yet impotent in the face of events. The Zionists could never be persuaded to moderate their attitude. One felt there would always be the constant outflow of demands and protests which, set beside the acts of terrorism, lost their sincerity in the eyes of the world. And so long as certain members of the Jewish community gave shelter to the terrorists, the outbursts of anti-Semitism in the Western world would continue. Both Arabs and Jews made incompatible demands. The Jews would not agree to partition. The Arabs would never cede Palestine to the Jews. The political picture had had blood splashed on its canvas, but its composition was still the same as when the first farming colonies were established following the Balfour Declaration. The personal picture — one which people outside Palestine did not see — had become a panorama of distorted unhappy lives. The women who went about their work in the cities and villages, the farmers on the settlements, the children at school — each was personally affected by the tense unhappiness of the country and none could face the future with confidence.

"What can we do?" I heard this question on all sides. "What can we, ordinary Jewish men and women, who have come here from Europe, do to bring peace to Palestine? We can't go out and fight the terrorists. We can't influence such powerful bodies as the Zionists to change their policies and lessen their demands. We can't give information to police when we are afraid our people may be arrested and exiled without trial. Our militant nationalists have alienated the authorities. And we are even denied the right of self-defence against the traditional depredations of the Arabs."

How real and reasonable these statements seemed! How one longed to be able to present the viewpoint of the ordinary Palestine Jew to the world, to by-pass officialdom and try to save something from the wreckage of these people's lives!

There was neither time nor opportunity. Each week brought with it some new event to worsen the situation.

* * *

November closed with the trial of two colonists charged with the illegal possession of arms. They were David Epstein and David Solomon, both under twenty-five. Each pleaded guilty to the specific charge of carrying, separately, a pistol and ammunition, but denied the joint charge of possessing three more pistols, two hundred and fifty rounds of ammunition and sixteen hand grenades. Epstein, the younger of the two accused, made an impassioned plea for mitigation from the dock, saying he had reasonable and full moral excuse for carrying arms. "We

263

have been most careful to keep our arms sacred for one moral purpose — self-defence," he said, and went on to explain that his settlement was in the Beit Dajan neighbourhood,[116] where murder and robbery were rife. The settlers had been unable to harvest their crops owing to Arab marauders; the authorities had been approached for help but had given an evasive reply. To refrain from carrying arms would have meant giving up their lands, said Epstein.

David Solomon told how the settlement had applied to the authorities for arms and for the establishment of a Jewish Settlement Police post, since they were in danger and their farm-work constantly hampered. They were told that such a post needed a room with iron grating on the windows and an iron door. The material provided for this purpose had then been stolen by the Arabs. The settlers had no choice but to carry unauthorised arms, declared Solomon with conviction. "We were caught by the police while on guard on our lands."

The defence called as its first witness Eliahu Golomb, the Jewish labour leader. He reviewed the numerous attacks on Jewish settlements since the beginning of the British occupation of Palestine. The authorities in Palestine had never been able to give full protection to the Jewish settlers, he said, and referred to the murderous attacks in Hebron and Safad in 1929, when, because there had been no men trained in self-defence almost the entire Jewish community had been massacred.

When the president of the court asked Golomb if he advocated that where there was no protection Jewish youth should arm themselves, he replied fearlessly that that had always been the way since the new Jewish settlement of Palestine began.

Whenever a Jewish settlement was in danger, it was necessary to supply arms for its protection. Golomb went on to declare that the Palestine Police knew of the presence of arms for defence in Jewish settlements and on several occasions there had been arrangements with them in this connection. In some cases, the police had authorised the settlers to use their unauthorised arms to hold off attacks. He cited the case of the colony of Tirat Zvi[117] where Arab attackers were beaten off by the use of hand grenades.

The next morning the prosecution called a deputy superintendent of police who said he was satisfied the accused were not terrorists, but members of a party opposed to terrorism. Asked by defence if the authorities knew that Jews had used illegal arms to defend themselves during the Arab disturbances, he agreed that he did.

Another deputy superintendent described how a group of men and women from the colony of Epstein and Solomon had thrown themselves on the bonnet and beneath the wheels of the police truck in an attempt to prevent his leaving with eight prisoners. On instructions from Jerusalem, he drove away from the colony without making arrests. By that time, about five hundred Jews from Rishon-le-Zion had arrived to support the colonists. Epstein and Solomon later voluntarily gave themselves up to the police.

The court concluded its findings. Epstein and Solomon were both pronounced guilty and given sentences of seven years each.[118]

The previous week the military court had tried and sentenced four Arabs to imprisonment ranging from six months up to two and a half years for the illegal possession of a Sten sub-machine gun and ammunition.

The *Palestine Post* published the two stories next to each other — without comment.[119]

* * *

Clues gained during the Moyne investigations in Cairo led to the arrest of many more alleged terrorists as November closed. Thirteen were taken in Nathanya, nine in Tiberias, seven in Jerusalem and three in Haifa. At the same time twelve bales of cloth, out of the hundred thousand pound's worth stolen by the Irgun Zvai Leumi from the Department of Light Industries, were recovered from a Jewish truck driver in Tel Aviv.

Such police activity, far from easing the internal situation, provoked greater tension. Were these men to be detained indefinitely, without trial until the authorities chose to exile them? What was to be their fate? The Jewish press asked: "What proof have the authorities that these men are associated with terrorism?" "We demand a trial for these suspects…"

Side by side with this rising flood of distrust, there was the bitterness of the colonists at the government denial of their right to self-defence. Epstein and Solomon sentenced to seven years — Epstein and Solomon, young Jewish farmers, anxious to bring in their crops after the months of toil — denied that right by the authorities.

And as a footnote to the colonists' claim that they should be allowed to carry arms, news was released of the arrest of Sharif el-Noubani, one of the notorious gangsters who had led the armed Arab bands in the Jerusalem District during the 1936–1939 disturbances. He had been at large for more than eighteen months since his escape from Latrun detention camp in 1943 and was finally run to ground near the Arab village of Ramallah.

Chapter Eighteen
December 1944–early 1945

Zionist recruiting campaign — More arrests and military court trials — Cairo trial of Lord Moyne's murderers — New Irgun Zvai Leumi activity — Husseini party issue declaration to Arabs — Arab assassination of District Commissioner recalled — Thoughts from England.

Hanukkah, the Feast of the Lights, was again drawing near. With the blackout lifted, the seven-branched candelabra could be lit not only in Jewish homes but on the rooftops of public buildings, on synagogues and colony water-towers. But the symbol of the Perpetual Light commemorating the victorious struggle of Judas Maccabaeus seemed an ironical expression of Jewish hope and achievement as the last weeks of the critical year moved towards their end. Although attempts were made to keep up the Feast of the Lights as a soldiers' festival, the lack of response to the recruiting campaign for the Jewish Brigade cast gloom over the celebrations.

That December, Moshe Shertok made two separate appeals for men to join the Brigade. At a Zionist meeting on Mount Scopus, he coupled his appeal for support for the Brigade with that of active cooperation in the eradication of terrorism. But the most important part of his speech dealt with Arab aspirations in the Middle East. The Arab world, he said, was groping towards unity and as agreement on positive issues was more difficult, it was uniting first on the negative platform of opposition to Zionism. The Jews had a clear conscience on the Arab problem. They had not come to Palestine to uproot or destroy but to plant and build. The myth about the displacement of

Arabs by Jewish settlement had been exploded and now a new legend was being disseminated that a Jewish state would result in the complete uprooting of the Arabs. Jewish political aspirations were strictly limited to Palestine and Zionism was opposed to the dispersion of Jewish settlers outside Palestine. If an Arab federation would lead to positive policies of development and reconstruction, the Jews would be ready to make their contribution to it. The Jewish Agency memorandum to the British Government contained all arguments against any possible partition proposal. Immediate Zionist demands were for a clear decision designating Palestine as a Jewish state and the transfer of immigration control to the Jewish Agency.

Arab leaders throughout the Middle East were at this time formulating their policies for a renewal of the discussions begun at Alexandria with the possibility, if not of federation, of bilateral agreements in which an Arab Palestine figured prominently. Shertok's statement that Arab unity was at the moment only on a negative platform was greeted with derision, particularly by Iraqis who had more to gain by bilateral trade agreements than the Arabs of the other countries of the Middle East.

In Palestine, Muslims treated the declaration of Zionist policy as yet another Jewish attempt to offset the White Paper, and scoffed at the denial that the Arabs were being displaced.

"How can Shertok make such an assertion," they said, "when official Zionist bodies are all the time trying to get round the law against land being sold to the Jews? We've already protested about this to the authorities but no steps have been taken to prevent further Jewish acquisition of some of the richest Arab lands in the country."

The Christian Arabs, holding themselves apart from Muslim and Jewish argument, pointed out meanwhile that if the Muslims really cherished their right to the Palestine soil no bribe or price should be high enough to make them sell.

While the political canvas became more vivid, the authorities impassively continued their campaign against terrorism. In Tel Aviv, police swooped on an Irgun Zvai Leumi printing press and seized illegal pamphlets. Another twenty-one thousand pamphlets were confiscated from a bus on the main Tel Aviv–Jerusalem road. In the Ramat Gan area, nine more suspected terrorists were arrested.

A few days later, foot and mobile police carried out what was officially described as "their largest anti-terrorist operation for several weeks." The seaside resort of Bat Yam, south of Jaffa, was cordoned off at dawn and several hundred men escorted to interrogation centres. Twenty-five were detained, among them David Levin, one of the Stern gang escapees from Latrun. Throughout the operation, British troops stood by. They were not called.

In Jerusalem also, arrests continued. On one night alone, five Jews suspected of terrorist activities were taken into custody when police mobile units and CID officers searched the General Zionist Club and Students' Billet in Jaffa Road. In Tel Aviv another suspected terrorist, Aaron Aaronblat, was arrested while trying to board a bus by a policeman who recognised him from photographs. He struggled to escape, and the police officer who made the arrest was injured by passers-by who went to Aaronblat's aid.

Though the majority of suspected terrorists were detained pending further enquiries, the military courts dealt that month with a spate of cases involving both Arab and Jews in the illegal possession of arms; and the General Officer Commanding confirmed many sentences passed by the court in previous weeks. Among ten sentences on Arabs, one of six years was confirmed for the illegal possession of an American military rifle, a British service rifle and forty-two rounds of ammunition. A few days previously, the military court had sentenced a twenty-three-year-old Jewish student to ten years' imprisonment for possession of an Italian anti-personnel hand grenade and detonator.

It seemed, during those last weeks of one of the most poignant years in the history of Palestine that the police had only to select at random a Jewish colony or an Arab village in order to fill their cells with suspected terrorists or traffickers in arms. If Christmas 1943 had brought with it no message of peace for the people of the Holy Land, Christmas 1944 seemed more a festival of mourning than of rejoicing. The crowds which swarmed out to Bethlehem to celebrate the birth of the Prince of Peace returned to a capital city labouring under the oppression of a two-edged fear — terrorist bombs and police swoops.

* * *

As the old year moved into the new, and Palestine Police continued to round up more suspected terrorists, the dramatic eight-day trial of Lord Moyne's assassins opened in Cairo. Elaborate precautions were taken by the Egyptian police to ensure that no eleventh-hour attempt was made by members of the Stern gang to rescue the two men who had confessed to the charge of premeditated murder. Unused rooms below the court were guarded day and night to prevent bomb planting.

When the prisoners, Eliahu Hakim and Eliahu Bet-Zuri, were brought into their iron-grilled dock, they faced the battery of press photographers who had been allowed inside the court with immense composure and confidence. Neither Hakim nor Bet-Zuri seemed representative members of the Stern gang. In quiet but firm voices, they both refused to speak in any language but Hebrew. "Hebrew is the official language of my country," Hakim stated.

Four prominent Egyptian lawyers conducted the defence, with Asher Levitsky — who had defended Rachlin at the Jerusalem arms trial — holding a watching brief for the family of Eliahu Hakim. Later, Levitsky made a dramatic withdrawal from the trial after being unable to persuade Hakim not to base his defence on political grounds. As Levitsky left the courtroom to return to Palestine, the second prisoner, Bet Zuri, called to him: "Tell my father not to think too badly of me."

The next day, Bet Zuri made a two-and-a-half hour statement telling how he had carried out the assassination. He began by saying: "We appeal to a law that has not yet been written. We believe that this case should be tried by a forum of absolute justice which is not tied to the boundaries of any one country." He continued to speak in English, declaring that the court translator was not sufficiently competent to express in Arabic what he would have preferred to say in Hebrew. Bet Zuri stood upright with his arms folded throughout his long statement. After finishing an analysis of the thoughts in his mind as he fired at Lord Moyne, he began to outline the political motives behind the crime. Only then did he exhibit emotion. When he began to read extracts from Victor Gollancz's pamphlet "Let My People Go", the court president ordered him to confine his speech to relevant points and forbade note taking in court of any political utterances Zuri might deliver. Zuri then denied that his motives had anything to do with Zionism and stated that his actions had been dictated solely by the fact that he was a son of Palestine.

Hakim, in the box the following day, laughed when the president asked him if the court could know how he received instructions for the murder. Later, police witnesses revealed that the revolver with which Lord Moyne had been assassinated had been traced by the Palestine CID to shooting incidents extending well over five or six years. The same weapon had been used in one of Jerusalem's main streets to assassinate Assistant Superintendent Wilkins. In May 1944, it had killed a Jewish constable in Tel Aviv.

Bet Zuri had already described the weapon as reliable, and although it was not proven at the trial, there is reason to believe that Bet Zuri was responsible for both the death of Wilkins and the police constable.

Counsel for Bet Zuri based his defence mainly on the sufferings of the Jews. He was stopped by the president who declared that he had received letters protesting that the defence amounted to a defence of Zionism, and added that the Court was not dealing with a case between Jews and Arabs. Hakim's counsel attempted to show that the murder of Lord Moyne had been a political crime involving wild appeal to the emotions. He asked for mitigation on the grounds of the youth and inexperience of his client.

The Public Prosecutor, summing up his case, pointed out that if the two accused claimed to be serving their countrymen, the body which spoke for the Jews had denounced them and their act, and asked for their punishment. He read statements made by the Executive of the Jewish Agency and went on to say that the accused had wronged by their act their own cause so that Mr Churchill, one of the leaders of democracy, threatened to revise his policy towards the Jews. "If I demand the heads of the two accused," he said, "and I insist on doing so — I am not doing so in order to satisfy the families of the victims whose loss is irreparable. I demand this penalty in order to eradicate this evil which has crossed into our country, thereby disturbing its peace, endangering its security and causing it disrepute."

The trial ended with the passing of sentence of death on both Hakim and Bet Zuri. Neither man showed emotion as the sentence was read. They both left the court without incident. Escorted by numerous police they were taken back to their prison cells to await execution.

So the trial ended. In Palestine, illegal pamphlets and documents circulated by the Stern gang attempted to arouse Jewish opinion to plead for the lives of the two men. No reaction came, despite the fact that certain pamphlets claimed that the assassination had been justified because it was Lord Moyne, as Minister of State, in the absence of Palestine's new High Commissioner, Lord

Gort, who had signed the deportation order sending two hundred and fifty-one Jews into exile.

The Palestine press gave full and detailed accounts of the trial but in editorial comment showed immense restraint. Side by side with the trial of the Stern men in Cairo, events of more immediate importance were taking place in Palestine. The New Year had brought with it no easing of the tension. Throughout Palestine, police activity continued to be intense. Protests were made to the government as more colonists and city-dwellers were arrested and taken to detention camps. Although the police had now begun to release some of their detainees after satisfying themselves that they had no connection with the terrorist gangs, this served only to inflame those who had claimed all along that there had never been any proof of the guilt of those arrested and they should have been given a fair trial. In one or two cases, it was found that the released men, far from having dealings with the gangs, had been active anti-terrorists.

That January, the police seized increasing quantities of illegal weapons in both Arab villages and Jewish colonies. In Tel Aviv, three separate police swoops hauled in more Irgun Zvai Leumi pamphlets dealing variously with the deportations to Eritrea, demands for the release of suspects arrested during December and appeals for action to force the government to abandon its White Paper policy.

The military courts worked overtime on a succession of cases. Two Jews, one aged seventeen, the other eighteen, were sentenced to seven years' imprisonment for illegal possession of one hundred and forty-six sticks of gelignite and four hundred and fifty-three rounds of ammunition. An Arab was sentenced to one year's imprisonment for illegal possession of a pistol and five rounds of ammunition. The *Palestine Post* published the two stories in the same column.*

*21 January 1944.

273

Meanwhile the Irgun Zvai Leumi was developing a new form of activity, which was to bring more suffering to the ordinary people of the country while ensuring a steady flow of loot into the coffers of the organisation. Dressed in police uniforms, Irgun Zvai Leumi gangsters started a series of searches in the main cities, confiscating people's possessions and robbing them of money and food. In Jerusalem, on one afternoon while official police parties were searching one district, an Irgun Zvai Leumi gang dressed in police uniform conducted a swoop on another, and caused damage estimated at several hundred pounds in Ben Yehuda Street.

This form of terrorism, while providing none of the drama of bomb outrages, was effective in preventing the Jewish community from trying to cooperate with the police. Now that uniforms no longer represented the arm-of-the-law, and a policeman on the doorstep might be an Irgun Zvai Leumi gangster, the majority of people began to refuse admittance to their flats. Fear breeding on fear, rumours of kidnappings by the gangsters and ransoms paid without question by rich families, robberies and loot-ing — this was the picture of Palestine as the year so pregnant with political decisions regarding the fate of the country moved into its second month.

* * *

February was to see more swift and successful police action. While the mayor of Tel Aviv condemned the out-bursts of kidnappings, and Petach Tikvah carried out a three-hour strike in protest against the shooting of a Jewish girl by a police night patrol, the authorities threw more cordons around Jewish colonies and city areas and roped more suspected terrorists into the net. A large-scale anti-terrorist drive was conducted on the Jaffa-Tel Aviv boundary including part of the Florentin quarter where Abraham Stern had been run to death. As usual, military and police surrounded the area at dawn and searched all

274

buildings. Six hundred people were interrogated, forty-nine detained. A new feature of this action was the precautions taken by the searchers to prevent recriminations from the townspeople. The dawn search began with the awakening of members of the Committee of the Jewish Quarter of Jaffa who were asked to accompany the police and later to sign declarations attesting that the police had conducted themselves correctly.

Such a step revealed only too painfully how tense was the situation and how even the authorities themselves could not move without covering their actions. Now that the end of the war in Europe could be glimpsed on not too distant a horizon, every happening in Palestine, every police action, was becoming food for hungry politicians of the peace. But while the Zionist bodies prepared their post-war campaigns and concerned themselves with rumours of great decisions to be made by Britain regarding the entire Middle East question, the Arabs did not linger behind in political activity. The Middle East was coming up into the front rank of problems to be settled by the victorious powers. A peaceful and contented Middle East was essential for ultimate peace in South Eastern Europe. The Balkans, with their sprinkling of Muslim minorities, were indirectly affected by events in the Arab countries. Now was the time for the Arabs to build anew on the decisions of the Alexandria conference, and for the Arabs of Palestine in particular to make clear their minimum demands.

At the beginning of February, the Husseini party in Palestine addressed a declaration to the Arabs of the country, stating: "In view of the recent declaration by the Colonial Secretary that it was hoped to reach a solution satisfactory both to the Arabs and Jews, and in view of current rumours about specific proposals regarding Palestine, the Palestine Arab Party declares that the Arabs, who are the rightful owners of Palestine, will accept no solution which conflicts with their national aspirations. The Arab nation which has for the past twenty-seven years struggled for Palestine's independence, sacrificing its most cherished

275

possessions in the attempt to preserve the national character of the country, will not be diverted from its basic demands."

This, in effect, constituted a refusal to consider any partition scheme that Britain might propose. Palestine — from Dan to Beersheba, from Jaffa to Jericho — was to be an Arab country, unpartitioned and complete.

Following Shertok's statement that the Jews would not tolerate any partition proposal and that they wanted a decision designating Palestine as a Jewish state, the wheel of Palestine seemed to have turned full circle. In 1936, the Royal Peel Commission after weeks of careful and scrupulous deliberations recommended a partition plan as the only possible solution to the problems of the country. That plan had been dropped as impracticable. Since then, it had been raised from time to time, only to meet with violent protests from both sides. Now it was coming again into the picture and again causing declarations of policy which proved its impracticability.

Not only were obvious political reactions forthcoming. Questions in Parliament at the beginning of February elicited a reply from the Colonial Secretary which stressed that although Jewish terrorism might have concerned the House on many occasions during the past few months, Arab terrorism before the war had been no less countrywide or brutal. Colonel Oliver Stanley described how responsibility for the assassination of the District Commissioner for Galilee, Lewis Andrews, in [July] 1937, had been ascribed to the Arab Higher Committee, which together with all Arab national committees had been declared an illegal organisation. He went on to say that four members of the Committee and another leading Arab politician had been arrested and deported, and nearly two hundred Arabs, believed terrorists or political undesirables, had been arrested and interned.

Four days after this forcible reminder in the House that the Arabs had been no less ruthless in their terrorist activities than the illegal Jewish terrorist organisations,

276

Jerusalem was the scene of a demonstration by the wives of the Jewish deportees who protested in front of the Jewish Agency offices over their husbands' exile and the conditions at the camps where they were detained.

* * *

Could there be any hope for Palestine?

That was the question I asked myself as I saw the sufferings of the people of Jerusalem deepen in those unhappy winter months, and felt the atmosphere of mistrust and bitterness which gripped the capital as cruelly as the blizzards which swept over the Judean Hills. The government, which had acted ruthlessly in certain situations and with lack of courage in others, was now trusted by neither Arab nor Jew. Salvation for Palestine, I felt, lay no longer in any action the government might see fit to take but in what the ordinary people of the country themselves could achieve.

Would Arab and Jew ever mix and settle down peaceably with each other? Individual Jews and Arabs were adamant that the two peoples could achieve happiness together. Who was to blame for the increasing turmoil in the country? Since Britain had freed Palestine from the Ottoman yoke, the Arabs of the country had regained their liberties. In the years that followed, the bulk of the Arabs, illiterate fellahin, had been content to scratch the soil with their wooden ploughs and live peacefully under a regime in which the constant threat of imprisonment and beating for the smallest offence no longer existed. But the Arab politicians, men from the minority of wealthy bureaucratic families had quickly developed intense feelings of nationalism incompatible with the promises Britain had made in the Balfour Declaration. These Arabs had set up illegal committees which organised and subsidised bandit gangs to attack the Jewish colonies and murder Jewish men, women and children. As each new colony was founded, as further immigrants were allowed into the country — refugees from torture camps, starving orphans, old people broken in health and spirit — Arab

277

indignation mounted. At the beginning of the present war, the Arabs had stopped actively opposing the Mandatory power out of respect for the gigantic struggle in which Britain was engaged. By 1944, the Arabs had begun to prepare for the post-war period. Arms were being collected; nationalist feelings stirred. It was obvious that once the British wartime garrison of Palestine was reduced, the Arabs would be ready to strike again with all their accumulated power and this time backed by nationalists in surrounding Arab states.

During the 1936–1939 outburst of Arab gangsterism the colonists had set up their Haganah organisation and prepared for self-defence. These arms had later found their way into the hands of Jewish youths, who, embittered at the White Paper stoppage of all immigration from Europe had organised themselves into gangs and committed bomb outrages and assassinations. For this the Jews as a body were blamed. But despite all Arab contentions it had been proved that the Zionists wholeheartedly opposed and condemned the activities of the Jewish gangs. The Zionists rightly preferred to fight with passive weapons for the establishment of a Jewish state. But passive weapons can be as disruptive as bombs. And the eloquence of the Zionists had created unnecessary unrest. Jews assimilated into other countries were angered by Zionist insistence that the Jews were a race apart; some had been provoked into becoming anti-Zionist.

And no one could deny that the Zionists on many matters such as education, had allowed their ardour to dictate to them when their better judgment should have prevailed. The Zionist bodies — the Jewish Agency and National Council — had been insistent in many demands. The Jewish labour bodies were too nationalistic to allow Jews to employ Arab workmen. Yes, for much unnecessary tension one could blame the Zionists while not forgetting that the goad which made them intolerant was the massed cry of European Jewry for the right to escape from hell to the sanctuary of the Holy Land. Was it wrong to force immigrants to go onto the colonies rather than allow them to settle down in towns and cities and upset the perilous economic balance? Was it wrong to conduct a worldwide political campaign for the establishment of a Jewish state in Palestine, when this was the only means by which state-less Jews could hope to regain their self-respect and liberties? Was it wrong to insist that Palestine, which had been the birthplace of the Jews, should now be returned to their descendants?

Those winter days as I visited friends in the Jewish res-idential quarter of Jerusalem I found the atmosphere overladen with such questions. While many stood firmly by Zionist ideals and aspirations, there were others who were convinced that if the Zionists could be induced to lessen their demand for a Jewish state there was greater hope for peace in Palestine, and for the setting up of the National Home. Towns and industries, colonies and farms had come into being since the Balfour Declaration. Was it not possible to allow more Jews to enter the country with-out displacing the Arabs?

To that question, the Arabs gave an unequivocal "No." Muslims I visited bluntly refused to consider the possibil-ity of any further Jewish immigration. "The Arabs will rise in revolt if one more Jew enters the country," a fierce nationalist assured me. Against this rigid and uncompro-mising attitude, what could the Zionists hope to achieve? And what was to be the fate of the Jews already in the country should Arab feelings be deliberately stirred in anger against them? That there was disagreement and dis-sension in the ranks of the Jews themselves I knew only too well, after five years of living in the country, but it was not unnatural between Jews of varied nationalities and varied shades of the Hebrew faith, Zionists, anti-Zionists, Orthodox and not Orthodox — each had his own viewpoint and not a few showed their bitterness towards each other. But one felt that disagreement amongst the Jews them-selves and the censurable actions of some of their leaders should not provide an excuse for claiming that Zionism had failed. The Arabs likewise had dissension in their own ranks.

Where was the solution?

* * *

I felt then — and I feel now since my return to England — that the hope of any settlement in Palestine lies no longer in the hands of the spiritual or political leaders, but in the hearts and minds of the people themselves. The ordinary Jews and Arabs who form the population of the country cherish no hereditary hatred for each other. It is political aspirations and idealist yearnings which have promoted distrust and the feeling that Palestine faces only two possible futures — that of an Arab or a Jewish state. If the ordinary people could be allowed to express their feelings by free vote, I believe Palestine could become both a refuge and a home for stateless and Zionist Jews, while at the same time continuing to support its present Arab population. If there is to be any chance of such a free expression of the desires of the people of the country, then all threats of unrest and civil disturbances must first be removed. If that is to be achieved, it must be achieved quickly — before the militant elements in both Arab and Jewish ranks condemn the country to more bloodshed and acts of violence.

Acknowledgements

My thanks go above all to Nina Rodin, Curator of Hadera's Khan Museum, for her loan of photos, her search for people in Hadera and her encouragement; and to Abed Aljariq Jebara, the P.A. to the Mayor of Tulkarm, who, my mother's manuscript in hand, took photographs of present day Irtah and tracked down the son of the mukhtar who hosted my mother one momentous evening. He was also responsible for a repeat performance in November 2007, with the sons of Hassan ibn Issah, when I made the journey to the Palestine Territories.

At various stages people have provided or searched for precious information. My thanks to Shmuel Shlimoni, late of the Hadera Burial Society; Gaby Kiwarkis, who runs the Assyrian Levies website; Steve Holland, John Herrington and Richard Simms who tracked down the birth, marriage and death dates of the elusive Michael Roy Hastings.

My thanks go to helpful staff at the Colindale Newspaper Library, especially Christian Algar; at the Jabotinsky Archive; the Jewish National and University Library; the Bir-Zeit University Library; Dr Orayb Aref Najjar of Northern Illinois University who sent me information about the Arabic newspaper, *Falastin* and to British Airways for information on flying-boat landing places during the Mandate.

Thanks also to those who have taken a personal interest in my mother's story: Nicola Rayner for her feature in the *Dorset Echo*, Clare Kinberg, editor of *Bridges*, for publishing "Editing my Mother" to coincide with this publication, and Dorset County Library for helping me put on an exhibition about their local writer in her home town, Weymouth.

Finally, among the many people who have helped in different ways and whom I cannot attempt to list, a very special thank you to Amitai Spitzer for help with reading Hebrew newspapers, and to Youssef abou Samra from Birzeit University for help with the Arabic press, to Marianne Colus for rereading the manuscript and to my publisher Ross Bradshaw.

Barbara Board is sadly no longer here to apologise in the usual way for any errors that may have crept into her manuscript. I have corrected those I found, mostly in the footnotes, but realise others may have slipped my attention.

J.K.

Notes

1 See also *Mandate Days*, by A.J. Sherman, 1997.
2 Tom Segev, in particular, *The Seventh Million: The Israelis and the Holocaust*, 1993 and *One Palestine Complete: Jews and Arabs under the British Mandate*, 2000.
3 The word *hadera* comes from the Arabic *al-khodra,* "green". The settlement was built on unhealthy marshland bought from Turkish landowners in the 1890s.
4 Hotel Ophir, in Hagalil St. The building has been renovated and is now a Yemenite restaurant, but the penthouse is still on the roof.
5 The hotel belomged to the Yarmolovsky family. Mr Yarmolovsky was a blacksmith, whose workshop was in the backyard of the hotel.
6 In Hebrew: Lohamei Herut Israel, abbreviated to "Lechi" or "Lehi"; founded by Avraham Stern in September 1940; called Stern gang or group by the British.
7 The Palestine Police, established at the beginning of the Mandate (1920), was a military force made up of British servicemen.
8 Yehoshua (Joshua) Zettler was responsible at the time for the Jerusalem branch of the Lechi.
9 This contemporary version of events has been disproved. Stern was captured, then shot in the back by a CID officer.
10 The Irgun in fact dates back to 1931, but the organisation split and was re-founded in April 1937 by Zeev Vladimir Jabotinsky (1880-1940).
11 *Mukhtar*, originally the Turkish word for an official, remained in the post-Ottoman era as the word for "official", a colony manager, and in Palestine, for a village chief.
12 A hot desert wind that blows for fifty days, from Arabic *khamseen,* "fifty".
13 To be more precise, Hebrew is a Semitic, Afro-Asiatic language.
14 The week of April 19–25.
15 The singular should be *matzo*.
16 Did Board understand the Hebrew plural, *matzot,* as a singular collective, like English "bread" and the Yiddish *matzie* as its plural? Or was it a reflection of usage in polyglot Hadera at the

time?

17 In fact, many early pioneers were secular Jews.
18 This section is from an earlier draft of the manuscript.
19 This section is from an earlier draft.
20 A common variant at the time, among non-Turks, for the historic centre of Istanbul, which had officially replaced Constantinople in 1930.
21 His full name was Hans Bargebor. He is still remembered today.
22 Arabic, "guard", "policeman".
23 On 25 November 1940, the Haganah planted a bomb on this refugee-laden ship in Haifa harbour to prevent its departure for Mauritius. It went off (unintentionally), causing heavy casualties.
24 We now know that the boat was torpedoed by the Russians. See Nicholas Bethell, *The Palestine Triangle*, for a detailed analysis.
25 Sir Charles Tegart (1881–1946), adviser to the Palestine Government on terrorism suppression, began the construction of this barbed-wire fence between Palestine and French-mandated Lebanon and Syria in 1938.
26 Board uses the French transcription for the Lebanon border post. (English transcription: Ras El-Naqura or Ras el-Nakura.)
27 The *Palestine Post,* founded in 1932, an English-language daily, became the *Jerusalem Post,* in 1950. During the Mandate, it spoke in favour of the Jewish National Home and against British immigration policy.
28 *Palestine Post*, 18 July 1943
29 This term, devised by Franklin D Roosevelt, and used after 1 January 1942, date of the "Declaration by the United Nations", which committed the Allies to the Atlantic Charter, predates the United Nations Organization.
30 Board refers indirectly here to the similar struggle by non-Conformists and Roman Catholics to be given equal voting rights and university access in nineteenth-century England.
31 David Ben Gurion (1886–1973) Chairman of Jewish Agency 1935–48 before becoming Israel's first prime minister.
32 Dr Arieh Altman (1902–1982), headed the Revisionist movement in Palestine from 1938. He later joined the Herut (future Likud) party and was elected to the Knesset in 1955.
33 18 July 1943.
34 20 July 1943, "Reflections" column.
35 Today's spelling: Irtah, just south of Tulkarm (Tulkarem).
36 Carp was farmed on Lake Tiberias.

[37] www.world.war-2.nt places this event on 9 September 1940, and mentions one hundred and eleven casualties.

[38] The former name of Prime Minister Golda Meir. An interview Board had with her in 1936 appears in her *Newsgirl in Palestine*.

[39] Representing, with his uncle Ragheb, the anti-Husseini faction, the National Defence Party, at the 1939 Round Table conference, Fakhri Bey Nashishibi, also spelt Nashishabi, was gunned down in Baghdad on November 9, 1941 by a member of the opposing Palestine Arab Party.

[40] Abraham Rachlin was sentenced to seven years' imprisonment, Leib Sirkin to ten.

[41] Jamal al Husseini, also at the 1939 conference, leader of the Palestine Arab Party, and member of the Arab Higher Committee, founded in 1936 to represent the Arabs of Palestine under the Mandate.

[42] Dr Chaim Weizmann, (1874–1952) President of the World Zionist Organization and first President of Israel.

[43] Arabic, "never mind", "it doesn't matter".

[44] The Boustanis were an important Haifa family. In the 1890s, a Boustani was Archbishop of Haifa, and the city has a street named after him.

[45] Also known as the "Anders Army" after its general, Wladyslaw Anders, who in 1942 led this seventy thousand-strong army of Polish refugees, soldiers and civilians, from Uzbekistan through Iraq and Palestine to join the British High Command in the Middle East. Jewish soldiers deserted en masse in Palestine; among them, future Irgun leader and Prime Minister, Menachim Begin.

[46] A Jaffa-based Arabic newspaper, founded by the al-Issa brothers in 1911; by 1930 it was a daily paper. Its English-language edition was first edited by Azmi Nashashibi. After 1948, it was published from Jerusalem. In 1967, on orders of the Jordanian government, *Falastin* amalgamated with *Al-Manar*, and moved to Amman, where it is still published under the name *al-Dastur*, "The Constitution".

[47] Iraq Petroleum Company

[48] Preacher and pacifist, (1876-1956).

[49] Today the forest is called Kefar ha Horesh.

[50] 1892-1944 After losing the 1940 presidential elections to F.D. Roosevelt, Republican Wilkie travelled to Europe and the Middle East as Roosevelt's personal wartime representative.

[51] Republican Governor Dewey stood against F.D. Roosevelt in the 1944 presidential elections.

[52] *Yedioth Ahronoth*, "The Latest News", a privately owned

paper founded in 1939 and run by the Mozes family, is still a major Israeli newspaper.

[53] *Haboker,* "This Morning", published from 1935–1965, was a politically-sponsored paper geared to the centre and non-Revisionist right and aimed at the middle class. Critical of the Mandatory power, it was also often at odds with Jewish Agency policies.

[54] *Davar,* "Word", was a Hebrew daily, with a weekly English language edition, that ran from 1925-1994. Edited first by Berl Katznelson, then by future Israeli president, Zlaman Shazar, it belonged to the Histradut labour union. During the war, it was reduced to two editions a week, on account of paper shortage.

[55] Moshe Shertok, 1894–1965, later known as Moshe Sharett. Prime Minister of Israel (1954-55). He guided negotiations between the Zionists and the Mandate administration.

[56] Tuesday, 23 November 1943.

[57] *The Palestine Post* also records for the same period many instances of suicide attempts ending in the courts, with the unhappy persons being bound over to hold the peace for several months.

[58] Described in Board's first book, *Newsgirl in Palestine*, Michael Joseph, 1937, p.108

[59] Monday, 14 February 1944 was one of the rare occasions when local news moved from the back page to the front of the *Palestine Post*, still mostly taken up with the Soviet advance on the Baltic front.

[60] Wednesday, 23 February 1943.

[61] 1894–1959 American journalist, later known as Gershon Agron. Founder in 1932 of the English-language daily *The Palestine Post* (renamed *Jerusalem Post* in 1950); Mayor of Jerusalem from 1955 until his death.

[62] Editorial entitled "Hurt and Redress", Friday, 3 March 1944.

[63] Emir Abdullah I, 1882–1951 (assassinated); Emir of Transjordan (1921–1946), King of Transjordan (1946-1949), and King of Jordan (1949–1951).

[64] Wadi Sarar, 13 November 1917.

[65] Board had been to Amman on several occasions; in 1936 when she was writing her first book, and again in April 1940, shortly after arriving from wartime England.

[66] Arabic, "headband".

[67] Taufiq Pasha abu al Huda, Prime Minister of Transjordan from 1939–1935.

[68] February–March 1939. The conference, properly called the St James Conference, in which Arab and Jewish delegations

refused to meet, resulted in the White Paper that limited Jewish immigration, published in May of the same year.

69 The banner was held by the RAF museum but was destroyed in a fire at the Officers' Mess at RAF Akrotiri in 1963.

70 Sir John Bagot Glubb, know as Glubb Pasha, was commanding general of the Arab Legion, 1939–1956.

71 Frederick Peake, Commander of the Arab Legion until 1939.

72 The Jewish population of Palestine under the Mandate.

73 Paul Emrys-Evans (1894–1967), Under-Secretary of State for Dominion Affairs from 1942 to 1945.

74 Senator Robert Wagner (Democrat, New York) and Senator Robert Taft (Republican, Ohio). This front-page news item only appeared in the *Palestine Post* on 3 March 1943, despite being dated "Feb. 2" but marked "Palcor delayed." Palcor was short for the Jewish-run Palestine Correspondence News Agency.

75 Emir Abd al Ilan was regent from 1939–1953, during the minority of King Faisal II.

76 Editorial of 9 March 1944.

77 *Bourse Egyptienne*: French-language Egyptian daily, published 1939–1948 in Alexandria; founded in the nineteenth century and initially published in Cairo, it was at times also called *Le Journal d'Alexandrie*. Continued publication until at least 1967.

78 Mustafa Nahas Pasha (1876–1965).

79 Editorial, Sunday, 26 March 1944.

80 26 March 1944.

81 "The Land"; moderate liberal newspaper, today often critical of government policy, founded in 1919. Its editorial policy was shaped by Gershom Schocken, editor from 1939–1990.

82 26 March 1944.

83 "On Guard". Left wing daily which published from the 1940s until 1995.

84 26 March 1944.

85 Also transliterated *Al-Difaa* — "Defence"– owned by Ibrahim Al-Shanti, an important intellectual figure in Arab journalism, who started publication in 1934. The British frequently closed it and imprisoned his owner. It was closed for good in 1948, and Al-Shanti sent into exile. But by 1950 he had revived the paper in Jerusalem. After the 1967 war, Al-Shanti moved his paper to Amman, where in 1971 the Jordanian government also closed the paper, on account of an article that displeased it.

86 Tuesday, 28 March 1944.

87 Tuesday, 28 March 1944.

88 1893–1945, founder and leader of the underground Zionist

military organisation, the Haganah.

[89] Poppy anemone, Lat. *anemone coronaria*, Hebrew, *kalanit*. *Kalaniyot* was a nickname for British paratroopers (the Airborne) during the Mandate, on account of their red berets.

[90] Hebrew, "Madam."

[91] Letter from W. Edelstein, of the Middle East Forces, published in the *Palestine Post* on Friday, 28 April 1944.

[92] Auxiliary Territorial Service, the women's branch of the British army in World War II, created in 1938. About four thousand women served in the Middle East.

[93] *Palestine Post,* Friday, 12 May 1944. The article is headlined: War Office Praise For Palestine ATS and sub-headed: Jewish Nationality Not Mentioned

[94] Born Hillel Kook (1915–2001), a name he used again after 1948.

[95] Aryeh Ben Eliezer (1913–1970), founder member with Menachim Begin in 1948 of the Herut movement. Exiled in Africa by the British, he escaped to France in 1947.

[96] In April 1942, the British Overseas Airway's Corporation's flying boat services started landing at Kallia on the Dead Sea instead of on Lake Tiberias.

[97] Large fish probably referred to by Jesus in *Matthew* 17, 24-27, when he suggests finding money in fishes' mouths. Musht swallow pebbles and even coins to prevent their young re-entering their mouths after spawning.

[98] 9 August 1944.

[99] Reported in *Palestine Post*, 30 August 1944.

[100] The *Palestine Post* for 11 August, in an article entitled "More messages to HC" quotes the Arab paper *Falastin* and Hebrew press *Davar* and *Hamashkif*. On 22 August, the Reflections column writes, "The verdict of the Assistant District Commissioner, in finding the inhabitants of Givat Shaul guilty of withholding information from the police concerning the attack on the High Commissioner, will cause grave concern."

[101] Spread over two columns of page one of the late edition Wednesday, 9 August 1944.

[102] Mustafa al-Khalidi, Mayor of Jerusalem 1934–1937 and 1938–1944.

[103] Daniel Auster, appointed Mayor for the first time from 1944–1945.

[104] Italian philsopher and politician, (1866–1952). After initially supporting Mussolini, Croce opposed him and became a popular figure in post-war Italy.

[105] *Haaretz*, Thursday, 21 September 1944.

[106] 21 September 1944. *Hamashkif*, "The Observer", was founded

by the Revisionist movement in 1938 and appeared until 1949.

107 *Times*, 20 September 1944. The same edition notes that the *Times* for September 18th was flown out by RAF transport Command to Cairo on September 19th, at the start of plans for a regular flight now that the greater part of the Continent was cleared of enemy forces. Hence Board's first reference to the London paper? The following day carried a letter from Colonel Robert D.Q. Henriques, stating that as a British Jew he could not regard the formation as distinctively Jewish — an expression which would have territorial meaning to Palestinian Jews but could only have religious significance to British Jews in the British army.

108 The RAF levied an Assyrian battalion in Iraq in 1940. Internet searches have enabled me to name him: Sliwo Dawid, Rab-Emma X/62, buried at Ramleh War Cemetery. He was in fact a captain, not a corporal. For more information about the Assyrians: http://assyrianlevies.com

109 Founded in 1936 by the British Mandatory Authority, the PBS broadcast in English, Arabic and Hebrew. In 1939, it moved to Jerusalem.

110 Ottoman unit of area. Corresponding to 919.3sq.m. until 1928, it then became metric, equivalent to 1000sq.m. The dunam is also still in use in adjacent former Ottoman territories.

111 *Palestine Post*, Editorial for 12 October 1944.

112 As an Irish peer, Earl Winterton was not entitled to sit in the House of Lords. He was MP from 1904–1951.

113 HM Forces' store.

114 Friday, 20 October 1944.

115 6 November, 1944.

116 An Arab village nine kilometres east of Jaffa.

117 South of Beit Shean (Beisan).

118 The sentence was confirmed, then reduced by two years.

119 28 November 1944.